THE SON OF GOD

BY THE SAME AUTHOR

THE SPIRIT OF CATHOLICISM
CHRIST OUR BROTHER
CHRIST AND THE WESTERN MIND

THE SON OF GOD

By KARL ADAM

TRANSLATED BY PHILIP HEREFORD

SHEED & WARD
NEW YORK

Copyright, 1934, by Sheed & Ward, Inc.

First Printing, May, 1934

Third Printing, May, 1947

MANUFACTURED IN THE UNITED STATES OF AMERICA

CONTENTS

I

CHRIST AND THE MAN OF TO-DAY

Dostoevsky, in the draft for his novel *The Possessed*, makes his hero declare that the most pressing question in the problem of faith is " whether a man, as a civilised being, as a European, can believe at all, believe that is in the divinity of the Son of God, Jesus Christ, for therein rests, strictly speaking, the whole faith." To Dostoevsky, therefore, the problem of faith is essentially the problem of the Godhead of Christ, and the racking question of the present time is whether the man of to-day can venture such a belief.

Dostoevsky's question is in great part that which we shall have to consider in these pages, though it is certainly not the whole question. For the mystery of Christ does not lie in the fact that he is God, but that he is God-man. The great wonder, the incredible thing, is not only that the majesty of God shone in Christ's countenance, but that God became true man, that he, the God, appeared in human form. The Christian gospel announces primarily not an ascent of humanity to the heights of the divine in a transfiguration, an apotheosis, a deification of human nature, but a descent of the Godhead, of the divine Word, to the state of bondage of the purely human. This is the kernel of the primitive Christian message. " The

Word was made flesh and dwelt among us "; he
" emptied himself, taking the form of a servant, being
made in the likeness of man, and in habit found as a
man " (*Phil.* ii. 7). Hence it is just as important to
establish that Christ is full and complete man, that for
all the hypostatic union with the Godhead, he possessed
not only a human body but also a purely human soul,
a purely human will, a purely human consciousness, a
purely human emotional life, that in the full and true
sense he became as one of us, as it is to establish the
other proposition, namely, that this man is God. Indeed,
the doctrine of the divinity of Christ first acquires from
the other doctrine—Christ is full and perfect man—its
specifically Christian imprint and its specifically Christian
form ; its essential difference from all pagan apotheoses
and saviour gods.

The belief in a divine Logos operative throughout
creation was not foreign to enlightened pagandom.
Moreover, the belief that the Godhead could manifest
itself in human form is not infrequently a constituent of
pagan mythologies. But in all these pagan incarnations
the purely human loses its individual significance, its
individual value. It becomes an empty husk, a phantom
of the divine. Docetism runs in the blood of all those
mythologies. Of quite another kind is the Christian
mystery of the Incarnation. The humanity of Christ
is here not an illusion ; its purpose is not merely to
make the divine visible ; it is not simply the perceptible
form in which the Godhead presents itself to us, the
perceptible point at which the divine flames forth. On

the contrary, the humanity of Christ has its own distinctive form, its own distinctive function. It is precisely in virtue of its human quality that it is the way, the means, the sacrament by which God draws near to us and redeems us. In the whole range of religious history we can find no analogue to this fundamental Christian doctrine of the redemptive significance of Christ's humanity. The redeemership of Christ rests on the fact that he who previously was "with God" had now become perfect and complete man and in this humanity and by virtue of it is the source of all blessings. Not one of the apostles has seen this more clearly or stressed it more emphatically than St. Paul. Since God's own Son took to himself human nature, he entered, sin always excepted, into the association, into the solidarity of the human race. By becoming man he became our brother, indeed the first-born of the brothers, not merely a man like us, but *the* man, the new man, the second Adam. All that this new man thinks and wills, suffers and does, he thinks and wills and suffers and does in solidarity with us, really sharing in every way our destiny in life, in death, and in resurrection. Fundamentally regarded his thoughts, actions, suffering, and resurrection are ours also. And our redemption consists in this, that by the mysterious process of baptism we are linked in the very essence of our being—therefore not merely in our thoughts, intentions, acts, but in what we are—with this incarnate God, through the whole range of his historical reality from the crib to the Cross, the Resurrection and the Ascension.

This is what it means to be redeemed, to be a Christian ; to be taken up into mutual participation in his life, passion, and resurrection ; with the first-born of our brothers, with the Head of the body, with the totality of his redemptive activity ; to become a real unity, a new community, a single body, his fulness and completeness. The Redeemer is that Man who by virtue of the mysterious relation of his being with the Godhead, through the oneness of his person with the Eternal Word, assumes and bears within himself the whole of humanity with its need of redemption. He is the living unity of the redeemed, that ultimate supreme principle on which the body of the redeemed is founded and in which it is united. This is why the Incarnation of the Eternal Word stands at the very centre of Christianity. In this world era, Christian interest, properly speaking, is focussed not in the sphere of the Godhead, nor in that of the pre-existent Word purely as such, but in this Man Jesus, who through the union of his being with the Godhead has become by his death and resurrection our Mediator, our Redeemer, and our Saviour. St. Paul gets to the heart of Christianity when he solemnly declares : " There is one God, and one mediator of God and men, the Man Christ Jesus, who gave himself a redemption for all " (1 *Tim.* ii. 5 *sq.*). In his epistle to the Hebrews (iv. 14 *sq.*) he enlists liturgical images to help describe this same essential core of Christianity. " Having therefore a great high-priest that hath passed into the heavens, Jesus the Son of God . . . we have not a high-priest who cannot have compassion on our infirmities, but one tempted in all things like as we are, without sin."

So long as this world endures, the divine majesty of his Godhead will not to Christian piety be the out-standing feature *in the figure of Christ*. I say "in the figure of Christ." It is true that the infinitely exalted Godhead, the triune God, he whom we men call our Father, Creator of heaven and earth, is and will ever be the unique and most sublime object of Christian devo-tion and Christian worship. "Our prayer should always be directed to the Father," is the way St. Augustine formulates this primary law of the Christian liturgy. "The hour now is when the true adorers shall adore the Father in spirit and in truth" (*John* iv. 23). But the adoration of the Father takes place through Christ our Lord. Of this adoration the incarnate Son is the mediator. "Through Thy Servant" was the primitive Christian formula. St. Paul prayed "in the Name of Jesus," and our liturgy still raises its voice to heaven "through Jesus Christ our Lord." Almost all the liturgical prayers of the Church are addressed not directly to Christ but through Christ to God the Father. And even in places where they supplicate Christ directly they have not in mind the pre-existent divine Word purely as such, but the Mediator, the Word made flesh.

Here is the decisive point where the true essence of Christianity is most brilliantly illuminated and where all distortions and perversions of the Christian teaching are at once revealed. Since the essence of the Christian faith culminates in the paradox, God's Son is true Man ;

since the sublimity and daring originality of the Christian confession consists precisely in this, that the two antithetical components of the Christ figure are embraced in one view and seen as one, a misrepresentation of Christ, and of Christianity, threatens directly *one* of these components is seen and affirmed by itself; and whenever in the mystery of Christ his human or divine nature is exclusively or falsely stressed, the mystery of the Redemption is misrepresented and therewith the whole of Christian devotion is distorted and misdirected.

In the list of such distortions a prominent place is taken by the *Jesuanismus* [1] of liberal theology. It fails to recognize the Divine in the Christ figure. It does not see Christ the God-man, but only Jesus the Man. All testimonies to the Divinity of Christ it sets down as fables imagined by the Christian community or regards as mythical. It has for its explicit aim to snatch from the shoulders of the simple Teacher of Nazareth the " heavy mantle of gold brocade " which the veneration of his disciples has woven for him; that is to say, the glory and splendour of his Divinity. According to *Jesuanismus* it is sufficient for true Christian piety to see in the bare humanity of Jesus God's creative love at work. Since Jesus is wholly and completely Man and nothing but Man, his sublime appearance has the effect of a transparency of the Divine. Thus he redeems us not by

[1] The word *Jesuanismus* has no precise English equivalent. The meaning is obvious—emphasis on the Man Jesus at the expense of the Christ.—*Tr.*

virtue of a mystical, incomprehensible act of sacrifice, but by his simple service to God and to men. Jesus is the bringer of a new religious sentiment, of a new morality. He it was who gave to humanity a new heart and a new conscience. Only in this sense can and may we call him our Redeemer.

Plausible and pious as all these statements about Jesus sound, and cleverly as they are assimilated to certain formularies of the Christian faith, they have nothing to do with Christianity and its dogma. *Jesuanismus* stands outside the orbit of Christian teaching and, as we shall see, outside that of historical reality. If Jesus were merely man and not God-man, then historical Christianity, which in its fight against Arianism defended as jealously the identity of the Son with the Father as, against the Monophysites, it did his identity with us, would have been one colossal illusion. And it would have been an idle playing with empty words still to talk of Redemption. If Jesus were merely man and nothing else, what he could give us would be only human, human with all its limitations and fallibility. No, *Jesuanismus* is an emptied soulless Christianity, a faith from which the heart has been cut out.

Though there is no such deformation of the Christian message, there is, nevertheless, a slight but definite distortion of it when, even though the old gospel of Christ the God-man is believed and preached in its entirety, a wrong stress is placed on the redemptive significance of the divine and human elements in Christ, and when the accent is laid exclusively on the divinity and the import of the humanity of Christ both in itself and in its redemptive power is ignored. When the Græco-Russian and certain oriental liturgies in the struggle against Arianism, which denied the consubstantiality of the Father and the Son and would make of the Son a divinity of the second order, wished to give expression to this consubstantiality in liturgical prayer, they deleted, in significant difference from the Roman liturgy, the closing phrase, " through Christ our Lord," lest the " through " should seem to imply an inferiority of the Son to the Father. By so doing, however, they struck out the mediatorship of Christ, or rather, they based this mediatorship solely on his divinity, not on the God-Man Christ Jesus. They saw the Redeemer not " in the form of a servant " but in that of God. They failed to recognize, therefore, they emptied, the redemptive significance of the humanity of Jesus. This humanity was to them only the earthly garment in which the God-Redeemer becomes visible. He who really redeems us, he who dies for us on the Cross, he who comes to us in the Blessed Sacrament, is for them not the God-Man but the Eternal Word in the veil of humanity. According to this way of thinking, therefore, the Redeemer does not appear as the new man, the first-born of many brethren, the one High-priest between God and man, but since he is regarded only as the God-Redeemer, he stands beside God alone. Between God and man an empty space is opened out which is filled by the multitude of the saints. In the Eastern liturgies the saints usurp more and more the place of the divine and human

Mediator. Hence in the devotions of the Christian East the more the Godhead of Christ engulfs, so to speak, and absorbs his humanity, the more monophysite does their attitude towards Christ become and the more important the mediation and intercession of the saints. Their liturgical prayers are no longer closed by the ancient Christian supplication " through Jesus Thy Servant," but by an invocation of the saints. Without going further it is clear how by this the whole attitude of prayer suffers a dislocation which threatens the Christian devotional life at its very root. The devout soul feels himself to be at an infinite distance from God and from Christ. " The Man Christ Jesus " is no longer by him, with him, in him. The sure infrangible foundation on which his life of prayer and love must rest is taken from under it. Faith, a childlike love and trust, are now no longer the highest expression of his piety, but are replaced by dejection and anxiety, fear and dread, even where the redemptive love of Christ touches us most directly, in the Sacrament of his Flesh and Blood. It is significant that Græco-Eastern theology takes a delight in translating the Eucharistic mystery into a mystery of awe and dread.

Nearly related to this picture of Christ revealed in the Eastern liturgies is that of certain exponents of Protestant theology. With the rest of Christendom they acknowledge that Christ is the appearance of God in man. But in this true proposition they, too, lay incomparably more emphasis on the first term, which speaks of God's appearance, than on the second, which speaks of his appearance in man. That God, the just and merciful, was revealed in Christ is for this theology the all-important fact. The significance of the humanity of Christ merely lies in the fact that we meet this God in it ; that the great transcendent God appears to us in the Christ figure with his words of judgment and forgiveness. Here, too, the humanity of Christ is threatened with the loss of its import *per se*, of its significance in the scheme of redemption. Here, too, monophysite tendencies may be traced. The humanity of Christ is not much more than the sensible garment of the Godhead, the visible point where God's justice and mercy flash forth. It follows from this that Christ stands only where God stands. Between us and this God who was revealed in Christ there yawns an infinite abyss which nothing can ever bridge, since no bridge has been built by God himself.

Our Christ, the Christ of Christianity, is perfect man as well as perfect God. Hence he is not only with God but also among men. Precisely because he is at once perfect God and perfect man, he is able to be the Mediator through whom we come to the Father. Since the eternal Word of God came down to us not in the form of God but in that of a Servant, we receive in him the new Man, the creative principle of a new humanity. A new humanity came into being in him, a new mode of human existence, by which our human nature is brought into relation with God, into union with him, and is fulfilled by him. With Adam's sin our humanity, which in germ was in Adam, lost this relation to and fulfilment by God, this intense positivity. The languishing and withering of our moral and religious powers set in as the gloomy consequence of the first sin and weakened and emptied our nature under the sinister stress of a negation, ever driving it towards the extreme limits possible, to the point where stand Satan and the damned, where the human ego has no other positive being than this : not to sink completely into non-being, but by the sustaining Will of God barely to succeed in clinging to the brink of being. Such was human existence before Christ, languishing and withering under the weight of original and inherited guilt up to the extreme limit of possible annihilation. And the new manner of existence, which in Christ is prepared for all his brothers, is to be taken up into his most sacred humanity. Thereby is sin taken from our nature. Man and sin are no longer identical. No longer are atrophy and decay our inevitable lot, but growth and development up to the full stature of Christ. In the human reality of the only begotten Son we have therefore received a new life principle, a new sphere, a being united to God and completely positive. Hence Christ is our Redeemer, not in so far as he is God, nor in so far as he is Man, but because he is God-man, the new Adam. Hence in the following pages we shall not only deal with the Divinity of Christ, but speak of the God become Man, who stands before us in the form of a Servant, of that Christ who on the first Easter morning said to Mary Magdalen in the Garden, " I ascend to my Father and to your Father, to my God and your God " (*John* xx. 17). Our concern will not be only with the

eternal Word in his divine nature, with the Second
Person of the Trinity, but with the Son of God in
human form, with the Son of Man who was exalted and
sits at the right hand of the Father, with him whom
" God hath made both Lord and Christ " (*Acts* ii. 36),
whom " God hath exalted with his right hand to be
prince and saviour " (*Acts* v. 31), with him who became
Man and of himself confessed, " The Father is greater
than I " (*John* xiv. 28). Only when we keep in view
Jesus as God made Man, only when his divinity and
his humanity are always seen and honoured side by side
can we be sure that the essence of Christianity is preserved, and the true kernel of the Christian message.

*   *   *   *   *

In the essence of Christianity there are three marks
to consider. Firstly, its eschatological aspect, its
orientation towards the last things. Christianity is not
something finished or completed. Christianity is a
growing, a becoming. Christianity is a sowing, is a
Messianic time of transition. It is a growing, a becoming,
because Christ, too, is this in his fulfilment as the
Mystical Christ. Christianity is the unfolding in space
and time of the humanity of Christ. For ever, at all
times, in all places the Incarnate Son, the Head of the
Body, joints new members to himself, till his consummation, his fulness, his πλήρωμα is reached (v. *Eph.* i. 23).
To the end he bears in his members the form of a servant.
Only when by the Will of the Father this world-era,
this Messianic interval, is closed, when the day of the

harvest, the new world-period dawns, everlasting and imperishable, only then will there be an end of this eschatological and Christological tension. In the place of the Messianic, the Christian era, there will arise that of the Trinity, the era of the triune God. As Head of the Body Christ will give back his Messianic power into the Father's hands. "When all things shall be subdued unto him, then the Son also shall be subject unto him that put all things under him, that God may be all in all" (*I. Cor.* xv. 28). Christianity is essentially an eschatology, a pressing forward towards future perfection.

The second mark of Christianity is its unique Sacramentalism. Christianity is not simply a revelation of the Spirit ; Christianity is the manifestation of God in things visible and human. In Christ the Divine enters into operation through his humanity. Theologians, therefore, rightly characterize the humanity of Jesus as an *instrumentum conjunctum*, as the perceptible, visible medium substantially united to the Eternal Word, through which God bestows his grace on us. It accords with the Sacramental primary essence of Christianity, that its individual blessings and graces also wear a visible cloak. Plainly visible is above all the sacred process by which the believer is once and for all made a member of Christ, namely, baptism. So, too, the mystery of our real and enduring union with the Head of the Body is visibly expressed in the Sacrament of his Flesh and Blood. It follows at once that the Christian Sacraments are not supplemental borrowings from the ancient practices of the mystery cults or from that of the Mandaeans, but were from the beginning a necessary part of the Sacramental essence of Christianity. To the *instrumentum conjunctum* of the humanity of Jesus there correspond the *sacramenta separata*, the visible signs of salvation. Over the relative importance and number of the Sacraments there may have arisen differences of teaching in the Christian body, but never has their essential connection with the visible appearance of Christ been doubted. Since they, too, belong to the Messianic interval they, too, point to that end of time when the Son of man shall resign his Lordship into the Father's hands. Christianity, then, as it is eschatological, so also is it Sacramental. There is no other Christianity.

The third mark of Christianity is its sociological form. Because the Man Jesus, the personified " We " of the redeemed, embraces in his Person the whole multitude of those needing redemption, Christianity is essentially a union of the members with their Head, a Holy Community, a Holy Body. There is no such thing as an isolated and solitary Christian, for there is no isolated and solitary Christ. This interior and invisible union of the members with the Head necessarily presses for an exterior unity equally close-knit. Hence Christianity in the world of time and space has existed always as an exterior unity, as a visible community, as a Church. Christianity has always demanded that its interior unity should be embodied and exhibited in an exterior unity. Christianity has ever been an ecclesiastical Christianity ; it has never been anything else.

We have had to establish this essential quality of Christianity with its several marks in order to arrive at a safe point of departure and a clear formulation of the problem for our later chapters. In our inquiry into Christ only this Christ, the Christ who is God-man, can be seriously and intelligently considered. It can only be concerned with the Christ of dogma. This Christ alone has been the stay and basis and content of historical Christianity. Here alone is the common fatherland, the place of our common origin, the one birthplace of all Christian professions of faith. No other Christ but this one has from the beginning lived in the hearts of the faithful. He alone has founded the Christian community and created their creeds and their sacred books. He alone gave to all the inner movements of Christianity, to its struggles, its cleavages, and reforms, to its worship and liturgy, to its science and to its art, their decisive stimulus and their ultimate signification. The Christ presented by dogma, as is objectively demonstrable, has alone operated in history and through history. It is the Christ figure of history. In his history of research into the life of Jesus, Albert Schweitzer remarks : " The Jesus of Nazareth who . . . proclaimed the moral code of the Kingdom of God, founded the kingdom of heaven on earth, and died in order to consecrate his life, has never existed. It is a figure projected by Rationalism, made animate by Liberalism, and clothed in an historical garment by modern Theology." It is no small merit of the so-called Mythological School of religious history to have shown conclusively, even for those outside the faith, that the whole corpus of primitive Christian literature in question knows of and confesses no other Christ figure but that of the God-man. From the beginning men knew only the one Christ of the Resurrection and the miracles. " It is wholly correct to assert that the representation of Christ in the Gospels from beginning to end is displayed in the light of the Easter experience. Not a single one of the primitive Christians wrote a line that was not based on the certainty that the Lord rose from the dead, ascended into heaven, and is ever present. ' The Christ according to the flesh,' whether in his heroism or in his tragedy, might have been burnt for all the men of primitive Christendom cared. If there was nothing else but he, then were they the most wretched of men."

From the purely scientific point of view the position of Christology to-day is as follows : We must either give our consent to the historical existence of the whole Christ, the Christ of the miracles, or openly in the face of all the historical evidence venture the assertion that the Christ of the Gospels never existed. The escape from the dilemma by differentiating the Christ of faith and the Jesus of history, that is to say by accepting the historical existence of the Man Christ while denying the supernatural in his appearance and in his works, is in the light of our present knowledge no longer practicable. Adolf von Harnack would not to-day have the courage to answer the question, *What is Christianity* ? by deliberately turning his back on the divinity of the historic Jesus. What he described might, with far greater justice, have been published under the title " What is Judaism ? " An unprejudiced and conscientious examination of the historical documents, especially of the New Testament books, has made it clear beyond any doubt that there is no such thing in history as a purely " historic " Jesus—that is to say, a merely human Jesus. Such a figure is pure fiction, a literary phantom. In history it is the " dogmatic " Christ, the God-man who lives and works in continuous existence. He has been the great reality of history, the turn of a new era, the beginning of the new Man. It is for his sake that tears and blood have been shed. From the beginning men's minds have been divided about him ; they are divided about him still.

Hence we can have no use for a picture of Christ which this or that littérateur, a Renan or an Emil Ludwig, has conceived and created from arbitrarily chosen texts. Our inquiry concerns the objective, the historical Christ, the dogmatic Christ. Dare we, must we, speaking for European thought, give our assent to this dogmatic Christ ? We will keep to Dostoevsky's question, " Whether a man, as a civilized being, as a European, can believe at all." The civilized European of to-day is far removed from the closing years of the antique world, from the men who actually heard Jesus and his message. Since the days of Copernicus and Kant, he has become prosaic, matter-of-fact, critical, indeed blasé and " knowing." What excites and occupies his thought is not the background of his world but the foreground, the world of phenomena. This is all he sees and contemplates. Inquiry into the nature of these phenomena, into the ultimate cause of their effects, into the ultimate meaning of their existence, seems to him misguided and sterile. His metaphysical capacity is stunted. Plato would say that he lacked an eye, the eye for the invisible. And similarly his sense for the supernatural and the divine is weakened. This lies still deeper below the surface than the supra-sensible. Hence he has a secret antipathy towards anything which, claiming to be divine, unconditioned, absolute, breaks into the world of phenomena as something entirely new. If for the mass of antiquity signs and wonders were the natural garment of the Godhead, the visible proofs of its presence, to modern thought they are anathema. If the world of antiquity had a mania for miracles, the modern mind shuns them. In the patchwork of numbers and measures, in the ordered relations of the world of phenomena it can find no room for supernatural forces. True to its whole make-up, modern thought reacts against any supra-sensible, especially against any supernatural, world. The world of faith makes no appeal to it whatever, indeed it has an aversion to it, if it be not actually hostile.

In this lies the immense danger for the Western European faith in Christ, that not only individual thinkers but thought itself has consciously turned from God and become atheistical; and this is even true of Christian thought in Europe. All our thoughts and opinions move in ruts which only have a meaning on purely naturalistic presuppositions, in as much as they are deliberately and on principle limited to sensual experience. Chesterton says somewhere, " The natural can be the most unnatural of all things to a man." Thought which deliberately confines itself to natural occurrences is actually the most unnatural, for it takes the smallest section of reality to be the whole reality, and ignores or denies the ultimate roots of this reality, its profoundest relations, its connection with the invisible, the superterrestrial, the divine. Our thought is now divorced from the totality of being, from the wealth of all the possibilities, since it has isolated itself from the creative thought of God. Too little attention has been paid to what Etienne Gilson, in his great book *La Philosophie de S. Bonaventure*, has told us about the literally passionate hostility shown by that brilliant Franciscan towards the Aristotelian epistemology taken over by SS. Albert and Thomas Aquinas. At that time in the fight against the Platonist-Augustinian illumination theory, which referred every ultimate and absolute certainty to an inflowing of divine light, and thus linked in the most intimate union created and divine knowledge, human perception was thrown on its own resources, and consequently knowledge and faith, the natural and supernatural, were neatly separated, and it was then that the primary conditions were created in which a world, which was more and more rapidly breaking loose from the primacy of faith, could emancipate all human thought from the creative thought of God. Men artificially mapped out a particular field of reality and called it Nature. They thus awakened and encouraged the evil illusion that the other reality, that of the supernatural, of God, had been brought into apposition with it from without, and that it was a more or less secondary reality. Nature was secularized by being released—from the epistemological standpoint—from its actual union with the supernatural, and the fiction was favoured that Nature was a thing *per se* capable of complete explanation independently of any outside factor. Thus we have all become secularized in our thought and we have schemata in our hands, or rather in our minds, which do not lead to the Divine, to Christ, but away from him. The obstruction does not lie only in our bad will. Our whole mentality is warped, and faith is therefore made incomparably more difficult for us than it was for the ancients or the men of the Middle Ages. Western eyes are grown old, and can no longer see the whole reality; or rather they have been ruined by long and bad usage. By having been concentrated on the world of mere phenomena their capacity to see the superterrestrial and the Divine has been weakened. Hence the evil does not so much lie in our bad will, certainly not in the difficulty of the Object, in the mysterious, paradoxical nature of the Christian message, but in the fundamental make-up of the modern European. He has forgotten how to see.

What is the consequence? It is that for him the Christological question is not simply one for his intellect, but for his whole spiritual being; further, that if he has lost belief in Christ or has his belief set about with obstinate doubts, certain ideas and arguments are no longer of any service. The real need above all others is for a new orientation towards the superterrestrial and the supernatural. We must again take the certainty seriously that the possibilities of the modern man do not exhaust God's possibilities, and that our thought is conditioned and bounded in time and therefore in no sense the absolute thought of God. We must again become little before God. It must be our first concern to cleanse ourselves from the time-conditioned prejudices of the Western mind, from the spirit of arrogant autonomy and autocracy, from narrow-minded rationalism and sickly enlightenment, from the purely materialistic habit of thought. We must broaden and open our minds to all God's possibilities, to all significant revelations and formations of the real in heaven and on earth. We must bring under subjection the European in us, cramped as he is by the influence of his peculiar history, in order to set free the original, genuine, true, living man from the smothering undergrowth which encompasses him. We must again return to ourselves, to our true nature, to the child in us. Never in the whole history of the West was the word of Jesus so full of significance, so charged with fate as it is to-day, that word which he spoke to his own disciples : " Unless you . . . become as little children, you shall not enter into the kingdom of heaven " (*Matt.* xviii. 3).

II

THE WAY OF FAITH

Since our eye for the invisible, for the holy and the Divine has become blurred, we people of the present day have need first to order and prepare our whole mind before turning to our inquiry into the reality of Christ. In our case this implies that our Christological investigations must be prefaced by a critical examination of our means of knowledge—in the sense, at any rate, that we must first consider what attitude is fitting when faced with the possibilities of the Divine.

In what follows, therefore, we are going to ask what the disposition of soul in the man of to-day must be, what subjective conditions must be postulated, if he is to hear the message of the Christ not merely with his outward ears but also inwardly. What is the essential basic disposition which the religious act presupposes, in our case the full acknowledgment of Christ? It is idle to speak of Christ before we are clear in our minds in what particular way he must be apprehended.

It is no small achievement of the Phenomenological school to have called our attention to the essential relation of act and object, to the inner relationship in which our act of apprehension stands to the object apprehended. Every act of cognisance of a given object postulates a particular attitude of ours towards it. If we apply this to the question how we come to believe in Christ, we arrive at the following conclusion : If the possibility exists that God did appear in Christ, if accordingly the Divine in Christ is taken as a *possible* object of inquiry, then this possible divinity must and will, in its distinctive and unique quality, colour the act, the whole series of acts, and thus the very method of our attempt to approach this divine object. The peculiarity of the divine, even if we only take into consideration its essence and not yet its actuality, lies in the way it presents itself as wholly unconditioned and forces us, the inquirers, to realise the bounds of our absolutely conditioned state, the impotence ethical and otherwise of our state as creatures. Where the divine looms into sight, though as yet only as a mere possibility, then man, even before he has reached a decision as to the existence of this divinity, will be compelled to abandon the purely objective, impersonal, scientific method of approach for one that is personal and subjective. This question is necessarily one of salvation, a practical question, not, that is, of a kind to be mastered by theoretical considerations only, not a mere problem of thought and knowledge, but one involving our very existence, by the solution of which our whole being is determined. The mere possibility of having to do with God himself lays man under the compulsion to listen to hear whether God is really speaking ; for if he is really speaking, it is not any ordinary person to whom we could quite well be indifferent, but the Lord, my Lord, to whom I, if he really exists, am in bondage to the last fibre of my being. The mere possibility that God may have disclosed himself in human nature, disclosed himself in its very depths, going to the length of surrendering his Son to us, has for man something so rousing, so compelling, so awful, so miraculous, that, if he would not sin against the very foundations of his being, he can never simply dismiss it with a shrug of the shoulders. The inquiry into the Incarnation of God is at the outset not in the same category as that, say, into the structure of the ant or the habits of insects.

What influence has this fact on our inquiry, our research into the nature of Christ? We must in the first place try to form a clear conception of the fundamental attitude proper to the inquirer. Afterwards we shall have to investigate how the concrete act, the seeking for and finding of Christ, must be constituted.

Since in this inquiry our concern is not an ordinary question of knowledge, but one which affects our conscience and our salvation, it follows that moral seriousness and a strict regard for truth are demanded of us, both in the presentation of the problem and in its solution; and these are not only scientific but also ethico-religious prerequisites. A superficial toying with vapid ephemeral hypotheses and conceits, a parade, not free from literary vanity, of destructive theories, an undisciplined violation, distortion, and perversion of the original texts, which makes mock of all sober criticism, a wild exegesis, all this is not only a profanation of historical truth and reality, but is a frivolity, a blasphemous playing with the possibility of abusing and denying the Word of God, the Word of God become Man. If we judge the " radical " research into the life of Jesus since the Wolfenbüttler fragmentists with this one question in mind—namely, whether the theories have been formulated with the moral seriousness and the reverence which their sublime object demands as the strict duty of every conscience alive to a sense of decency, we cannot avoid the conclusion that here in far too many cases violent hands have been laid, with appalling levity, on most holy things. We are not now speaking of the theologians themselves, on them we have not to pass judgment ; we refer to their methods. Consider first how that so many theories once advanced with such confidence, as, for example, that of the purely literary and anonymous origin of Christianity, of the contradiction between the synoptic and Pauline picture of Christ, of the purely eschatological character of Christ's message, have crumbled to dust ; consider further that the immoderation of their textual criticism of the Gospels has made an understanding of historical Christianity not only difficult but absolutely impossible, so that this criticism itself is lost in a labyrinth of its own fabrication, and feels it must flee from the *débris*-strewn field of the historical picture of Jesus to a meta-historical image of Christ ; all these facts must make us suspect that critical theology, in its method of sifting and examining the Biblical texts, is not governed by that scrupulous and conscientious care which the investigation of the divine demands.

The sources of error concealed in this criticism, the

absence from it of all piety and religious reverence, were revealed as by a lightning flash when men like Kalthoff, Smith, Jensen, Drews, proceeded from its premisses to the inference that Jesus never existed. It is true that in this very school of criticism there was aroused a moral revulsion against the revolting manner in which these men, and especially Drews, combined an extreme, indeed a flatly imbecile scepticism of all Christian statements and interpretations, with a disgraceful absence of the critical sense in the case of their own discoveries and assertions. Yet, after all, these men had but completed the road which " critical " theology had broken. They were spirit of its spirit. Anyone who is blind to the nature of the religious and the divine is in advance incapable of estimating the full significance of religious documentary sources such as the Gospels. And anyone who because of his blindness to the distinctive value of holiness does not take seriously the claim of the Gospels to be the Word of God, the message of the Incarnate Son of God, and approaches the Jesus of the Gospels with the superior attitude of a magistrate having to pass judgment on a suspected prisoner, renounces in advance any possibility of penetrating into the mystery of the divine. Wherever the bare possibility of the divine looms up, however remote, the only sensible attitude towards it for the human being, the creature, the sinner, is one of humble and reverent inquiry, an inquiry called forth not by scientific curiosity, but by the need of our being for redemption and bliss, by the primary consciousness of our own essential insufficiency and ruin. To one who has not yet felt this in his very marrow the message of Christ will never have anything but an exterior appeal ; it will never be a message to the heart, to the inner being. The aroused conscience is the one fitting place, the one fruitful soil where the Gospel of Christ can strike root and blossom. And here, too, is the only place where a scientific approach to the Gospels promises success. An investigator and critic who does not pray, who does not cry from the depths of his heart, " Lord, teach me how to pray ! Lord, help my unbelief ! " should keep his hands off the Gospels.

The second prerequisite due to the distinctive character of the inquiry, as one affecting our conscience and salvation, is an attitude of honest openmindedness, of true and sincere freedom from prejudice when facing anything concerned with the possibility of the divine. In this sense he only is truly unbiassed who is prepared to admit all the supernatural facts connected with the appearance of Jesus immediately his intellect and conscience are convinced of their credibility, no matter whether they conform to the traditional mechanistic habit of thought or not. Here is a point where a further defect peculiar to the " critical " method shows itself. The principles governing secular historical research are carried over without reflection to the investigation of the life of Jesus. This betrays a failure to observe that a qualitatively different object of inquiry is in question, namely the divine. God, if we only regard him as a possibility, is essentially Beginning, essentially new, essentially unconditioned, never in essential correlation with created things and their coming into being. If this God appeared in Christ, then it cannot *a priori* be the case that by the law of correlation, otherwise valid for the historian, he can be made wholly intelligible by a consideration of his surroundings and antecedents. He must necessarily shine forth as something new, unprecedented, as the dawn of a new day in the history of the world. Again, it is vain to apply to Christ without further thought an historical principle elsewhere applicable, namely analogy ; that is to say, to explore whether there be any analogues to the life and work of Christ in the history of the world. If Christ is of divine nature, his being and work must, at decisive points, transcend the human and the created and burst apart all norms of experience. The aversion to what is different, to what is wholly new in Christ, arises from a serious misconception of the nature of the divine. The historian faced with this novelty can stop and explain that his scientific means forbid a further advance. He can also, in fact he must, carefully test whether he cannot, on his hypotheses, place this new thing in a historical content and thus explain it by them. But he may not in advance and on principle refuse absolutely to admit the possibility of a direct incursion of the divine into the realm of created beings ; otherwise he will run the danger of doing violence to historical facts and divine realities in the name of his preconceived opinions and blind, implicit faith in his own philosophic creed. Hence in the denial on principle of the miraculous in history, of the *Deus mirabilis*, there lies a third great source of error in any inquiry about Christ. If we carefully examine the fundamental intentions underlying the critical formulation of the question and the solutions propounded, we shall in general come up against an aversion to the miraculous dictated by deistic-monistic prepossessions. Indeed, we shall find that this horror of the miraculous has become for many critics a decisive principle of judgment, the real criterion by means of which they can detach, so they imagine, the original deposits from the secondary and legendary strata obscuring it. By doing so they as a matter of fact extract the heart of the Gospel documents before investigating them. A conception of God is proposed which at no time or place when a living religion has flourished has been either known or accepted. Wherever a man has prayed there the God of miracles has stood before his soul, that God whose fire once, in the days of Elias, consumed the burnt offering, and " when all the people saw this they fell on their faces and they said : The Lord, he is God ; the Lord, he is God " (*III. Kings* xviii, 38 *sq.*).

*   *   *   *   *

The fact that the question of Christ is one of salvation not only determines the fundamental attitude of the inquirer in general, but must also influence the act of apprehension ; that is to say, the act by which I apprehend Christ. It differentiates religious apprehension specifically from every kind of secular knowledge. This is, above all, because, since it involves the whole man, not simply his dispassionate mind, it enlists his emotional as well as his rational powers in the process of cognition. The secular sciences follow a purely rational method, since questions and answers derive solely from the object. They set aside on principle all consideration of subjective requirements and interests. Secular knowledge proceeds from the impulse towards the truth, from the need to determine and elucidate the interior and exterior world of experience. In the religious inquirer, on the other hand, the impulse for the truth is not the only one at work. Since he is concerned with the possibility of the Divine, the Holy, those impulses and dispositions, which are directed towards the Divine, will also be enlisted. The human soul is no mere *tabula rasa*. As a conditioned, finite entity it is of its very nature attracted towards an Absolute which is unconditioned and final, and in the depths of its consciousness it is aware of this attraction as an unrest, as a nostalgia for eternity and completeness, as a state of sickness for God. St. Augustine clothes this fundamental human experience in the sentence : " Our heart can have no rest until it rests in God." This metaphysical distress in man is born of a sense for the wholeness of the cosmos, for its first cause, and for all that is at the back of it, for the complete vision of its individual parts in an ultimate unity of meaning and value. In other words, our metaphysical distress postulates a metaphysical sense or at least a metaphysical impulse. This metaphysical distress and this metaphysical impulse undergo in normal people, in whom the moral consciousness has been awakened, a peculiar colouring, or rather an intensification, a deepening, through the intrusion of a feeling of guilt, of an inner distress when faced with moral holiness, of a clear consciousness of having fallen from that highest personal dignity which has been given to our nature and set up as a model for it. As this metaphysical and this ethical distress permeate one another, the awe of the Supreme Being and awe of the supreme Value, they arouse in man the religious feeling, that which the ancient philosophers and theologians called "innate belief," that distinctive sense of the holy and divine, which is different in quality from all other human emotions; it reacts only to manifestations of the divine, and when this appearance is genuine is taken captive by it and persists.

Without burdening ourselves here with the question whether the sense for the holy born of the fusing of the metaphysical and moral impulses is a gift of Nature, or has only been acquired in the course of many thousands of years, we will content ourselves with the remark that it has in point of fact been active in historic man at all times. It was so active that, as the history of religions proves, it was actually creative, and out of itself brought forth imaginary realities. The metaphysical impulse gave rise to the gaily-coloured figures of the gods of the old cults and to their still richer mythology, which on its part stimulated the thought of antiquity and fructified it. And the moral impulse, or the sense of guilt whipped into activity by it, had its result not only in the widespread habit of penance among the primitive races, but above all in that remarkable yearning for redemption which in almost all religions led to rites of expiation and sacrifices, and of which the belief of the earlier and later mystery cults in a saviour and mediator was born. So strong and fruitful was this interweaving of the meta-physical and ethical impulses, in a word, religious feeling, that it shook itself loose from all sober thought and restraint, and the person dominated by it believed, as in a delirium, that the longings and ideals which it inspired had actually been realized, though this was never the case. It may indeed be said to be a characteristic of pagan religious sentiment that it only proceeded from this impulse, that it was a mere wild growth, rising rankly to a purely emotional, irrational structure.

What cognitional value attaches to the religious impulse, and how far does it affect religious knowledge, faith in Christ ?

We need not to-day bother ourselves with that theory, propounded by Schleiermacher and elaborated by Ritschl, which held that the one unique organ of all religious experience must be looked for in religious emotion. We need only say that the emotional theory of value with the consequent purely psychological value of revelation is now a thing of the past. It was primarily the champions of dialectic theology who overthrew it by a sharp frontal attack. On both wings, the epistemo-logical and the theological, their position was equally untenable ; it carried its death in itself ; on the epistemo-logical side because mere valuations which do not rest on solid ontological findings necessarily remain within the subjective sphere and thereafter can engender no objective certainty. In the grasp of reality the primacy belongs not to value, but to being. Hence it is not the evaluating emotion, but the reflective perception which holds the tiller. And the position was untenable on the theological side because it made a purely human and creaturely fact, the religious experience and not the eternal reality of God's Word, the basis and content of Christianity. God's Word would thus be debased from its sublime transcendency to become the handicraft of man. Hence the picture of Christ would not be the revelation and act of God, but of our own religious emotion, which like that of a synthetic *a priori* category would be to give a religious shape and interpretation to the material of experience which crowded upon it from the Gospel story. An objective picture of Christ was impossible on this method. Precisely because in the question of Christ I am concerned with the objective determination of a world of facts exterior to myself, the lead must be taken not by my subjective experience, but only by that human faculty which was created and developed to make possible a grasp of reality, for its positive cognition and critical appraisement, namely, the sifting intellect, in other words, critical thought. The question of Christ stands, therefore, in the clear, bright, cold light of the Logos, not in the insecure twilight of groping emotion.

On the other hand, it is equally certain that religious perception, precisely because it is perception of concrete reality affecting the whole person, is most intimately intervowen with the appraising religious emotion. This interweaving is found at the beginning as well as at the end of the act of perception. At the beginning since the religious emotion steers the desire for truth in a definitely determined direction, to that place where the holy and divine are to be sought. It addresses, in other words, certain definite concrete questions to the world of phenomena. It suggests to the mind certain possibilities and causes it to stretch out towards those possibilities. Hence, humanly speaking, it introduces the act of cognition and gives it a definite orientation. Directly the inquiring intellect comes up against traces of God, against certain facts of the case which lead it to suspect the action of a power which is above all creation, when, that is to say, the intellect finds itself facing things un-intelligible, a break in the series of cause and effect, a vacuum in creation, facts which it cannot explain on natural grounds, it is the religious emotion which steps in, surmises this new thing emerging from the vacuum as an act and working of God, as a manifestation of the divine, and appraises it as a revelation of God's omni-potence, justice, and love. While therefore the reason determines simply the actuality of occurrences, their connection with what has gone before and what follows, their actual and possible place in the totality of experience —even when it can only determine their place negatively as a vacuum, as an hiatus in this experienced reality— the religious emotion gets an inkling of their supra-sensual significance, their transcendental meaning and value. The intellect, for example, can appreciate the

Resurrection of Christ so far as this appertains to space-time experience, has, that is to say, an external history. It can also plainly discern the point where all possible correlations with normal experience are broken, where the vacuum yawns, where the unheard of, the miraculous comes into sight; indeed, it can of itself attain the certitude that here and now there is present an operation which is not explicable by any natural series of cause and effect, a dynamic supernatural intervention. It cannot, however, penetrate into the inner religious content, into the awakening power, into the overflowing treasury of the Resurrection. It is here that the religious emotion enters to complete its work. It grasps the deeper bearings of the facts which the intellect has made evident. It sets free their inner life, their warmth and glow, and thus establishes an intimate point of contact, a union of the object and subject reaching to the core of the personality. Humanly speaking, it is in the depths of the religious emotion that the decisive inner passage through the ascertained truth is first achieved. The philosophical or historical insight opened up by the intellect is changed through the religious emotion from a purely objective, impersonal cognition to a personal realization. From a truth *per se* it becomes an experienced truth, my truth, your truth.

Religious emotion has therefore a specific function in the process of religious knowledge. It does not, however, play a leading but a complementary, perfecting *rôle*, and it is therefore in constant inner dependence on the intellectual judgment which precedes it. When the emotional function is divorced from that of the intellect, as in the redemptive experiences of the pagan mysteries, it necessarily loses its anchorage in assured facts, its truth and reliability, and thus surrenders the character of a genuine, true, and enduring experience. What differentiates the Christian world of experience from the non-Christian is that the former does not rest on itself, but has a rational foundation, and is thus able to exercise a permanent binding power on the mind.

* * * * *

With this fact, that in religious knowledge, as distinct from profane, emotional elements are interwoven with the guiding rational ones, and that not until there is congruence of these elements and a concord is established between them will a personal realization of, a complete penetration by the truth, be guaranteed, the nature of the religious act is by no means exhausted. Indeed, to speak accurately, with this fact only the human prerequisite for a true religious knowledge is established, a necessary instrument sorted out, which on the human side first makes possible the occurrence of the religious act, of belief in Christ. The religious act itself cannot be understood by a human explanation, but only a divine. Since the object of the religious cognition includes the possibility at least of the divine ; since the specific aim of theological investigation is to inquire into the unfathomable depths of the divine life, to discover the love of three divine Persons for men, a love revealed in space and time as the incarnation of the divine Word ;

since therefore we are concerned with the establishment of realities which clearly transcend the bounds of purely human experience and are due solely to the spontaneous and incalculable will of the divine love, the knowledge of these facts can by no possible means proceed from man, but only from God himself. In other words, the way of knowledge cannot lead from earth to heaven, but only from heaven to earth. Since God alone knows his divine essence, the infinite richness of his inner life, "the mystery which was kept secret from eternity" (*Rom.* xvi. 125); since it rests on him, on his free, gratuitous grace, how far, if at all, we may learn this divine mystery, knowledge, if it is to exist at all, can only come to pass by grace through the revelation of himself on the part of God and by faith, the gift of grace, on the part of man. God is ever the Subject, ever the Creative Giver, ever the One who of his grace communicates himself. Towards him no other attitude is possible for us, if his Word reaches us, than one of belief and trust in him. Revelation by God's grace on the one hand, on the other our faith—these alone are the ways by which Christ can meet us.

From this it will be plain without further comment how perverse it is when "critical" research makes the claim, or at any rate behaves as if it does, that by the sole use of philological and historical methods, that is to say, by means of known terrestrial quantities, it can reach a definitive and decisive judgment on the mystery of Christ's divinity and of his redeemership. Their critical boring tool breaks off when the real question first emerges, that of the supernatural being and activity of Christ. Their method organized only for the plane of experience necessarily stops on this side the line. It simply cannot push forward to where the supernatural reality, the reality of God and his Christ, is to be found, if it can be found at all. This is why " critical " theology found itself forced to detach the " historic Christ " from the " Christ of the faith," indeed to set the two in an irreconcilable antithesis and to relegate to mythology the full and complete Christ, who lived in the hearts of the early Christian worshippers. It may be said that critical theology went on the rocks because it on principle employed on the problem of Christ a method which, from its very nature, could only reach to the threshold of the true mystery. Its tragic offence was that it presented without further consideration the scanty knowledge which lay to its hand as the sum of all possible knowledge of Jesus, as the definitive, exhaustive information obtainable about him. It ended at the very beginning and mistook the middle for the end.

It follows from the unique character of the object that we can only come to know about Christ and his mystery, if this can be revealed to the world at all, in the measure in which God himself has disclosed himself to us in his Word, and hence only by the way of revelation and of faith. The primitive confession *Credo Deo Deum* becomes a *Credo Christo Christum*. It is by faith alone that we can apprehend Christ.

And even this faith in the mysteries of Christ, the eternal generation of the Son by the Father, the Incarnation of the eternal Word and the redeeming death of the God-Man is not in every respect our own act. Externally indeed it is human. It is the human will, smitten by the Majesty of the divine Revealer that enables our understanding to utter a firm assent to the mysteries of Christ, though even after the revelation the latter remains dark to it. For our intellect could not be accessible to this influence of the will, had it not been rendered receptive of it by a special supernatural endowment. This is what theologians understand by the infused habit of faith (*habitus fidei infusus*). And our will could never decide in favour of a supernatural sphere of reality, unless God's grace had inwardly prepared its decision. That is why St. Thomas calls grace " the sovereign and most active cause of faith," and the knowledge of faith a certain " foretaste " of the beatific vision. And this gratuitous character of faith is even more evident in the soul already justified. It is the " gift of the Holy Ghost," imparted together with infused charity which " renders our understanding and knowledge," so to speak, " akin to divine things," and so strengthens the firmness of our faith that it becomes an experienced certitude.

Thus at the beginning of every true, full, and complete recognition of Christ there stands as its supernatural antecedent that fundamental fact, to which Jesus himself bore witness in the words, " Flesh and blood have not revealed it to thee, but my Father who is in heaven " (*Matt.* xvi. 17). Belief in Christ is not the direct and obvious result of laborious study, nor is it the easy deduction from any premisses. As regards the mystery of Christ there is in the strict sense no convincing, demonstrative theology. Belief in Christ in its becoming and being is an act of God, a kiss from his freely bestowed love, it is his creative word to us. There is no true belief in him except through the agency of the Holy Ghost. All purely scientific knowledge can be only a preamble, a preparation. It can only build up, or rather lay bare, the steps to the sanctuary. It can never lead into the sanctuary itself. This can only be done by the Father in Heaven and his Holy Spirit.

A question forces itself on us here. Is not then belief in Christ something clearly irrational, an incomprehensible mystical occurrence, which God directly induces in me, without any foundation given to it on my side by human insights and experiences, by insights into God's extraordinary attestations, into his signs and wonders ? From the fact that belief in Christ is in its essence *fides infusa*, God's own direct act, do not all the purely human, natural, historical attestations—what the theologians call *motiva credibilitatis*—sink into unimportance ?

Dialectic theology, in the persons of some of its exponents, thinks that this deduction must be made. In arriving at an understanding on this point, we may perhaps be able in some measure to make clear the relation of the rational and emotional elements of belief to its supernatural essence.

In order to combat as effectively as possible the psycho-experimental theology taught by Schleiermacher and his school, the Dialectic school's concern is at all costs to safeguard the idea of the transcendence of God, his objective reality, having no dependence on any subjective experience. In thus striving they are on common ground with the noblest intentions of Catholic theology, but part company with it at once owing to the methods by which they describe and assure God's transcendence. Here they hark back to the original Calvinistic heritage. If Luther and Calvin twisted the old truth of an all-operative God into the proposition of an alone-operative God, the Dialectic theologians in the spirit of Calvin have carried the exaggeration further : the fact that God is alone-operative is based on the infinite qualitative difference between him and the world, a difference which makes any collaboration between divine and human forces, any form of incarnation, metaphysically impossible. The world and all that it connotes, all ethics and culture, all theological science, the visible Church, the scriptures, even the humanity of Christ, in so far as this is a piece of the world, all this is set in a bracket with a negative sign prefixed, as being ever questionable ; so that from this side, the earth's side, no bridge of knowledge or experience across the gulf dividing it from the God on the other side can in any sense be thrown. In so far, too, as the evangelists are in bondage to space and time the mark of the problematical, the questionable attaches to their bare text, to the literal meaning of their words, and therefore also to their picture of Christ. From the world's point of view there exists no reason for judging the historical appearance of Jesus, and in particular his signs and wonders, save by the analogy of the rest of the founders of religions, and consequently in great part as the offspring of myth and pious imagination. Hence the attempt to construct an historical picture of Jesus Christ by purely scientific and human efforts from the text of the Bible and to proceed from this historical foundation to a belief in the divine Christ, that is to say, every attempt to find bases in the Gospel accounts for belief, can have no prospect of success and is the wrong road to take to attain to belief. It is all the more hopeless and unfruitful since man, burdened by the weight of Original Sin, remains, even when justified and absolved, a sinner and as a sinner no longer possesses a sense for the holy and divine ; and from this consideration also he cannot in the Gospels discover or recognise or experience the traces of the divine. According to Dialectic theology the matter stands thus : Not alone the mysterious realm of Christian belief, the contents of revelation, but also the revealing act of God himself, the fact that he has revealed himself, cannot with certainty be ascertained by human knowledge or experience, but solely through the grace of God. For the purely human eye there lie only scattered *débris* on the plain of the Gospel story. The seeker is like one who has been ship-wrecked in the Arctic Sea, who can only seek an escape over unstable, broken up, and piled-up infloes, and who has to make the attempt with eyes blinded and hands crippled. If, nevertheless, he find his way out he thanks for this " nevertheless " the *Deus solus* and the *gratia sola.* Hence his belief has nothing human in it, has no human knowledge or experience ; it is a pure act of God, a metaphysical occurrence worked by God in the soul, with no sort of psychological context or foundation.

This is not the place to go fully into the concept of belief held by the Dialectic theologians. We will here merely establish the fact that primitive Christianity, indeed Christ himself, never and nowhere recommended this way of *gratia sola.* The whole teaching of Christ, his signs and wonders, are governed by his purpose to summon men to test for themselves his dicta and claims. " Search the Scriptures . . . the same are they that give testimony of me " (*John* v. 39) ; " If you do not believe my words, believe my works " (*cf. John* v. 36 ; x. 38 ; xiv. 10–12). Again, with the disciples at Emmaus, the risen Christ does not appeal to *gratia sola,* but to their bounden duty to search the Scriptures (*Luke* xxv. 25). The purpose of the Gospels themselves is only to set out those characteristic elements in the historical life of Jesus which will guide the thoughtful mind to the mystery of Christ. They deliberately subserve the needs of missionary apologetic in order, as the prologue to *Luke* (i. 4) tells us, to convince the believer of " the verity of those words " in which he has been instructed. In this connection it is extremely significant that the apostles after the suicide of Judas laid stress on the point that only such a disciple should be chosen to fill his place as had " companied with us, all the time the Lord Jesus came in and went out among us, beginning from the baptism of John until the day he was taken up from us "

(*Acts* i. 21, 22), and had been an eyewitness to all that had occurred. It is obvious that they knew no other way of approach to the mystery of Christ than through his historical life and words. Thus the faith which Jesus and his evangelists have in mind is not without solid roots. As surely as the divinity and Redeemership, to which Jesus lays claim, belong of their very nature to the supernatural and superhistorical sphere, so surely does the claim itself, with the testimonies to himself which he gives in proof, belong to historical fact and therefore, like every other historical phenomenon, needs critical investigation and confirmation. As a rational being conscious of my responsibility I may only give assent to the revelation of God in Christ when the historical fact of this revelation is established to my satisfaction, when it is made credible to my mind and conscience. Or, to use the words of the theologians : the supernatural, God-given belief in the mystery of Christ postulates a rational insight into the credibility of the " historic " Jesus, into the *motiva credibilitatis*. It is only when I have become historically certain that there once was a Man, who knew himself to be the Son of God and the Redeemer of mankind, and when, furthermore, I am historically certain that this Man was absolutely worthy of confidence, that I shall be warranted, nay bound, before my intellect and my conscience, to place my trust in that testimony weighted with mystery which this Man gave to himself, and which reaches to the profound depths of the triune God, a testimony which historically I am unable to check. The road to the *mysterium Christi* leads not across the uncontrollable secret places of the transcendental, past the precipices of the paradoxical and incredible, but over the bright open plain of the historical life of Jesus. This is the way of the faith, *per Jesum ad Christum*, or more plainly with St. Augustine, *per hominem Christum tendis ad Deum Christum*.

On the other hand, resolutely as sober contemplation defends itself against every extravagant form of mystical faith, so, too, is it as far removed from the temptation to put its trust exclusively in a purely natural insight into the *motiva credibilitatis*. Here, too, it steers a safe middle course. *Gratia sola* does not suffice, but neither does *ratio sola*. Rather do God and man, grace and contemplation here collaborate. It is true that man's natural thought without any superhuman aid, if healthy, properly directed, and kindled by religious feeling, can of itself make certain safe assertions concerning Jesus and his works, and reach certainty as to the trustworthiness of his Person and of his statements about himself. But it is also certain that a conscience which is illuminated by this clear insight will be immediately and freely drawn towards that complete conversion, that renewal of the inner man, which is one of the claims made on us by belief in Christ. It is equally certain, on the other hand, that man, being weighed down beneath the burden of original sin and evil desires, stands in need of the healing power of divine grace before he can hope to rise above his natural state and to escape from the web of sensual images and desires in which his spirit is entangled. For only thus could he reach a standpoint of complete independence and emancipation from all those hindrances which enable him to make, with absolute freedom, an act of faith in Christ and his Kingdom.

It is only when that mysterious motion and power of the divine love opens our spiritual sense, with its particular manner of feeling, perceiving, and willing, to the specifically supernatural in the historic event, when we are endued by this love with a new and deeper perceptive power for the special ways in which the Divine reveals itself, with a kind of *discretio spirituum* for the forces working deep beneath the surface of history, that we are enabled in the context of the natural, the historical and the mutable to apprehend in any way that supernatural, eternal and immutable factor. In the babel of a thousand voices, created and human, we are able, *inspirante gratia*, to pick out, because it has given us an ear for the distinctive quality of the holy and divine, the Voice of the Father, and to confess : *Amen, Amen, Dominus dixit, Dominus fecit.*

Summing up what has gone before, we arrive at the following conclusions :

1. It is only by the way of faith, not by that of knowledge, that we can arrive at the supernatural mystery of Christ, that we can know the complete Christ. This faith is wholly and solely the act of God, supernatural, in its origin and object a " gift of God." The method of apologetics never affords conclusive proof nor does it convince ; it is never anything but a pointer, like the

outstretched index finger of the Baptist in Grünewald's picture.

2. This supernaturally begotten belief in the mystery of Christ is by no means devoid of solid roots, but rests on clear, historical insight into the credibility of Jesus and his works. *Per Jesum ad Christum.* We theologians when demonstrating the credibility of Jesus can prepare the way for the supernatural belief in him, though we are unable ourselves to implant it.

3. This judgment on the credibility of Jesus, based as it is on historical and rational considerations, first gains its overpowering, compelling force from the fact that it is informed and illumined by the grace of God.

At the beginning, therefore, and at the end of our road to Christ there stands Grace, there stands the Father of Lights, there stands not man in face of the problematic character of all history, not the apologist, but divine love alone.

Once upon a time the disciples were rowing in their ship over the Sea of Genezareth and at about the fourth watch of the night they saw Jesus walking upon the sea. " They all saw Him " (*Mark* vi. 49) ; they saw him plainly. And yet fear came upon them, was it an apparition, a spectre ? " And they cried out . . . and immediately he spoke with them, and said to them : Have a good heart, it is I, fear ye not." We, too, in the following pages will be passing over the stormy sea of purely human, though religious knowledge. We shall see Jesus. We shall see him plainly. And yet, fear may at times come upon us : is this figure perhaps in the end an apparition, a mere phantom ? Wherever there is anything purely human there will illusion be possible. It is only when Jesus himself speaks, only when his divine Word and his grace touch us, only then will all possibility of illusion, all fear vanish. "Have a good heart ; it is I, fear ye not ! "

III

THE SOURCES FOR THE LIFE OF JESUS

The road to the divine Christ leads across the historical appearance of Jesus. We cannot separate Jesus and Christ. Indeed, the primitive Christian body, by the use of the holy name Jesus Christ, made their solemn profession of conviction that Jesus is the Christ.

This intimate interrelation between Jesus and Christ has always, since the days of Bruno Bauer, been combated by those who thought it necessary to deny the whole Christ figure, the terrestrial as well as the celestial. Precisely because it was not practicable to detach the "historic Jesus" from the divine, the "spiritual Christ," those who could make nothing of the miraculous Christ, the divine Christ figure, had no option but to erase the whole picture of Christ. The critical negation of the divine Christ must involve a critical negation of the historic Jesus. To escape from the uncomfortable dilemma : Jesus or Christ, it was necessary to venture the opinion that the Jesus of the Gospels *de facto* never existed. What did exist were merely certain conceptions and ideals, which by their innate creative power gave themselves substance and expression in the figure of Christ. The origin of Christianity is, therefore, anonymous. The more the influence of Hegel's philosophy permeated historical research, the more open became men's minds to the possibility that Christianity was to be explained as deriving not from a creative personality, but from the victorious incursion of certain powerful ideas. According to one view the figure of the poor, crucified Jesus was the creation and idol of a Messianic mass movement of the proletariat. Others went so far as to refer it to mystery cults of the Near East, which in the pre-Christian era had worshipped a divinity which was called Jesus. Although definite proof was adduced that the mainstay of this contention, a reference on a papyrus, could not have dated before about the year A.D. 300, and that a true Jesus cult first arose with the beginning of Christianity, the attempt was, nevertheless, subsequently made to link this pre-Christian, anonymous Jesus cult with the myth, alleged to have been widespread in Asia, of a redeeming deity who died and rose from the dead, and thus to unmask the whole Gospel picture of Christ as merely legendary. Indeed, they went the length of advancing the theory that the Christian legend was nothing more than a repetition of the ancient Babylonian epic of Gilgamesh, that it belongs, in fact, to that group of parallel episodic systems which in the history of human thought are demonstrable as occurring over thousands of years, and have no relation whatever to real history.

In the light of the question thus put, Did the Christ of the Gospels exist ? our task is determined for us, namely, to subject to the most careful test those depositions in Christian and, wherever possible, non-Christian litera-ture which bear witness to the historical activity of

Jesus. Do these depositions lie in records which historically must be taken seriously? Are they records of the life of Jesus himself or do they merely reflect the history of the belief in this Jesus? Is what they have to tell living history or only the living faith of the followers of the cult? Since non-Christian depositions are free from all suspicion of being reflections, creations of the Christian faith itself, they will have special weight in countering the extravagances of the mythological school. Do such non-Christian witnesses, whether pagan or Jewish, exist?

When we consider, on the one hand, that the whole literary legacy of Imperial Rome up to the time of Tacitus and Suetonius has been lost, and, on the other, that the Messianic movement of an executed Carpenter of Nazareth, which at its very start seemed to be collapsing, must in the turmoil of the times have been much too petty and insignificant a thing to attract the attention of contemporary historians such as, for instance, Justus of Tiberias, who wrote a lost chronicle of the Jewish kings from Moses to Agrippa II., we must regard it as the most astounding good fortune that both Tacitus and Suetonius refer to Christ and to the early Christians. Tacitus in his *Annals* (c. A.D. 116), tells how Nero, to get rid of the report that he had set fire to the City, "fastened the guilt and inflicted the most exquisite tortures on a class hated for their abominations, called Christians by the populace." And he goes on to say : " Christus, from whom the name had its origin, suffered the extreme penalty during the reign of Tiberius at the hands of one of our procurators, Pontius Pilate, and a most mischievous superstition, thus checked for the moment, again broke out not only in Judæa, the first source of the evil, but even in Rome, where all things hideous and shameful from every part of the world find their centre and become popular." The passage is pure Tacitus in its concision and terseness. The characterization of Christianity as "a most mischievous superstition," as something "hideous and shameful," is only possible in the mouth of a non-Christian, and it cannot be an interpolation by a Christian hand. The precise indication of time and place, the references to the procurator Pontius Pilate and to the Emperor Tiberius, rule out any assumption that Tacitus got his report from nothing more than popular legend. Either he took it directly from the Senatorial records or, as is widely held, he got his information from the Consul Cluvius, who held office under Caligula. It is also possible that he got it from the Pro-consul Pliny, with whom he was on terms of friendship, and who, in a letter to the Emperor Trajan, had taken up the question of the spread of the Christian cult. At any rate, Tacitus knew nothing of any anonymous Christian movement with Jesus as its ritual deity. Moreover, such a ritual deity would not in any way have shocked his pagan mind. What he knew and set down was this: The Christian movement traces back to a certain Christus; it must be of a scandalous nature since its Founder was executed by the Roman magistracy. Following Tacitus is Suetonius, who in about the year 120 has something to say about

Christ. With his usual unreliability—in this he differs widely from Tacitus—his information is vague, revealing a very superficial acquaintance with the subject. According to him, in the time of Claudius, there were disturbances among the Jews *impulsore Chresto*, the same disturbances as those mentioned in the *Acts* of the Apostles (xviii. 2). Other sources also give the name Chrestiani for *Christiani*. It is therefore not surprising that Suetonius should speak of a Chrestus. He takes this Chrestus to be a Jew and Rome the scene of his activities. Erroneous as this assumption is, it yet reveals the fact that Christ must have been generally known at that time as the Founder of a Jewish sect. Here, too, therefore, the statements are based on historical facts of which the memory is, however, blurred. It is again significant that the allusion is not to a mystery god, but to a concrete Jew named Christus. The letter of the younger Pliny to the Emperor Trajan referred to above shows knowledge of this Christus and describes the spread of Christianity and its cult in Asia Minor. As far as he can gather, these Christians " assembled periodically at dawn and sang a hymn to Christ as to a god (*quasi deo*)." But Pliny also is silent about an alleged mystery god ; he only knows of a Christ whom his believers honoured as God.

If we now turn from pagan to Jewish sources reference must first be made to the notices in the Talmud on Christ and Christianity which Strack among others has collected. Since, however, these traditions, though their sources often date back to the time of Christ, were only put into literary form at a later period and accordingly allow of no definite dating, they cannot be adduced as historical sources. Still, they at least reveal this much, that in Jewish circles Christ and Christianity were regarded as intimately connected and that no one knew anything of an anonymous Jesus cult. " On the judgment day before the Passover," remarks the Babylonian Talmud, " they hanged Jesus of Nazareth because he practised sorcery, led men astray, and seduced Israel from her allegiance." Justin the philosopher, who, as a native of Palestine, was thoroughly familiar with the Judæism of the beginning of the second century, records a similar Jewish dictum. In his dialogue with the Jew Trypho he gives the Jewish verdict on Jesus thus : " Jesus the Galilean is the founder of a godless and lawless sect. We crucified him. His disciples stole his body from the grave by night and led the people astray, telling them that he was risen from the dead and ascended to heaven." As early as the first half of the second century the Rabbis used to revile the Christian evangel as *Avengillajon* (pernicious writings) or as *Avongillajon* (blasphemous writings). They must therefore have very early become acquainted with Christianity and its Gospel. Incomparably more important than these Talmudic texts as evidence of the historical existence of Jesus, is the question of the authenticity of the information which the Jewish historian Josephus gives about Christ. In his *Antiquities of the Jews*, which he published in Greek in about the year 93—94, he describes James the Less as the brother of " Jesus who was called Christ." The

passage is so soberly matter-of-fact that no suspicion
can arise of its being a Christian interpolation. It
presupposes, however, that the reader already knows
something about this Christ. As a matter of fact there
a circumstantial reference to Christ in the eighteenth
k : " Now there appeared about this time Jesus a
n of wisdom, if it be lawful to call him a man, for he
s a doer of wonderful works, a teacher of such men as
receive the truth with pleasure. He drew over to him
many of the Jews and many of the Gentiles. He was
the Christ." Is this passage genuine ? In contra-
distinction to the soberly phrased passage on James it is
a clear acknowledgment of Christ, a confession which
in the mouth of a Jew, one, moreover, who in all his
literary work was painfully careful to avoid giving
offence to his pagan patrons, Vespasian and Titus,
would be in itself very surprising. Literary arguments
have also been brought to bear against the authenticity
of this passage. The sources used by Josephus for the
Antiquities treated Pilate's administration from the
point of view of the continuous political disturbances
($\theta \acute{o} \rho \upsilon \beta o \iota$). Within such a scheme of treatment an
excursus of this kind, a purely dogmatic outburst on
Christ, unrelated to any disorders, would seem utterly
incomprehensible. The present text of the *Antiquities*
appears, therefore, to have been edited by a later Christian hand. The only question is whether we have merely
a Christian revision of the passage or whether it must be
regarded as a Christian interpolation. Seeing that
Josephus also speaks of the execution of James the

brother of Jesus and that he also mentions other important events in Jewish history, as, for instance, the appearance of John the Baptist, it would certainly be surprising
if he kept complete silence about the Christian movement.
Moreover, there is a similar remark on Christ in an
work of Josephus, in his *Jewish War*, in that
recension of this work, which Josephus himself in
own mother tongue (τῇ πατρίῳ γλώσσῃ), that is to say
in some Aramaic dialect, had dedicated to the " Bar-
barians of the East." Although we may not now have
this older version of the *Jewish War* in its original form,
it is nevertheless certain that the Old Slavonic translation of the work is based on this version. What is
important in this connection is that this translation also
has a longish reference to Christ, which begins quite
similarly to the parallel passage in the *Antiquities* (" At
that time there appeared a man, if indeed it is seemly to
call him a man . . ."). This passage, moreover, falls
in with the general plan of the work in a way which the
Christus reference in the *Antiquities* fails to do. The
life and work of Jesus are in fact presented as an influence
which let loose political aspirations and set on foot
agitation among the Jewish people. It is unquestion-
ably true that this Christus text in the Slavonic translation
of the *Jewish War* contains not a few obvious interpola-
tions of Christian origin. But its peculiar scheme of
composition, conforming so closely to that employed in
the *Antiquities* by Josephus when giving an account of
Pilate's administration, as well as the almost verbal
consonance with the first part of the Christus passage in

the *Antiquities*, makes it exceedingly probable that in this section of the Old Slavonic translation of the *Jewish War* we have that original ground plan before us which Josephus found in his sources and elaborated in is own way both for the first edition of the *Jewish War* book for the *Antiquities*. In view of this we cannot assent to the unqualified opinion that the whole of Josephus's witness to Jesus is a later Christian interpolation. It can in fact only be a case of a Christian revision, confined substantially to the dogmatic declaration, " He was the Christ " ; and possibly also to the other phrase : " A Teacher of such men as receive the truth with pleasure." All the rest of the account is supported by its consonance with the Old Slavonic text and can be readily put in the mouth of a Jew who was meticulously careful not to take sides with his nation. Every probability points to our having Josephus to thank for the earliest historical mention of Christ from a non-Christian pen. Since his *Jewish War* was written before A.D. 79, the sources used by him must be still older, and his witness to Christ takes us back to a time when, according to the mythological theory, an anonymous Jesus cult, a Christianity without Christ, must still have been in existence.

* * * * *

From the non-Christian we now turn to the Christian sources for the life of Jesus. At the outset it will be obvious to anyone considering the matter dispassionately, that the most complete and reliable accounts of Jesus must be looked for in the circles over which Jesus won

his influence, namely, among his disciples and followers.
They must, it is true, be given a searching examination
to see whether they deserve credence, whether we have
to do with mentally sound, morally unobjectionable,
reputable, and veracious witnesses.

The earliest reminiscences of Jesus are recorded in the
four Gospels. These exhale over wide stretches the
fresh fragrance of a personal experience, and, regarded as
a whole, directly reflect the original apostolic teaching.
Nevertheless, the literary fixation of these accounts of
Jesus are of later date than the writings of St. Paul.
From the purely literary point of view the earliest
testimony from a Christian source is to be seen not in the
Gospels, but in St. Paul's epistles, and in particular those
to the Romans and Galatians, and the two epistles to the
Corinthians.

What do we learn from St. Paul about the historical
existence of Jesus ? In putting this question we come up,
on the very threshold of the New Testament message,
against that significant duality in the knowledge of
Christ on which we have enlarged in what has gone
before. Paul has no historical interest in Christ in the
modern scientific sense. His view of Christ, that is to
say, does not lead him to gather together all available
reports about Jesus and weave them into a complete
narrative of his public ministry, not even to construct
a faithful historical picture of him. " If we have known
Christ according to the flesh (*i.e.*, in his purely human
appearance), now we know him no longer so " (*II.
Cor.* v. 16). Before his believing, adoring soul there

stands not the Ἰησοῦς κατὰ σάρκα, that is, Jesus in
his earthly human shape, but the Χριστὸς κατὰ πνεῦμα,
the divine Christ, the Christ of faith. But precisely
because for him this Christ of faith is at the same time
that Man Jesus, whom once he had persecuted in the
person of his followers : because for Paul the mystery
of Christ culminated in the fact that he, as God's " own
Son " (*Rom.* viii. 3, 32 ; *Gal.* iv. 4), appeared on earth
in the likeness of man, " taking the form of a servant "
(*Phil.* ii. 7) : because in consequence of all this his conception of Christ embraced the human and the divine
nature in equal measure : his dogmatic interest, the
interest of his faith, is not confined to the divinity but
also includes the humanity of Jesus, indeed his humanity
in its concrete, historical form, the Man Jesus, who was
descended from Abraham (*Gal.* iv. 16), of the seed of
David (*Rom.* i. 3), born of a woman, and made under
the law (*Gal.* iv. 4). Here, in this dogmatic interest in
" the Man Christ Jesus " (*I. Tim.* ii. 5), lies the true
motivation of the apostles' historical statements about
Jesus. It is not as if the Pauline picture of Christ bore
the pale, colourless, fleshless traits of Hellenistic speculation or of the apocalyptic visions of the Jews. It is,
on the contrary, a picture of a Christ of flesh and blood.
It is Paul we have to thank for the most detailed account
we have of the Resurrection (*I. Cor.* xv. 3–8). The
careful and exact nature of his enumeration of the
appearances of Jesus proves that historical trustworthiness is a matter of concern to him. In the same passage
he is careful to state that his knowledge of the matter is

derived from the reports of others (*I. Cor.* xv. 3). How anxious he is that his teaching should give a concrete, historical picture is shown by his remark in the Epistle to the Galatians (iii. 1), that he had set forth the crucified Christ before their eyes. Again, it is Paul who gives us *inter alia* a more exact account of the Last Supper, of the betrayal and apprehension of the Lord on that black night (*I. Cor.* xi. 23 *sqq.*). He returns again and again to the subject of the suffering Christ, whose stigmata he himself bore (*Gal.* vi. 17). He quotes verbatim various sayings of our Lord (*I. Cor.* vii. 10; *Rom.* xiv. 14), just as he gives in his own way the account of the Last Supper. He recalls scattered sayings of Jesus which the evangelists have preserved only in their general sense, *e.g.*, that they who preach the Gospel should live by the Gospel (*I. Cor.* ix. 14; *cf. I. Tim.* v. 18; *Rom.* xii. 14, 17). Indeed, he gives certain sayings of our Lord on which other sources are silent (*cf. I. Thess.* iv. 14). He forcibly calls to the minds of his flock the words of the Lord (*I. Tim.* vi. 3; *Acts* xx. 35), Christ's commands (*Gal.* vi. 2; *I. Tim.* v. 18), and is careful to differentiate between his own words and admonitions and those of the Lord (*I. Cor.* vii. 12). Again, in none of the Apostles do the great phrases of the Gospel message, the " Kingdom of God " and the " Father in heaven," recur so often as with him : and his Song of Songs on Love (*I. Cor.* xiii.) not only calls to our minds the sublime thoughts of Jesus, but also with sensitive brush paints for our souls the luminous picture of our Lord himself. Thus his whole teaching on Christ is

based upon the strictly historical picture of the Person
and teaching of Jesus.

Whence did Paul derive his knowledge of Jesus?
He was certainly not an actual disciple in the original
sense, and was therefore neither an ear nor an eye witness
of his ministry. But the Apostle's remark (*II. Cor.*
v. 16), that he knew Jesus according to the flesh, makes
it appear probable that he had seen and heard Jesus,
if perhaps only from a distance. He got more detailed
information from the mouths of the Christians whom he
had persecuted unto death (*Acts* xxii. 4). This information he enlarged three years later by personal intercourse
with the original Apostles, especially with Peter (*Gal.*
i. 15 *sqq.*). Thus Paul was able to throw no inconsider-
able light on the historical figure of Jesus, light so rich
and bright that by its rays alone we could attain to the
essentials of his historical message.

But is the testimony of St. Paul reliable? We can
answer without any misgiving that he displays the
highest degree of human trustworthiness, and that there
can hardly be another historical testimony existing which
has been so sealed with the very heart's blood of the
witness as this of St. Paul. In the beginning he had
taken violent measures against similar testimony,
" binding and delivering into prison " all who held to it.
He had persecuted them unto death. The Christ whom
they loved was alien to him, indeed an offence and an
outrage. True, in the apocalyptic hopes of his race the
Messias was presented to him as " the Man from heaven,
heavenly " (*cf. I. Cor.* xv. 48 *sqq.*), and in the Jewish

wisdom literature he knew the Messias to be described
as the " wisdom of God " (cf. I. Cor. i. 30 ; ii. 7). His
picture of the Messias must have borne, in contradis-
tinction to the ideal of the Pharisees, the traits of a
spiritualized, celestial being ; yet to him the picture
always showed a Messias of heavenly splendour and
glory, not a Messias who is crucified and dies. Thus he
felt the Christian Gospel of a crucified Christ to be a
scandal and a gross blasphemy. And now this *Christus
crucifixus*, against his most secret wishes, against all his
most sacred hopes, had come to him from without and
had conquered and overthrown him that day on the
road to Damascus, when " God shone in his heart and
gave him the light of the knowledge of the Glory of
God in the face of Christ Jesus " (cf. II. Cor. iv. 6). Not
one of the Apostles had resisted this testimony so fiercely,
so furiously, and no Apostle, not even Peter or John, was
thereafter so permeated and possessed by it. Hence-
forward Paul's proudest and happiest boast was to be
that he was " the Apostle of Jesus Christ " ; his " mes-
senger," his " slave," his " servant." What before he
had hated was now become his new and great love.
If hate has keen eyes, the eyes of love are keener. Thus
both in his hatred and in his love Paul is for us a faithful
witness to Christ.

* * * * *

From Paul we shall turn to the Gospels, and first to
the three synoptic Gospels of Matthew, Mark, and Luke.
It is all-important that we should be clear as to the
essentials of their genesis and literary form, since only

thus can we come to any decisive judgment on their value as sources. In forming a judgment we must begin with the recognition that they are primarily compilations. Matthew, Mark, and Luke had no idea of writing original works in which they shall set out their personal conception of Christ based on the material at their disposal. All they aimed at doing was simply and objectively to gather and arrange in order all the traditions about Jesus which were already current among Christians, and were derived from the narratives of St. Peter and the other Apostles or from information obtained from the Mother of Jesus. These narratives before they were written down had no literary existence ; but, since each of the Apostles was wont to tell them in his own particular way, they had already become set in characteristic turns of speech and sequences, and were passed from mouth to mouth in these characteristic forms. It is not, therefore, as if the evangelists only took over the content of the available narratives and moulded its form and shape by their independent literary labour. As a fact they took over in wide measure both content and form, so that we can gather from the synoptic Gospels not only what the first disciples had to tell about Jesus, but also how they delivered their message, and the manner in which they were wont to relate the various acts and teachings of Jesus to the faithful. However much they might agree in essentials, Matthew preached in another way than Peter, and Peter otherwise than James and John, and their disciples took over from their masters their special individual methods of presentation. Thus certain specific types of tradition took shape, exactly as had happened in the formation and development of the Rabbinical tradition when " the ancient Halakot were not taught in the schools in definite set words and in rigid sequence, but were presented by each Tannait in his own words and in the sequence favoured by him." The evangelists found this unity of tradition and diversity of type when they began to collect and arrange the material for their compilations. They were under the influence of this Rabbinical method of teaching in which they had been brought up ; their respect for the *ipsissima verba* of their Master as delivered to them placed them under an immeasurably higher obligation to hold closely to tradition. They could not do other than select those elements of the tradition suitable to the time and place in which they found themselves and faithfully unite them in a uniform Gospel according to the particular field of vision and interest of their audience. There is nothing more impersonal, more straightforward, more objective than the manner in which the Gospels were compiled. The literary personality of the evangelist counts for nothing; the matter delivered is everything. Even when, as at certain climaxes in the story of the Passion, the evangelist might be expected to show his partisanship or sympathy, he keeps himself in the background. In the light of this method of presenting the Gospel story the so-called synoptic problem loses its importance for the question of the credibility of the Gospels. Fundamentally its interest is only a literary one. If, for example, the

primary source of the present canonical Gospels were
the logia, written by Matthew in Aramaic, and the
Petrine Gospel of Mark ; if, that is to say, our canonical
Matthew in Greek as well as Luke each represented an
independent working over and elaboration of these two
alleged primary sources, these Gospels with their
special contributions would not on that account lose in
historical conclusiveness, for what they relate, as in the
case of the logia and of Mark's Gospel, was already
current knowledge in the Christian communities before
its redaction in literary form. Thus seen the value of
each one of the four sources—Matthew's logia, Mark,
the Greek text of Matthew, Luke—stands on a level
with that of the rest, while, in addition, not the slightest
trace of any attempt at improving or developing the
narrative is demonstrable. The traditions were reduced
to writing by the evangelists at different dates, some
earlier some later, but the traditions themselves are all
equally old, equally venerable, both in their content
and in their wording, for they contain all of them
reminiscences of Jesus preserved by the first generation
of Christians. Some scholars even go so far as to say
that the logia, the original Aramaic Matthew, were put
together during the lifetime of Jesus, since they make
no mention of his Passion, and since everything points
to St. Paul having known and used them. Now that
E. Littmann has established the fact that the primitive
Aramaic text of the *Pater noster* shows a four-stress verse
metre with end rhymes, it is reasonable to suppose
that this metrical form goes back to Jesus himself and

that in the Aramaic text of the Our Father we can hear
" our Lord's actual words as they originally sounded.".
The point of view of some expositors, that because they
are variously reported we cannot be sure that we have a
single saying of our Lord in its original form, is to-day
no longer tenable. Recently E. Sievers maintained that
he had proved, by the aid of rhythmical analysis,[1] that
the Apostles John and Peter in particular " had a large
hand in the formation of the text of the Gospels," and
that consequently their content and literary form derive
primarily from these two disciples.

Be this as it may, the fact is incontestable that precisely
those things which might be a stumbling-block to the
layman making a comparative examination of the separate Gospels, their numerous correspondences, parallels,
and interdependencies, on the other hand their divergencies in particular details, their doublets, further their
purely external structure, the method of presenting
their material, all these offer us a sure guarantee that we
have before us the primitive Apostolic and Christian
depositum of tradition. This strange form of narration
does not imply any awkwardness in the writers. On the
contrary it demonstrates, as nothing else could do better,
with a moving clarity, their faithfulness to tradition,
extending to the smallest element, the last word. It

[1] In German, *Schallanalyse*; for which, I am advised, no
English term has been as yet coined. It is a method of recording
the pulse or beat of a verse or passage when spoken into the
machine, by which conclusions can, it is said, be drawn as to the
authorship of various parts of a composition suspected to be the
work of more than one hand. *Tr.*

reveals the anxious pains which the evangelists took to reproduce the deposit of tradition current in the Christian communities, in so far as it contained Apostolic reminiscences, wholly unconcerned what inequalities or contradictions or doublets might be found therein. So conscientious were they in the faithful reproduction of the narrative, so sensible of their responsibility, that Luke, to take an example, who was a Greek, shrank from rendering into pure Greek those passages where, as in his account of the childhood of Jesus, he was drawing on Judæo-Christian, Palestinian sources. He preferred to give a strictly literal translation of the Aramaic, " so that his gospel over wide stretches bears a strong Palestinian character in its vocabulary and in the structure of the sentences." The curious result is that, although he was a Greek, it is actually Luke who has preserved the original wording of his Semitic sources with greater purity and more faithfully than those evangelists like Matthew and John, who, because of their greater command of the Palestinian idiom, might and could venture a freer translation. We may say that the precept which St. Paul so forcibly recommended to Timothy : " Keep the good thing committed to thy trust " (*II. Tim.* i. 14), that this profound respect for what had been delivered them from Christ, this inflexible purpose to hand on what they received in the most straightforward impersonal manner possible, was what inspired the evangelists in their work, and made them, even from the purely natural standpoint, the most reliable witnesses to the primitive Christian message.

It was due to this consciousness of their responsibility to hand on faithfully what had been delivered to them and not to any literary intention or art, that the synoptic evangelists not only depict accurately the external framework of the story of Jesus, the political, economic, and social relations of Judaism, even down to the tribute penny and the daily wage of a labourer, though this framework was once and for all shattered with the destruction of Jerusalem, but also reproduce the soul of the Judaism of that time, its religious and political ideals, its sacred and profane speech, with an exactness which could not have been recaptured a few decades later when, with the dispersion of the Jews over the world, that spirit was dead. It is significant that conceptions and expressions commonly current in the time of Jesus, such as Son of Man, Son of David, Kingdom of Heaven, are employed as a matter of course in the Gospels, though at the date when they were reduced to writing such expressions were but seldom used in the Apostolic communities and were ultimately quite forgotten. On the other hand, favourite ideas and phrases which appear in the Apostles' teaching after Jesus' death—the Holy Ghost and his charismatic working, the Church of the Saints, Redemption by Christ's most precious blood—do not occur in the Gospels, or occur but seldom. When we consider how easily such slight anachronisms could have crept in when the Gospels were reduced to writing, so easily that their inclusion would hardly have surprised us, seeing that the evangelists wrote them not in the lifetime of Jesus, but in the atmosphere of the faith and experience of the Apostolic communities, when we consider all this we must recognise in the historical purity of the style of the Gospels something utterly extraordinary and indeed unique. The ultimate explanation of this historical accuracy lies in nothing else than their inner subjection to Jesus and his Word, in their fidelity to Jesus, which made them take anxious care that nothing should be added to or subtracted from the words of the Lord current in their midst. Their historical fidelity was the expression of their faith in Jesus.

Up to now we have been speaking only of the synoptists. St. John's Gospel, however, is also a priceless and indispensable source for the life of Jesus. True, its literary style is entirely different, while its doctrinal purpose is not, like that of the synoptics, to lead the mind up from the humanity of Jesus to his Divinity, but to illumine the human life of Jesus by the light of his Godhead. For this reason, too, it is not simply a compilation, but is the product of the writer's personal feeling, his passionate desire to display the glory of the Only Begotten Son full of grace and truth in his actual earthly life and doings. Hence the detailed words of Jesus, which reveal the lively consciousness of his Sonship. Hence the description of his miracles as transparencies of the divine ; hence too the transfiguring lustre and the sublime splendour in which the whole of our Lord's ministry and passion up to the triumphant " It is consummated " is viewed. This is not the place to enlarge on the individuality of St. John's Gospel in detail, and we shall here only show very briefly the reliability and credibility of his account. When H. Müller, to his " no small surprise," found that metrical laws were dominant in the Fourth Gospel, just as they were in the Sermon on the Mount, in the Prophets, and in the Quran, and when C. F. Burney, by a systematic analysis of the characteristics of the Johannine language and style was able to adduce positive proof, that in St. John's Gospel we have the work of an Aramaic-speaking author writing in Greek, the contention that this Gospel had nothing to do with the Apostle John, but had sprung up in the soil of Hellenistic-Asiatic syncretism, lost its surest support. Again it was a complete error to regard Palestine—and not merely Galilee, whose chief towns were in fact only a few hours distant from Hellenistic regions, but also Jerusalem—as a kind of Aramaic island and not as a bilingual land where the majority were as familiar with the vulgar Greek tongue as they were with one or other of the many Aramaic dialects. When Christ was talking with the woman of Canaan (*Matt.* xv. 22 *sqq.*), or with the pagan proselytes at Jerusalem, it is exceedingly probable, if not certain, that he spoke to them not in Aramaic but in Greek. With the Greek language, Greek habits of thought and Greek ideas must necessarily have been almost native to the people as Aramaic. A careful comparison of the synoptic and Johannine Gospels leads to the definite conclusion that the author of the Fourth Gospel not only knew all the other three, but also followed a definite object, namely,

to supplement them and, here and there, when mis-
understandings threatened, silently to correct them.
But for John we should know nothing of the earlier
relations of individual disciples of Jesus to the Baptist,
of our Lord's many journeys to Jerusalem, of the exact
day of the Crucifixion. We should miss, also, important
glimpses into the mystery of Christ's interior life, into
the luminous clarity with which he revealed his pre-
existence and his consciousness of the fact that he was
the Son of God. The divine and the human in the
nature and consciousness of Jesus, which in the synoptic
Gospels appear side by side as more or less unconnected
attributes, attain first in John to a living unity and a
conclusive psychological truth. We can therefore say
that but for John the synoptic picture of Jesus would
have remained imperfect, in particular on its psychological side. It is his Gospel that first presents to us the
complete, the inner, the living Christ. Its relationship
to the other Gospels is not merely external but necessary and essential, and it cannot be conceived of apart
from them. Its author must have been a man who
was familiar not merely with the narratives about Jesus
current in the community, but with what lay behind
them ; and with rare tenderness and love he contemplates the interior life of Jesus, with whom his spirit was
so interwoven that his very language involuntarily
became that of the Master. Of this tender, affectionate,
yet restrained and reserved speech of Jesus we find in the
synoptic Gospels but a few detached fragments (*cf. Matt.*
xi. 25 *sqq.*; *Luke* x, 21, 22). If we want to know how

Jesus talked, not as a preacher among the peasants and husbandmen and fishermen, but as a friend among friends, as the bridegroom with the wedding guests, and his approach to the intellectuals of his day, we must go to John.

Who is this John, this disciple who thought in Aramaic but wrote in Greek, this man who, with unheard-of assurance, dared late in the day to write a fourth Gospel, when three had already been in circulation, for years who dared in this fourth Gospel to depart radically from the traditional Gospel style, and to draw his picture of Christ on an entirely new and bold design, who with the lightest touch of his brush brought long familiar Gospel narratives into new contexts, who made illuminating additions to them, who was able to tell quite intimate personal things about Christ, and who did all this with such fervour and tenderness and love that to this day the reader is moved by the tones of this soul ? Who is the author of the Fourth Gospel ?

The evangelist himself stresses the point more than once that he intends to set out only what he himself has seen and heard (i. 14; xix. 35), and does this in almost the same words as those with which the author of the first Johannine epistle calls attention to his personal testimony as an eye-witness (*I. John* i. 3). He betrays by numerous indications that he and the beloved disciple are one, and his own group of disciples support this testimony: " We know that his testimony is true " (xxi. 24). Christian tradition, too, as well as the Gospel itself, points to John as the " disciple whom Jesus loved." The witness of Irenæus is especially weighty, for Irenæus was a disciple of Polycarp, who at the end of the first century was a man of mature age and therefore counts among the witnesses of the first generation. Quite independently of Irenæus there also appear in support of St. John's authorship Theophilus, Bishop of Antioch, Clement of Alexandria, and, further, the oldest list of the writings of the New Testament known as the *Muratorian Fragment*. The judgment of Clement is the more worthy of attention in that he has a keen eye for the stylistic peculiarities of the Fourth Gospel. Against this testimony of tradition no valid objection can be raised. The conjecture that John had been put to death long before the end of the first century has not been able to maintain its ground in the light of historical evidence. As early as the time of the Council of the Apostles in the year 49-50 Paul names John among the pillars of the Christian community at Jerusalem (*Gal.* ii. 9). According to the oldest tradition John passed the last years of his life at Ephesus. Even if the evangelist had not come into touch with Hellenistic ideas in his own bilingual Galilee, this fact, vouched for by tradition, that during his later and most mature years he lived and worked at Ephesus, the meeting-point of Western and Eastern thought, would alone make intelligible the Hellenistic way in which John regarded and described Jesus. We must therefore say : Behind the last Gospel of Jesus there stands none other than the personality and mind of his beloved disciple, John. It may well be that John's own disciples first published his Gospel in complete form, and, as the last of the concluding verses suggest, made some additions ; but its essential content and its characteristic form derive without any doubt whatever from John himself.

We have, then, if we do not count the logia contained in Matthew and Luke as separate, four sources for the life of Jesus, four springs of which the water is fresh and undefiled. So far as these sources contain matter collected by the writers, they are in themselves a sufficient guarantee of the directness and genuineness of the accounts they give. No third factor, whether author or literary artifice, comes between them and Jesus. We have in them the naked, unadorned Apostolic testimony. As to the Fourth Gospel, while it is the record of a personal confession, its essential content derives from John himself, and therefore this Gospel, too, gives us first-hand news, the reports of an eye- and ear-witness.

Thus accepting the authenticity and primitiveness of these sources we find ourselves in the immediate presence of the earliest disciples. They are, so to speak, in the witness-box ; we hear them speak. May we, should we, must we believe their testimony ? Our question is no longer purely historical, but psychological and ethical. Properly speaking, it is now a question of what confidence we can place not so much in the Gospel texts in themselves, nor in the evangelists, but in those who stand behind them, their ultimate sponsors, all the early disciples. These, however, do not come up for our consideration as individuals, as isolated persons, as chance witnesses. From the beginning they give their testimony as disciples of Jesus, as members of a community sharing the same faith, as a unit and a whole. As far back as we go in the history of Christianity an apostle or evangelist never preaches or works on his own account detached from the body of the disciples. This is a mark of the Gospel literature from its very beginning and distinguishes it fundamentally from profane literature—its sociological spirit, the common solidarity of the witnesses, the close relation between all the individuals, making of all the I's and You's one single living " We." It is a message of the thousand who are one heart, one soul.

The position therefore is that in the Gospels it is not only the evangelists we are listening to, nor merely the earliest disciples ; for in them the pulse of the whole primitive Christian Church is beating. In them we have a confession of the Church, the credo of a single religious body gathered round the risen Saviour.

It is precisely this solidarity, this uniformity in the earliest expressions of belief in Christ, that gives them reliability in the highest degree. We should certainly be acting unjustly, indeed outrageously, if *a priori* we regarded every primitive Christian believer with mistrust and without further consideration put him down as a deceiver or half an idiot ; for judging by the earliest Christian documents, and in particular the Apostolic epistles, it is strikingly clear with what immense seriousness the first Christians took the question of the meaning of their existence and its duties, and how in the most difficult circumstances they risked their lives for duty's sake. Conscious deceit, wilful inaccuracy cannot be laid to the door of a group like this. However, if we consider the isolated individual, self-deception is not necessarily ruled out—in the sense, at any rate, that he may have been the victim of his ideals or dreams or ideas originating in the confused depths of his own mind or through the control over his mind exercised by an exterior agent, which lacked a rational basis and safeguard. The history of pre- and early Christian Gnosticism proves that solitary, isolated religious thinking always runs the danger of becoming confused and losing itself in wild speculations and dreams.

In contrast to this the Christian message was from the very beginning the affair of a close community, of a community, in fact, alertly conscious that its main mission was to preserve with the utmost fidelity the Apostolic doctrines, which long before the writing of the pastoral epistles, in fact before St. Paul's conversion, had been thrown into the form of a baptismal creed, enunciating the essentials, the kernel of the Apostolic tradition. Against any and every departure from the " way in Christ Jesus " (cf. Cor. iv. 17), from sound doctrine (I. Tim. vi. 3), this community made the sharpest possible stand. Its determination to hold fast to the Apostolic heritage was not the least of the causes of its veneration for the episcopal office, which by the imposition of hands was endowed with the special grace of truth (charisma veritatis), by virtue of which it could hand on unfailingly the norm of the faith, the regula veritatis. So far as we can grasp historically the primitive Christian movement, it was embodied in a community, held together by a teaching authority, which derived directly from the Apostles and was concerned to preserve inviolate, down to the minutest point, what had been delivered to it by the Apostles. It is this which distinguishes it from parallel phenomena in Buddhism and Islam. Within this community, which took its stand solely on the Word of Jesus and his Apostles, there was no room for individualistic speculation. In it there was continuous contact between the members, a continuous interchange of ideas, the possibility of steady reciprocal and official control, and with it an absolute safeguard against extravagances of individual minds or the influx of alien ideas and experiences.

In the fact that the primitive Christian message was never restricted to individuals or to individual groups or schools, but was always attached to the whole body, which was fast-anchored to the Apostolic teaching transmitted to it, and that this message was passed on as an Apostolic belief held in common by the body, lies the strongest guarantee that the Christian faith from its first beginnings invariably remained true to itself, and also that in its pre-literary period it was not tampered with, that we have therefore in the Gospels the primitive message of Jesus in all its wealth and purity.

Seen in this light, it is a psychological and historical outrage if, simply because we have in the Gospels the creed of a cult, we feel at liberty to talk of a " creative community dogma," or to entertain the suspicion that

in the Gospel narrative itself we already find exaggerations, transfigurations in the picture of Jesus due to
members of the cult. If we do we utterly fail to understand the clear conviction which banded together the
first believers, and in particular the disciples of the
Apostles and their successors, in a common adherence
to the Apostolic heritage, and the positively passionate
determination to preserve inviolate what had been
handed down to them, the deposit. But we should
fail to appreciate also the conserving, normalizing power
inherent in every religious faith held by a community.
So strong is this normalizing power that the danger was
rather that what is unessential and superficial in the
message of Jesus should be eliminated, or at any rate
attenuated, in order that what was essential and decisive
might be thrown into stronger relief. It is not without
some reason that the possibility has recently been suggested that this levelling tendency has, in the case of
certain Messianic attestations of Jesus, rather weakened
and disfigured their special purport than strengthened
and transfigured them.

Just as the inviolability of the primitive Christian
message is assured by the common holding of the same
faith, so is it also by the sublime object of that faith. It
was the concern of the Gospels as it was of St. Paul to
proceed to Christ through Jesus, through his historic
figure to his supra-historical divine nature. It was a
matter of faith in the Son of God made flesh, the living
God, who out of his love for us became Man. To-day
no reasonable scholar doubts that all the Gospels pre-

suppose that Jesus was truly Son of God, and that they were written in this belief. This, the true faith of the Christian community, is supernatural in the sense that it has and can have no natural roots either in the mentality of the Jews of those days, or in that of the Greeks, or in any other imaginable mentality; that historically it has no precedent, is something absolutely new and therefore cannot possibly be regarded as the offspring of the faith of the primitive Christian community itself. We can imagine, it is true, that the force of legend or pious belief and enthusiastic hero-worship or even conscious literary art might raise and transfigure a mere human figure to divine proportions, with the result that a natural or artificial process of apotheosis set in. But for such an apotheosis there is no place in the soil of Christian ideas. The concern of the Christian faith is not with a progressive transfiguration and divinization of a mere man, but with the recognition of a Being who is perfect and complete Man and whose mystery lies in the fact that in this his complete and simple human nature he is essentially One with God. In this paradox of a complete, real human Being who is yet the Son of God the true kernel of the Christian faith consists. The Evangelists, the Apostles, and their followers had therefore no dogmatic motive to transfigure the human image of Jesus in any way or to exalt it to the divine. On the contrary, their dogmatic interest lay much more in the lowliness of his humanity, in the fact that the Man Jesus was born and died as we, suffered hunger and thirst as we do, and like us was cast down and wept. There is no parallel in the whole history of religion to this full humanity of the Son of God. Wherever deifications have taken place, the human has always been swallowed up in the divine, has been dissolved into it. When Antinoos, the favourite of the Emperor Hadrian, was drowned in the Nile, he was at once worshipped as Osiris disguised. The same thing happened in the cults of Simon, Menander, and Elkensai. The result of the metamorphosis was not a God-man but Deity alone. Hence the κύριοι of the mystery cults do not stand between God and humanity as does the God made Man ; they are not the way to the Father, Mediators. They are themselves the apparition of the Deity : so that the ultimate end of pagan redemptive mysticism is not to become united to the Mediator and through him to attain to the divine, but the divinization in the absolute sense of the μύστης. The adept himself becomes Isis or Mithras. There was no place for divinization such as this in Christianity, since its Christ is and remains wholly, completely Man, and through his very humanity redeems his people.

Again, the God who is one with this truly human man is for Christians not one out of many deities, male and female, one of the thousand possible grades of being from the terrestrial to the super-terrestrial. The God Christ is, in his union with the Father and the Holy Ghost, the one, unique, solitary God of heaven and earth, *Deus solus*. The one, unique, solitary God of the Old Testament finds his continuation in the one, unique, solitary figure of the Son of God on earth. Nowhere in

the whole range of religious history is to be found any
counterpart to this unique God and this unique Christ.
In this Christian conception of God lies the second mark
of differentiation from all parallel conceptions in the
history of religions. Wherever in the legends of
antiquity a deity has appeared in human form it has been
as a god, not as the one unique God. All these divine
figures grew out of the conceptions underlying polytheism and pantheism. They were all natural forces
projected into the Infinite, an agglomerate Nature, but
not the Lord and Creator of Nature. Hence they were
all in thrall to their purely natural being, and, exactly like
all other creatures, were subject to the vicissitudes of
Nature, to Fate, to the εἱμαρμένη and their decrees.
It is quite other with the Eternal Word, which according
to the Christian confession appeared in Christ. He is
Deus de Deo, lumen de lumine. In the eternal divine
life-process he proceeds to-day, to-morrow, for ever
out of the bosom of the Father, whose essence he
expresses in substantial individuality as the consubstantial Son of the Father, his reflection and image. For the
Christian faith the mystery of Christ lies in the fact that
his human nature receives its substantiality, its existence,
its personality from this divine Word, which is of the
same substance with the Father and the Holy Ghost.
Christ is indeed full, complete man, but the utmost
depths of his reality are in the divine Word. When,
therefore, Christians call Christ God, this God is infinitely
different from all pagan deities. Of his very nature he
transcends all natural forces and created things, all gods

and goddesses, all angels and human beings, the absolute self-sufficient Being, which is unrelated to this world and can therefore never become a part of this world. It follows that the God of the Christians can never, like the Greek gods and goddesses, be transformed into the shape of other deities. He is with the Father and the Holy Ghost the great unique, and essentially exclusive God, *Deus solus*. There is no point of contact with heathen conceptions of deity. It is a gross misinterpretation, indeed a falsification of ideas, when the Hellenistic Θεός is incontinently confounded with the Christian Θεός. What they stand for is as different, indeed as antithetical, as Christianity and paganism, theism and pantheism. For three centuries Christians suffered the cruellest martyrdom on account of this sharp antithesis. And when the Hellenistic intellect tried to introduce itself in some veiled form into Christianity through this or that apologist, and afterwards, throwing off every mask, in Arianism, the old faith reacted against it with all its will to live and sacrificed the life, the home, the honour of its best in a seemingly prospectless struggle against the power of the State and subservient ecclesiastics, until the victory was won and the doctrine of the consubstantial Son of God attained general recognition. It is an offence against scholarship to overlook this and, simply because of the same term Θεός, to force the Incarnation of Christ into the context of pagan incarnations.

Again, it is as inexplicable that this belief in the Son of God should have sprung from Judaism as from Hellenism. For, in view of the earnest solemnity with which the Jewish people cherished its belief in God, the jealousy with which, in the midst of pagan polytheism, it preserved the strictest monotheism as its most precious national possession, the idea that this one God from all eternity should be living an eternal triune life, as Father, Son, and Spirit, must have been utterly alien to its purely human understanding. In the *shema* the devout Jew daily prayed, " Hear, O Israel, the Lord our God is one God." For centuries it has been deeply graven on their consciousness that Jahveh had neither wife nor child. Hence the tidings of the first Christians of a Son of God on earth, who as the Author of life had appeared among men and had been put to death at their hands, must have seemed to them a monstrous impiety, and so long as they only listened to their own thoughts they could do no other but cry out, " Blasphemy, blasphemy," and rend their garments. And the first Christians, the one-time Jews, would never of themselves have dared, or been able or have desired to risk, this confession, if the new belief had not entered their souls with overpowering force from without, from the historical Jesus. Just as the tidings of the Man Christ and of the Son of God differed specifically from all Jewish and pagan Messianic expectations, so too did the other divine message embracing both God and man, with its proclamation of the Redeemer, the God-Saviour. It cannot be derived from such sources. True, in a small collateral line of the Jewish people, in the circle of the apocalyptic writers, men dreamed of a celestial Son of

Man who should come on the clouds of heaven; and from time to time voices were raised which proclaimed this celestial Son of Man to be the servant of the Lord portrayed by Isaias, who entered the lists for his people. But all those voices died away unlistened to. The great mass of the Jewish people and, above all, its Pharisaic and Sadducean leaders, professed with all the force of their national egoism a Messias of glory who was to make the heathen his footstool. A suffering Messias was completely alien to the Jewish theological thought of that time. When therefore the Messias was dragged before them in fetters and ignominy and in spite of this spoke of his future coming with the clouds of heaven, they could only feel this to be blasphemy raised to the highest pitch; and "Crucify him, Crucify him!" was their one answer. The Cross of Jesus proves with cruel impressiveness how alien to the Jewish mind was the Christian belief in a Saviour; so that it is psychologically impossible that it should have been born of a Jewish womb, of the womb of the community of Jerusalem.

Nor had pagan Hellenism any part in it. What to the Jews was an offence to the pagans was folly and raving madness. For how could God's connatural Son, his only Son, whom the Christians confessed, suffer and die! It is true that in the mystery cults there had been saviour gods who suffered and died; but these myths were not compatible with the belief in the *Deus solus*, but sprang from the polytheistico-monist conception of gods and goddesses, the highest celestial powers, as imperfect, capable of transformation, subject to Fate. Moreover, these cults did not, as in Christianity, relate to a Redeemer of mankind who gives up his life freely for the many, but launched forth into vague dreams of unhappy celestial beings, to whom death and resurrection were a tragic fate imposed upon them by destiny, and who did not accept death of their own free will for the salvation of humanity, but suffered it under compulsion. And, lastly, all these redemptive figures had only a shadowy existence in the far-distant haze of legend. They had their beginnings in remote antiquity and there was nothing in them which could be taken hold of as historical. That the Christians would have nothing of such dreams, that in all seriousness they confessed a Redeemer-God, who had been a carpenter of Nazareth, a man of the most recent past, who had been crucified under Pontius Pilate as a malefactor, this seemed to the pagan mind incredible, unheard-of folly and madness.

Certainly neither the Jews nor the Hellenists could of themselves have arrived at the figure of Christ which glows in the pages of the Gospels. All talk of a creative communal faith and hero-cult is, historically regarded, false and deceptive. If the staggering reality, the uniqueness of an ineffably sublime event, had not painted the life of Jesus on the soil of Galilee, no human brain could ever have conceived it nor human art composed it. " Innumerable and terrible," says Lavater, " are the doubts of the thinking Christian, but the uninventible Christ conquers them all." In fact it would be impossible to invent this Son of God who on the

Cross cries out : " My God, my God, why hast thou forsaken me ? " (*Matt.* xxvii. 46 ; *Mk.* xv. 34). No one could ever have invented this All-Holy One, this *Solus Sanctus*, who was the companion of publicans and sinners and let himself be annointed by a despised harlot. Unimaginable is this risen figure, the Lord of Glory, who receives his betrayer's kiss and when they spit in his face keeps silence. . . . No Jew, no Greek, no Roman, no German could ever in his wildest dreams have shaped the image of such a Saviour. Have we really accustomed ourselves, we Europeans of the twentieth century, to this image of a Saviour ? To us is he not still to-day something quite apart, a strange lonely figure ? No, no ! this Messianic picture which the Gospels reveal has no earthly origins. We cannot explain it historically, still less explain it away. An awe-inspiring figure is the Christ of the Gospels, planted like a *tremendum mysterium* in our midst. He stands forth challengingly, a riddle which must be solved, a question which must be answered. He stands before us as our fate. Yet, thus it is. Jesus is our κρίσις, our judgment. The pleadings are written, the witnesses come forward. We cannot look away or close our ears, we must watch and listen. " Lord, incline my heart unto Thy testimonies " (*Ps.* cxviii. 36).

IV

THE MENTAL STATURE OF JESUS

In the Gospels we have the unadulterated Apostolic traditions about Jesus, traditions which, in what constitutes their essence, namely confession of a God-Redeemer, were of individual growth and were given shape and maintained in conscious opposition to all neighbouring Jewish and Hellenistic conceptions of belief. The Gospels are in their deeper purpose confessions of the faith, not of individual disciples, but of the whole primitive Christian community, quickened and sustained on the one hand by its passionate will to preserve and transmit the Apostolic heritage, on the other by an inner sense of profound hostility towards all that was non-Christian, whether Jewish or pagan. This individuality of the tradition forbids our explaining belief in Christ as deriving from Jewish or pagan roots. We have here nothing derived or secondary ; what we have is original, an original faith, an original confession.

What have these Gospels to tell us of Jesus ? To avoid making any false step let us first try to form a clear idea of everything in the historical appearance of Christ which may be taken as certain and definitely established ; that is to say, let us see what facts about his outer appearance, his spiritual nature, his interior life, his actions and influence in the field of history may be exactly determined. It is only when we have formed as clear and complete a picture as possible of the impression Jesus made on his disciples and on his contemporaries, when, that is to say, Jesus stands before us as his own people actually saw him, that we may proceed to inquire into the secret of his personality, what was for him the ultimate and most profound reality, what shaped his exterior and interior conduct of life. This latter is the inquiry into what Jesus was conscious of in himself ; and only when this question has been answered do we attain the region where the imperceptible, the supernatural, the divine looms up, where wonder upon wonder flashes on our view, and whence there will resound in our ears those words of reverence and awe heard of old by Moses : " Put off the shoes from thy feet ; for the place, whereon thou standest, is holy ground " (*Ex.* iii. 5). The question which will first occupy us, therefore, is that of the exterior and interior figure of Jesus.

Since the interest of the evangelists, just as in the case of St. Paul, hung not so much on the earthly, human appearance of Jesus as on the Christ of glory, the Son of God and Redeemer, it is from the outset vain to expect from the Gospels that they will draw for us a picture of Jesus in all its details, or that there will even be an attempt to bring home to our perception his historical figure in concrete form. In the eyes of his disciples and of the first Christians Jesus was the risen Lord, the transfigured, the heavenly Christ. Hence the evangelists described his life on earth only in the light of this his divinity. Yet they did describe it notwithstanding.

They described it simply and artlessly, with no subsidiary intention of transfiguring it, precisely because the glory of the Resurrection was thrown into more luminous relief against the background of the poor and lowly human life of Jesus.

As Kepler determined long ago, and as more recent investigations corroborate, the birth of Jesus falls in the autumn of the year 7 before our era. At that time the planets Jupiter and Saturn were in conjunction. According to the same reckoning the day of our Lord's death must be set down as April 7th in the year 30. Jesus was therefore thirty-seven years old when he was put to death, and if we assign three years to his public ministry, he was thirty-four years old when he left his home and betook himself to the Jordan to be baptized by John the Baptist. When he began his teaching he was therefore at the height of his powers.

The exterior appearance of Jesus must have been extremely attractive, indeed fascinating. If a woman of the people quite spontaneously broke out into praise of him with the words, " Blessed is the womb that bore thee, and the paps that gave thee suck " (*Luke* xi. 27), the answer with which Jesus corrected her, " Blessed are they who hear the word of God, and keep it," betrays the fact that the woman had his bodily excellences in mind as well as the spiritual. If at a later date Origen and, following his lead, the Greco-Egyptian monks, supposed Jesus to have been ugly in appearance or at any rate of no distinction, they came to this conclusion on purely dogmatic, exegetical grounds, since the prophet Isaias had foretold of the Servant of God that there would be no beauty in him nor comeliness: the lamentable picture which the prophet drew of the suffering Christ, as he was haled through the streets of Jerusalem, was applied by them to his normal appearance. What underlay this interpretation of theirs was their Hellenistic, Platonic mode of thought which regarded the body, every body, as something which ought not to be, as something infra-human, as the prison of the soul, and actually suspected any beautiful body of being a seductive device of the devil. They had no alternative therefore but to ascribe to the Redeemer an ugly body. The powerful impression which Jesus made at sight on ordinary people and especially on the sick and on sinners certainly owed something to his attractive exterior, which by its charm drew everyone to him and held them, even if it was primarily due to his spiritual and religious power. His eyes with their burning, wakening, reproving looks must have been especially striking. Does not he himself say " the light of thy body is thy eye. If thy eye be single, thy whole body shall be lightsome " (*Matt.* vi. 22). It is significant that Mark, when reporting some important saying of our Lord, not seldom uses some such expression as, " And looking round about on them he saith " (*cf. Mark* iii. 5, 34; v. 32; viii. 33; x. 21; xxiii. 27).

Coupled with this exterior comeliness we get the impression of health, power, energy and well-being in the appearance of Jesus. According to the unanimous witness of the Gospels Jesus must have been a thoroughly

healthy man, inured to fatigue and with a great capacity
for work. In this he is differentiated from other
important founders of religions. Muhammad was a
sickly man, tainted with an hereditary disease and with
a shattered nervous system, when he unfolded the
banner of the prophet. Buddha was mentally a brokendown and worn-out man when he died. We never
hear of Jesus that he was visited by any sickness. All
the sufferings which came to him were due to his calling,
to the privations and the sacrifices which his messianic
mission laid on him. His body must have been hardened
in no common measure. A proof of this is seen in his
habit of beginning his work in the early morning.
" Rising very early, going out he went into a desert
place, and there he prayed " (*Mark* i. 35). " When
day was come, he called unto him his disciples : and he
chose twelve of them " (*Luke* v. 13). His joy in nature
breathes the same fresh, healthy, unspent sensibility.
The hills and the lake were especially dear to him.
After a tiring day's work he loved to climb to some
lonely height or late in the evening get himself taken
on to the shimmering water of the Lake of Gennesareth and stayed out far into the night (*cf. Mark* iv.
35 ; vi. 36). We know further that the whole of his
public life was one of wandering, coming and going
through the mountain valleys of his homeland, journey-
ing from Galilee to Samaria and Judæa and even as far as
to the district of Tyre and Sidon (*Matt.* xv. 21). And he
made these journeys with the simplest provision for the
way, as he would also have his disciples do. " Take

nothing for your journey, neither staff, nor scrip, nor bread, nor money, neither have two coats " (*Luke* ix. 3). Hunger and thirst must therefore often have companied him. His last journey from Jericho up to Jerusalem is rightly pointed to as an astounding feat. Under a burning sun, along roads in which there was no shade of any kind, through a desolate rocky waste he had to mount some 3,500 feet in his six hours' climb. And the most astonishing thing is that Jesus was not tired. On the very same evening he took part in a feast which Lazarus and his sisters had made ready for him (*cf. John* xii. 2). By far the greater part of his public ministry was spent not in the comfort of a home, but in the open, exposed to all the rigours of the climate. Were not the spots where he was born and where he died apart from human habitation ? Between the manger of Bethlehem and the hill of Golgotha he spent a life more homeless and poor than that of the birds in their nests and the foxes in their holes. If he ever entered a house, it was one belonging to acquaintances or friends. For himself he had not where to lay his head (*cf. Matt.* viii. 20). There can be no doubt that Jesus must have spent the night in the open many hundreds of times and that it was not least this that made the birds of the air and the lilies of the field so familiar to him. Only an absolutely sound body could have been equal to such demands on it. Moreover, this wandering life was filled to over-flowing with labour and toil. Again and again Mark notes the fact that they had not time to eat (*cf. Mark* iii. 20 ; vi. 31). Till late in the evening the sick kept coming and going (*Mark* iii. 8). And with the sick there came malevolent enemies, the Pharisees and Sadduccees, and word wrestled with word, mind with mind, and racking disputes took place, leading to dangerous moments of tension and conflict. In addition there were the tiring explanations he had to make to his own disciples and the heavy burden which their want of understanding and their self-seeking laid upon him. Any sickly or even weak constitution must have given in or broken down under the strain. That Jesus never on any occasion gave in, not even in the most tense and dangerous situations, that, for instance, in the midst of a raging storm on the Lake of Gennesareth he went on peacefully sleeping until his disciples woke him, and that suddenly roused from his deep sleep he immediately grasped the situation and dealt with it, all this is proof how far his nature was from being excitable and temperamental, what complete control he had over his senses, how sound he was in body.

Was there also a sound mind in this sound body? This is a question which must be asked. In view of the extraordinary nature of his public activity and considering the unheard-of statements and claims which he made, it is quite intelligible that normal everyday people, wanting in the sense for the extraordinary and heroic, should have found in the appearance of Jesus a stumbling block and have over-hastily assumed that they were in the presence of something mentally abnormal. The first to slander him by saying "he is become mad" were his own relations (*Mark* iii. 21). And his adversaries among the Pharisees only put the same thing in their own way when they assumed that an evil spirit was working in him (*Matt.* xii. 24). This suggestion of an unclean and evil spirit has persisted through the centuries and has quite recently been eagerly taken up in order, in this simple and brutal way, to rid the world of the enigma of Jesus. For this reason, if for no other, it is necessary for us to get as clear a picture as possible of the purely human mental disposition of Jesus. It is only when we have adequately grasped the guiding lines, the main characteristics of his mentality, that we shall be able to give an answer to the question whether Jesus must be classed among the decadents or whether his mind possesses a high, indeed the highest, the incomparable, absolute, divine quality. How then did Jesus behave as a simple human being? What idea are we to have of his purely human mental disposition?

The evangelists give us unequivocal information on this point. What struck them most in his human nature and what they were always underlining was the tremendous clarity of his thought, the sure consciousness he had of his aim, and the resultant inflexibility and finality of his will. If one wished to attempt the impossible and to sum up his mentality in one phrase, he would have to set down this resolute virility and fixity of purpose with which Jesus sees his Father's will as his appointed task, and carries it through to the very end, even to the pouring out of his own blood. His very turn of phrase, with its ever-recurring " I am come," " I am not come," gives expression to the stern, determined Yea and Nay of his life and the inflexibility of his purpose. " I came not to send peace, but the sword " (*Matt*. x. 34) ; " I am not come to call the just, but sinners " (*Matt*. ix. 13) ; " The Son of Man is come to seek and to save that which was lost " (*Luke* xix. 10) ; " The Son of Man is not come to be ministered unto, but to minister, and to give his life a redemption for many " (*Matt*. xx. 28 = *Mark* x. 45) ; " Do not think I am come to destroy the law, or the prophets. I am not come to destroy, but to fulfil " (*Matt*. v. 17) ; " I am come to cast fire on the earth ; and what will I but that it be kindled ? " (*Luke* xii. 49). Jesus knows what he wills, and he knew it from the beginning. In the scene in the temple at Jerusalem, when he was but a twelve-year-old lad, he gave clear and plain expression to what his life's work was to be. " Did you not know that I must be about my Father's business ? " (*Luke* ii. 49). The three temptations in the desert are, psychologically regarded, a victorious settlement with the godless, satanic possibility of using his own messianic powers for his own self-glorification and selfish ends and not for the construction of the Kingdom of God. We can see here with the utmost clearness how plainly, at the very outset of his public ministry, Jesus sees the new way, and how resolutely he treads it, the way of self-surrender and of sacrifice for the heavenly Father's sake. In the days that followed it was not only his enemies who sought to divert him from it. On at least three occasions we can trace influences from within his own circle at work to force him to abandon the *via dolorosa* on which he had set out. At Capharnaum these are already vaguely in evidence in the secret opposition of his own kindred (*Mark* iii. 31 *sqq.*). They came to a head in Peter's determined protest at Cæsarea Philippi : " Lord, be it far from thee, this shall not be unto thee " (*Matt.* xvi. 22). And they led at last, when Jesus spoke of the eating of his flesh and the drinking of his blood (*John* vi. 57), to a mass-defection of his own followers. " After this many of his disciples went back ; and walked no more after him " (*John* vi. 67). But Jesus pursued his way, determined, if need be, to follow it alone and solitary. He has no reassuring words on this occasion for his disciples. He only puts to them the sharp, short question, " Will you also go away ? " (*John* vi. 68). Here we have Jesus, the man of clear will, whose every action reveals the fixity of his purpose. In the whole of his public ministry not one single instant can be found when he had to reflect on an answer, or when he hesitated in indecision, or when he reversed a statement or an action. And he demands the same inflexible and steadfast purpose of his disciples. " No man putting his hand to the plough, and turning back, is fit for the Kingdom of God " (*Luke* ix. 62) ; " Which of you having a mind to build a tower, doth not first sit down and reckon the charges that are necessary ? " (*Luke* xiv. 28) ; or what king minded to make war does not first make a muster of his troops " (*cf. Luke* xiv. 31). It is his own method quite personal to himself that he here enjoins on his disciples. Unconsidered, over-hasty action, vacillation, any coming to terms or compromising, these are not for him. His whole life and being are a Yea and Nay, nothing else. Jesus is always the complete man, always prepared, for he never speaks or acts except out of his whole clear consciousness and his own firm will. Hence he and he alone can venture the imperative " Let your speech be yea, yea : no, no : and that which is over and above these is evil " (*Matt.* v. 37). His whole nature and life are a unity, a completeness, a transparency, are fundamental clarity and truth. He bore so clearly the marks of the true, the upright, and the strong, that even his enemies could not escape this impression. " Master, we know that thou art a true speaker, and carest not for any man " (*Mark* xii. 14). Here, in the unity and purity and transparency of his interior life lies the psychological point whence started his life's struggle against the Pharisees, those " whited sepulchres," representative of the spurious, the finical, the purely exterior and the narrow in religion and life. From this point his way led directly to the Cross. It was, psychologically speaking, his tragic fate that he throughout remained true to himself, to that genuineness and loyalty to himself and his Father's will which was his nature.

Jesus is in every respect an heroic, epic figure, heroism incarnate. And it was this heroic spirit, this unconditional staking of their lives for the known truth, that he demanded also of his disciples. The heroic is to him a matter of course. To the rich young man who had observed all the commandments but one thing was wanting, that he should sell all he had and follow Jesus (*Mark* x. 21). The true disciple must be so valiant, so resolutely purposeful that he will not even take the time

to bury his own father. "Let the dead bury their dead"
(*Matt.* viii. 22 = *Luke* ix. 60). His concern must not
be for the dead but for the living. What makes a disciple
a disciple is that he "hate his father, and mother, and
children, and brethren, and sisters, yea and his own life
also "; that is to say, in the Aramaic figure of speech,
that he set all these aside in order to follow Jesus (*Luke*
xiv. 26 ; *cf. Matt.* xviii. 22 ; *Mark* x. 29).

This concentration and focussing of the will on his
goal, this initiative and energy, make Jesus the born
leader. He called Simon and Andrew, " and immediately
leaving their nets they followed him " (*Mark* i. 16 *sqq.*).
He called James and John "and leaving their father
Zebedee in the ship with his hired men, they followed
him " (*Mark* i. 20). He cast out them that bought and
sold in the temple and none ventured to resist him. His
is a masterful nature, a regal disposition.

The disciples felt this. Hence their diffident awe of
the Master, their strong sense of the gulf separating them
from him, which kept them at a distance. Again and
again the evangelists note how they wondered among
themselves at his words and actions, how these struck
terror into them (*Mark* ix. 5 ; vi. 51 ; iv. 40 ; x. 24, 26),
and how they did not dare speak to him (*Mark* ix. 3).
Mark describes the start of the last journey to Jerusalem
with the significant words : " And Jesus went before
them, and they were astonished, and following were
afraid " (*Mark* viii. 32).

This same timidity and awe also affected the multitude. " And they were afraid," " and all men wondered "

(*Mark* v. 15, 33, 42 ; ix. 14). He was not like one of them, neither was he like one of their own leaders, the scribes and Pharisees. He was one having authority. So strong was the impression of towering ascendancy in the figure of Jesus, that the people sought the loftiest images and names to find words to express it. Is he John the Baptist ? Is he Elias ? Is he Jeremias, or one of the prophets ? (*cf. Matt.* xvi. 14). Jesus was fully conscious of the essential difference between himself and all other men. We shall have to show later how dear to him their consciousness was, and how it gave motive and shape, ardour and strength to his whole life and to his death. Jesus knew that he was not as all the others were. Hence he loved solitude. So soon as he had spent himself in preaching to and healing the multitude, he withdrew into himself and betook himself to some lonely spot or on to some silent hill. Again and again this is noted by the evangelists. " And having dismissed the multitude, he went into a mountain alone to pray " (*Matt.* xiv. 23). We shall hear, too, that it was a solitude *in sinu patris*, that is to say, a solitude shared with the Father. But it was nevertheless a withdrawal from the multitude into himself, a silence of his concentrated forces, a silence whence as from some hidden well the living water gushed forth.

It was a psychological necessity that this tremendously concentrated and disciplined will, this pent-up spiritual power should discharge itself in stern language and bold action when powers of evil arrayed themselves against him. On such occasions Jesus could wax wroth and show his displeasure like any prophet of the Old Testament, an Osee or a Jeremias, or like Moses when he threw the tables of the law to the ground. This must be recognized, if we would get to know Jesus. In Jesus there dwelt not only mighty powers held in restraint and a disciplined will, but the fire of a holy zeal. We need only test his words and actions for their emotional content to verify this. " Begone, Satan," was how he frightened away the devil who came to tempt him (*Matt*. iv. 10). " Go behind me, Satan, thou art a scandal unto me," was how he rebuked Peter when the latter wished to break down his will to pursue the road which led to the Cross (*Matt*. xvi. 23). "I know you not whence you are : depart from me, you that work iniquity," is what he will profess to those who have neglected to do good to his suffering brethren on earth (*Luke* xiii. 27 ; *cf. Matt*. vii. 23). It is not quiet, peaceful reserve of spirit that we have here, but deep emotion and passion. Not a few of his parables breathe the same fiery spirit. In them the thunder rolls and the lightning flashes, as in the parable of the cockle : " The Son of Man shall send his angels, and they shall gather out of his kingdom all scandals, and them that work iniquity. And shall cast them into the furnace of fire. There shall be weeping and gnashing of teeth " (*Matt*. xiii. 41 *sq*.). Similarly, too, in the parable of the fisherman's net : " The Angels shall go out, and shall separate the wicked from among the just. And shall cast them into the furnace of fire : there shall be weeping and gnashing of teeth " (*Matt*. xiii. 49 *sq*.). The same angry sentence is also pronounced in the parables of the ten virgins, the talents, and the sheep and the goats (*Matt.* xxv. 1 *sqq.* ; 14 *sqq.* ; 33 *sqq.*). In the parable of the unmerciful servant the king " being angry delivered him to the torturers until he paid all the debt " (*Matt.* xviii. 34). Again, in the parable of the marriage of the king's son, the king " was angry, and sending his armies, he destroyed those murderers, and burnt their city " (*Matt.* xxii. 7). And when later on the king saw a man at the feast who had not on a wedding garment, he in unconcealed anger gave the order : " Bind his hands and feet, and cast him into the exterior darkness : there shall be weeping and gnashing of teeth " (*Matt.* xxii. 11–13). And in his similitude of the faithful and unfaithful stewards, the lord of the house returns unexpectedly and orders the latter to be " beaten with many stripes," and appoints him his portion with the unbelievers " (*Luke* xii. 46 *sq.*).

There can be no doubt but that the temperament which gave birth to these parables was charged full with emotion. Of sentimentality there is not a trace. As for the polemics against the scribes and Pharisees, against the ruling caste, against the teachers of Israel, and the judgments pronounced on them, they are downright feverish in their flaming indignation. " Wo to you scribes and Pharisees, hypocrites ; because you devour the houses of widows, praying long prayers. For this you shall receive the greater judgment. . . . You blind guides, who strain out a gnat and swallow a camel. . . . Wo to you scribes and Pharisees, hypocrites : because you make clean the outside of the cup and of the dish :

but within you are full of rapine and uncleanness"
(*Matt.* xxiii. 14, 24, 25). Here we can only picture
Jesus with flaming eyes and glowing cheeks. The same
temperamental vehemence and heat breaks out in not a
few of his actions, especially in the cleansing of the temple
shortly before his Passion, when "he cast out them that
sold and bought in the temple, and overthrew the tables
of the money-changers, and the chairs of them that sold
doves. And he suffered not that any man should carry
a vessel through the temple" (*Mark* xi. 15 *sq.*). And
it is also displayed in the malediction of the fig-tree
on which there was not yet fruit, "for it was not the
time for figs" (*Mark* xi. 13). In both these cases his
wrath took a form likely to alienate those who regarded
these events by themselves. The merchants in the court
of the temple thought that they were acting fully within
their rights; for they had, with the knowledge and
consent of the Jewish authorities, leased their trading
rights from Annas. Then again the fig-tree was quite
blameless in not having any fruit in early spring. Appealing to these two events, men have not shrunk from
talking of serious mental strain, of maniacal depression
pointing to an abnormal disposition. This can only be
said if the peculiarity of the Gospel traditions is ignored,
namely, the intention to display the life of Jesus only on
the basis and against the background of his prophetical
Messianic mission. A primary concern of the evangelists was the Messianic revelation of their Master, to
bring into relief everything in his life which might show
him to be the Lord of all the prophets and the Messias.

Now it was distinctive of the prophetic, and particularly of the Messianic method, to announce by apparent paradoxes, and by unintelligible acts, the new, unprecedented, revolutionary character of the Messianic message. The very paradox of his actions will necessarily call attention to the prophet and his revolutionary influence. Hence the evangelists have a special interest in the cleansing of the temple, and each of them gives an account of it (*Matt.* xxi. 12 *sq.*; *Mark* xi. 15 *sqq.*; *Luke* xix. 15 *sqq.*; *John* ii. 14 *sqq.*); and in telling the curse put upon the fig-tree Mark is careful to add the words, " for it was not the time for figs " (xi. 13). It is in the unusual that the Messias is manifest to them. In the seemingly unfair and inconsiderate casting out of the merchants from the temple, they see the solemn proclamation of the newly arisen Messianic worship of God in spirit and in truth, of the new Messianic temple and of the destruction of the old, a proclamation destructive of all merely earthly human ambitions. The apparently senseless curse put upon the fig-tree is to their minds, precisely because of its harsh unintelligibility, a prophetical symbol of the approaching sinister curse on Israel, that fig-tree which the Lord had himself planted, and which had remained unfruitful in good seasons as well as bad. Both events, therefore, mark the end of the Messianic work of Jesus and lead up to the catastrophe, to the downfall of the old covenant and to the death of the Messias. There is hardly another place in the Gospels where the Messianic background, against which the life of Jesus as related in them is enacted, is

more evident. Whosoever does not see this background can only misunderstand Jesus.

Certain as it is that Jesus here acts as the Messias is
expected to do and that he wishes to be judged as the
Messias, it is nevertheless equally true that he knows
himself to be the Messias of the wrath of God in the
sense of the prophets of the Old Testament, and therefore anything but a fair-weather Messias. The evangelists make other references to the " anger " of Christ, as
for instance when he showed his displeasure with his
disciples for wanting to hinder the little children from
coming to him (*Mark* x. 14), or in particular when the
Pharisees in the " blindness of their hearts " stood out
against any new and higher vision of truth and stub-
bornly held their peace (*Mark* iii. 5). It may well be
that his displeasure, rising from a wounded love of truth
and honesty, found relief in stern severe words, so that
Jesus spoke of hypocrites, serpents, and of a generation of vipers (*Matt.* xxiii. 33), and that he did not hesitate to call his own ruler, King Herod, a " fox " (*Luke*
xiii. 32). Jesus was not one to tread delicately, he was
no timid weakling when the need arose to bear witness
to the truth. His was a fighter's nature. But here, too,
in the midst of the fight, he always remains himself, he
never forgets himself, never loses control. His anger
is always an expression of supreme moral freedom, the
act of one having full knowledge, of one who could
say, " for this came I into the world, that I should give
testimony to the truth " (*John* xviii. 37). It is because
he was so consistently true to his Father's will, because

he was only "Yea and nay," that he reacted with unequalled severity against anything that was ungodly or hateful to God, whether this found expression in perverse theological formularies or in the decree of a ruler. And the story of his life proves that in harmony with his uncompromising words he was ready to stake his own life for the truth and to die for it. ∨

*   *   *   *   *

The purposeful virility, the absolute genuineness, the austere uprightness, in a word the heroic in the personality of Jesus, is the first thing in his human character to strike the eye of the psychologist. It was this, too, which first bound the disciples to him. The iron Yea and nay of his nature finds emphatic expression in his terse, compact sayings. They are with the parables the direct outpouring of a will bent on completeness, on consistency, on spiritual orderliness. They are instinct, as we rightly feel, with the very breath of genuine originality. "If thy eye scandalize thee, pluck it out" (*Matt.* xviii. 9) ; "He that shall lose his life for me, shall find it " (*Matt.* x. 39) ; "No man can serve two masters" (*Matt.* vi. 24).

From the heroic Yea and Nay of his nature it might seem as if Jesus ought to be considered as being of the thoroughgoing radical type, or at any rate should be classed with those dreamers living in a world of their own removed from the actualities of life, to whom the drab, work-a-day life around them is swallowed up in the glow of their obsessing ideal, or at most but casts a shadow on the borderland of their consciousness. Is this really the case? In what relation does Jesus, that lonely, supremely heroic figure, stand to the men and affairs of his time, to the emergencies and demands of the moment, to the here and now? The answer to this question will open up a new vista into the breadths and depths of his human nature, and we shall become aware that we cannot compare the humanity of Jesus with ordinary humanity, that it would be vain effort to try to class him under any given type, that in him we have an absolutely unique human figure, which can only be explained by itself, never by any historical analogue.

We shall inquire, therefore, into his sense of the actualities of existence, into the measure of his approach to the life around him. What attitude did Jesus take towards the men and affairs of this earth? Were his thoughts and purpose those of a dreamer or enthusiast, or perhaps of an ecstatic?

To deal with this last point first : Jesus was no ecstatic like Muhammad or even like Paul. Muhammad spent a great part of his life in a state of somnambulism. Paul describes with joyful pride his transports when he was " rapt even to the third heaven . . . and heard secret words, which it is not granted man to utter " (*II. Cor.* xi. 2, 4). We hear nothing of this kind about Jesus. High as the primitive Christian community rated the ecstatic gifts, the visions, the speaking with tongues, and the prophesyings—and Paul most strictly forbids any attempt to extinguish the overflowing of the spirit

(*I. Thess.* v. 19)—and clearly as they recognized in these
" the showing of the spirit and power " (*I. Cor.* ii. 4),
they never ascribe this extraordinary exaltation to Jesus,
a decisive proof that ecstatic vision and prayer and
speech had as a matter of fact no place in his life, a
proof also of the further fact that it was entirely foreign
to the mind of the early Christians to foist their own
ideals on Jesus and to paint his picture in their own
colours.   True there was one hour in his life when his
figure stood out from all terrestrial mists and shadows,
when his garment shone white " as no fuller on earth can
make white " (*Matt.* ix. 2), and when the enraptured
eyes of the disciples saw Elias and Moses " talking with
Jesus " ; but what occurred on this occasion was not an
interior rapture, a transporting of the spirit of Jesus, a
true ecstasy, but a superterrestrial transfiguration of his
outward appearance.   It was an anticipation of the
miracle of the Resurrection, sent by God to support the
disciples through the grievous hours of Christ's Passion
which was so imminent.   It was a revelation not in the
subjective but in the objective sense.   Of what went on
within the consciousness of Jesus we learn nothing.   If
we must speak of an ecstasy, it is not to Jesus that the
term may be applied but to the disciples, and especially to
Peter, who was moved by this sudden revelation of the
divine in Jesus to utter the ecstatic words, " Rabbi, it is
good for us to be here, and let us make three taber-
nacles " ; " for he knew not what he said, for they were
struck with fear " (*Mark* ix. 4, 5).

If we take ecstasy in its original strict sense as a con-

dition of the soul in which not indeed consciousness, but
all the activity of the senses is eliminated, so that we
might speak of a condition of depersonalization, in which
the soul is in a state of suspense and passive submission,
where, however, in reality there is the most alert consciousness and the strongest possible concentration of
the affective faculties on the divine, and the soul is so
overmastered by the divine communication, that it
beholds, experiences and touches it in a pure immediacy ;
if we take ecstasy in this strict sense which excludes all
sensible activity, then Jesus was assuredly not an ecstatic.
The Gospels tell us of no single moment in the life of
Jesus when this man of driving activity renounced this
activity and in a purely passive rapture became one with
God.

Hence it certainly does not do to talk of ecstasies of
vision or audition in the life of Jesus. It is true that he
saw and heard things which are hidden to the ordinary
man. At his baptism in the Jordan " he saw the heavens
opened " and heard a voice from heaven saying, " Thou
art my beloved Son, in thee I am well pleased " (*Mark* i.
11 = *Matt.* iv. 17 = *Luke* iii. 22). In the desert he
settled matters with the devil who came to tempt him,
and immediately afterwards " angels came and ministered
to him." Shortly before his Passion a voice from heaven
again promised him imminent glorification (*John* xii.
28), and on Mount Olivet an angel strengthened him in
his agony (*Luke* xxii. 43). Supernatural phenomena are
certainly to be seen in the life of Jesus. Angels and devils
come and go ; sensible celestial influences intervene,

and these are as directly accessible to his perception as the things of the visible world are to us.

What is to be thought of these phenomena? The Gospels do not offer the slightest support to those who would give a purely psychological explanation of them based, shall we say, on the supposition of a state of excessive emotional excitement, with a concomitant splitting of the ego. It is precisely when they appear that Jesus least gives us the impression of being a man inwardly rent by severe spiritual conflict with himself. It is on such occasions that he is most entirely absorbed in himself, his task, and vitally set upon its fulfilment. The finality and perfect unity of his will is especially evident on the banks of the Jordan when, after his baptism by John, "coming up out of the water, he saw the heavens opened." He is here the complete man, prepared at all points, who with all his senses alert sets about the great work in front of him. Again, his dealings with the tempter in the desert do not betray any hesitation and uncertainty, there is no vacillation between opposing possibilities, but an immediate, clear, strong, determined ἄπαγε σατανᾶ, "Begone, Satan!" And if on the Mount of Olives the fear of death overtook him and "his sweat became as drops of blood trickling down upon the ground" (*Luke* xxii. 44), his moral will in this grievous hour was notwithstanding firmly anchored to the will of the Father. "Not as I will but as thou wilt" (*Matt.* xxvi. 39). It is no sickly, brokendown mind, but a healthy, vigorous, heroic spirit which is manifested in these strange meetings with angels and devils. These phenomena in the life of Jesus differ consequently from all the ordinary visions and auditions with which the psychiatrist has to do, just as Jesus himself with his will of steel and fully conscious personality differs from every broken, mentally afflicted human being.

There is a further important observation to be made here. In the Gospel narratives these singular occurrences do not appear as in any way fortuitous, exterior events, as baroque volutes stuck about his image, but stand in the most intimate organic connection with all that was extraordinary and singular in his person. They have their necessary place in the totality of his exceptional appearance. They are seen, namely, at the turning points and climaxes of his ministry : when this begins with his baptism at John's hands ; when at the temptation in the desert he of set purpose ranges himself against everything which is hostile to God ; and lastly at the beginning of his Passion when his ministry is reaching out to its climax. They are therefore organically bound up with the marvellous and supernatural course of his life. Where such a miraculous Christ exists it cannot be astonishing, indeed it is *a priori* to be expected, that there should be visitations of angels and devils in his life. Our attitude towards these phenomena is therefore in the last resort determined by our view of the miracle constituted by the very life of Jesus, and it is only in the light of that miracle that the phenomena can be properly viewed. The extraordinary in a phenomenon is in no way a justification for summarily refusing it any objective reality in the name of so-called tried experience, nor does it justify the attempt forcibly to explain it away as the result of mental disorder. On account of the numberless possibilities of error exact research, precisely for the sake of exactness, has every reason to abstain from a summary rejection on any matter in the realm of the occult. It is under obligation to investigate each separate case with the greatest possible care. It is a serious error, a sign of a naïve rationalism not yet outgrown, to wish to force the vast realm of reality with its tremendous deep-lying strata within the scope of preconceived categories of perception and thought. The real will always be richer and deeper and more comprehensive than can be contained by all the network of strands with which philosophers seek to fetter it, so as to bring order into the chaos. In supernormal psychology we are to-day facing phenomena to which our traditional methods of thought give us no clue. The reality of everyday experience is not the whole of reality, and this is especially true of the reality of religious experience. Wherever there has been a living religion, that is to say, wherever living people have existed, there has always been the question of super-sensible phenomena, of the impressions of some unearthly supernatural existence. In such cases a reality appears which cannot be determined and understood by the ordinary standards of earthly experience. Here the *homo religiosus* is alone entitled to be heard. So, too, the extraordinary events in the life of Jesus can only be properly explained by a consideration of this *homo religiosus* in his totality. In view of this we must hark back to the historic figure of Jesus.

We will again take up our question as to the attitude of Jesus towards the men and affairs of his day. His virility, his purposeful and determined pursuit of his goal, are characteristics which will not allow us to class him among the dreamers and enthusiasts. They presuppose rather a markedly rational disposition. Intuitively artistic as is his vision in its comprehension of a reality as a whole with its ultimate and profoundest meaning, his thought is severely rational and soberly logical when he is engaged on the determination of causal connections and relations, on the establishment and safeguarding of individual truths. Often as his opponents try to catch him in argument, they have always to retire discomfited, since they can find no reply to the deductions contained in their own premisses, which his keen understanding and penetrating vision enable him to expose. For example, he is able out of their own mouth to convict the Sadducees, who denied the resurrection of the body, by appealing to their own conception of God. If they confess God as the God of Abraham, Isaac, and Jacob, this confession can only have any sense if Abraham, Isaac, and Jacob are still living; for "he is not the God of the dead but of the living" (*Matt.* xii. 27). Similarly, against the Pharisees he used their own interpretation of the verse in the *Psalms* (cix. 1), "The Lord said to my Lord," in order to prove the supernatural origin of the Messianic Son of

David by the fact that David here calls his own descendant Lord. "If then David call him Lord, how is he his son?" (*Matt.* xxii. 45). And as Jesus on this occasion uses the clear, acute logic of his thought in the regular framework of a Rabbinical demonstration, so too in general he adapts it to the circumstances of the moment and the questions arising from them, so that almost invariably his solution had the effect of a dazzling *demonstratio ad oculos*, which reduced his opponent to silence. When the Pharisees were scandalized by his healing of the sick on the Sabbath-day, he reduced the whole problem, which to Pharisaic thought was simply impossible to unravel, to the simple question : "Is it lawful to do good on the Sabbath-day, or to do evil?" (*Mark* iii. 4). "Which of you shall have an ass or an ox fall into a pit; and will not immediately draw him out on the Sabbath-day?" (*Luke* xiv. 5). Indeed, it may be said that his whole fight against the Pharisaic passion for the strict letter of the law was a struggle of clear, simple, straightforward, logical thought against the obscurations and senseless subtleties of casuistical dialectic and against an incredibly narrow and ossified interpretation of the Scriptures. All the maxims he employed against Pharisaism had as their object the reduction of ethico-religious demands to their essentials and concentration on the latter. It is with a ruthless hand that Jesus strips the veneer laid by human hands on holy things, all "doctrines and commandments of men" (*Matt.* xv. 9 = *Mark* vii. 7), all "tradition of the ancients," as he puts it (*Matt.* xv. 2 = *Mark* vii. 3, 5), in order to clear the view into the very heart of holiness and morality. "Wo to you scribes and Pharisees, hypocrites: because you tithe mint, and anise, and cummin, and have left the weightier things of the law, judgment and mercy and faith" (*Matt.* xxiii. 22). In freeing holiness from all human trimmings and encumbrances he brings to light its profoundest depths, and shows how he can seize the whole man and lay bare his most secret thoughts and his most hidden impulses. "You have heard that it was said to them of old: Thou shalt not commit adultery. But I say to you, that whosoever shall look on a woman to lust after her, hath already committed adultery with her in his heart" (*Matt.* v. 27 *sq.*). "You have heard that it was said to them of old: Thou shalt not kill. . . . But I say to you, that whosoever is angry with his brother, shall be in danger of the judgment" (*Matt.* v. 21 *sq.*). The eye of Jesus cannot rest on the surface of human action; it sees and follows up all action to its roots, to the point whence it emerges from the heart. "From within out of the heart of man proceed evil thoughts" (*Mark* vii. 21). Hence his determined fight against the superficial juristic formalism with which the Pharisees understood and expounded the decalogue; hence his passionate plea for "more abounding justice" (*cf. Mark* v. 20), which far from tolerating any laxity would not have anyone "break one of the least of these commandments" (*Matt.* v. 19), but which at the same time will have every commandment seen and fulfilled from within as a demand of the heart. The man who in his actions follows his native uncontaminated conscience, the man of moral personality in other words, is the man whom Jesus wants to see, and not the man of external laws and precepts, the mere legalist, the " whited sepulchre," as Jesus calls him. If we consider the tremendous paralysing weight which a centuries-old tradition, " the tradition of the ancients," had laid on the conscience, warping its simple, unadulterated sense for the moral and the holy, so that men could no longer think of them but as ritual legal formularies mingled with a confused mass of secular ideas, we shall see very plainly how uniquely sound and clear and penetrating, how independent and free the mind of Jesus must have been to rise superior to all these prejudices which were become the set rule of life of his people, and to lead humanity back to its real self, to its innate, healthy, moral perception, to the simplicity of a child. This return to the child-like which characterizes Jesus' teaching, the decision with which he holds up the child to his disciples as the measure and model of all discipleship (*Mark* ix. 35 *sq.*; x. 13 *sqq.*), is born of a mind which forces its way through and beyond all the veneer of culture, through all the knotted skeins of a tangled theology, to true first principles, a mind which is ever actual, and to which all excess, all that is fantastic and extravagant is as alien as it is possible to be.

This eye for the substance and core of a thing presupposes in Jesus the gift of acute observation, an unusual faculty for clear seeing. Heroically, epically as his mind is devoted to the sublimest remotest ends, he yet gives his attention dispassionately and without reserve to the quite small things in life. We have only to call to mind his parables to see this. With a few quick strokes he describes so graphically and with such life and warmth the doings of the peasants, the fisherfolk, the vintagers, the pearl merchant, the tenant farmer, the trader, the day-labourer, the builder, the gardener, the woman of the house, the lonely widow, and on up the scale to the judge, the military officer, and the king; and so picturesque and variegated are the descriptions of the work-a-day world, the child playing noisily in the street, the broad phylacteries of the scribes with their long fringes, the wedding procession in the cool of the night, the gay meal, the strict etiquette of the ceremonial board, the poor beggar on the roadside, the workless standing at street corners and by the hedgerows because no one has hired them, the humble publican " standing afar off " in the temple, the poor woman in her chamber who lit a candle to seek a groat she had lost, the happy woman who, seeing her new-born babe, remembered no more the anguish she had undergone, the rich peasant who went to sleep hugging himself because his barns were full;—so picturesquely and concretely does the everyday life of his time down to the last details stand out in the parables, that from them alone it would not be difficult to construct a faithful picture of the homely middle-class world of his day. How close Jesus' thought was to the life around him and how direct was his response to it, is shown among other things by the clearness with which his own calling as builder and carpenter may be recognized, as for instance when he speaks of the beam and the mote in the eye or of the corner-stone which the builders rejected, or of the house built upon a good solid foundation which no wind or rain or flood could endanger, or again of the charges which must be reckoned if one were minded to build a tower.

The same sense of reality and the same close approach to life dominate Jesus' attitude towards the current social, economic and political conditions. He sees them and accepts them as they are, not as they could be or as he would have them. It never enters his thought violently to destroy the channels in which the life of his people ran its course. To the tempter in the desert who would suggest to him a political revolution, the erection of a worldly empire, over which as the Messias he should reign in magnificence and glory, he flung his " Begone, Satan." And on another occasion his injunction is, " Render unto Cæsar the things that are Cæsar's " (*Mark* xii. 17) ; and when Peter wished to offer resistance to those who came to seize Jesus, the rebuke comes instantly, " Put up again thy sword into its place." On principle he refused to intervene in matters of law. " Man, who hath appointed me judge or divider over you ? " (*Luke* xii. 14). Indeed, even in the sphere which most truly was his own, in that of religious worship, he acquiesced in the old Mosaic dispositions and regula- tions : the temple, the services in the synagogue, fasting, circumcision, and the rest. Did he not himself wear the fringes on his garment prescribed by the law (*Num.* xv. 38 ; *Matt.* xiv. 36 = *Mark* vi. 56), and pay

his temple tax (*Matt.* xvii. 26)? He is indeed well
aware that "no man seweth a piece of raw cloth to an
old garment" or "putteth new wine into old bottles"
(*Mark* ii. 21, 22). He knows that the new man whom he
is going to bring into being, that "the new testament in
his blood," will and must create for itself a special kind
of corporate body. Hence it is that he speaks of the
Church which at a future time he will build upon the
rock of Peter (*Matt.* xvi. 18). But it is significant that he
only promises this Church for the future, that he does
not found it in due formality in the present. The new
men, his "brethren" (*Matt.* xii. 50 = *Mark* iii. 35), his
"household" (*cf. Matt.* x. 25), his "children of the
marriage" (*cf. Mark* ii. 19), and table companions (*cf.*
Luke xxii. 30) must first be chosen and prepared, the
mighty wind of Pentecost must first have swept over their
souls and kindled them, for only then will the new community be able to live. It is not from without but from
within, from the new living members, that the new body,
the new community, the Church, must come into being
and grow. Jesus Christ is much too objective, much
too closely in touch with the realities to expect salvation
to lie in empty ideologies packed with new regulations
and dispositions. These are to him not the primary
consideration, but only secondary. When the wine is
new, new skins are needed, and only then. Nothing
was farther from his thoughts than a rigid, lifeless form
of public worship laden with regulations. Not new
forms, but the living man alone, is the supreme goal at
which his teaching aims.

The living man. With this we come to speak of the relation of Jesus to men, of the particular way he regarded them and judged them, and of his attitude towards them.

There can be no worse misunderstanding of Jesus than to detach his immortal Gospel of love, the sublimest and tenderest message that was ever uttered by human lips, above all his exhortation, " Love your enemies, do good to them that hate you," from the total context of his mind and outlook, and to judge it thus detached as heroic indeed, but, nevertheless, as high-flown and extravagant, the impossible demand of his benevolent heart, the message of a man than whom, as Nietzsche once expressed it, " no man had ever flown higher or gone astray in a more lovely manner."

This Gospel of love, indeed it above all, has also its place in his sense of reality and in his closeness to life, and it is only in this context that it can be properly understood and explained. His charity is anything but a dreamy, transfiguring, idealizing love. It is no mere humanitarian cult. Jesus, in fact, sees humanity in all its weakness and wickedness. It is to him " a wicked and adulterous generation " (*Matt.* xvi. 4). Those " Galileans whose blood Pilate had mingled with their sacrifices," those " eighteen upon whom the tower fell in Silom and slew them," were not " debtors above all the men that dwelt in Jerusalem " (*Luke* xiii. 1, 4). Thus he sees all Jerusalem in bondage to sin. Even in the case of his disciples, where some self-deception would have been very easily intelligible, nothing that was warped or

perverse in their natures ever escaped him, so that it
was at times difficult for him to bear with them (*Matt.*
ix. 18; viii. 17; vii. 18). Even in the most trusted of
his disciples, in Peter, he discovers wickedness and
indeed devilishness (*Matt.* xvi. 23). Seldom as he
speaks explicitly of original sin, in the way for instance
St. Paul does, he nevertheless sees the all-too-human, the
infra-human at work in mankind, and it is as a matter of
course that he pronounces all his hearers " evil " (*Matt.*
vii. 11). Even for the weaknesses of children, whom he
loved so dearly, their capricious, wilful, playfully superficial ways, he has a very clear eye (*Matt.* xi. 16). For
him the entire immaturity of his time is mirrored in
their childish natures. Hence the very first word he has
to say to mankind is, " Do penance " (*Matt.* iv. 17).
It cannot be passed over in silence that in the love which
Jesus had for mankind there was a certain reserve, in
fact at times something like an element of vexation and
disgust. Jesus suffered from people. His love bears
secret wounds. It is an understanding love.

But precisely because it is an understanding love it
penetrates not only to the dark depths of the human
heart, but beyond them to every corner of it. It knows
all about human limitations and frailty. Therefore it will
not judge. " Judge not, that you may not be judged "
(*Matt.* vii. 1). " Why seest thou the mote that is in thy
brother's eye; and seest not the beam that is in thy own
eye ? " (*Matt.* vii. 3 = *Luke* vi. 41). He rebukes his
disciples for wanting to call down fire on the unbelieving
cities (*Luke* ix 55). The cockle in the wheatfield must

not be pulled up prematurely and without discretion (*Matt.* xiii. 29). When the day of the harvest shall come God himself will do it through his angels. When the scribes and Pharisees brought to Jesus the woman taken in adultery and demanded a judgment of him, he bowed down and wrote with his finger on the ground. And when they plied him with questions, he answered : "He that is without sin among you, let him first cast a stone at her" (*John* viii. 7). It is a saying saturated with knowledge of human nature, with contact with life, and with complete objectivity. And it is not merely one of his sayings, it is of his essence. He himself is this word. When the soldiers spit upon him and buffet him and set a crown of thorns on his head, he is silent. There is nothing more eloquent than this silence. The eye of Jesus sees through the veil of illusion, through the dense veil of human passions, right through to the poverty and nakedness of man as he really is, man in his incompleteness, in his dependence on a thousand bodily, spiritual, and social influences, man in his pupilage and immaturity. And therefore Jesus will not judge, even though they torment and abuse him. This is why he will only forgive, forgive again and again, not, as he says to Peter, "till seven times, but till seventy times seven times" (*Matt.* xviii. 22).

Again, it is in this objective insight into the psychological conditions affecting all human actions and not in a morbid, overwrought mental state that this love of Jesus for his enemies is rooted. When he says, "If one

strike thee on the right cheek, turn to him also the other "
(*Matt.* v. 39 = *Luke* vi. 29), there lies behind this
abrupt, extreme utterance a deep insight into the irrational, animal element in every blind expression of
emotion. An emotion which does violence to love has
its origin in the depths of animal nature, in the gloomy
caverns where the dogs bay, not in the lightsome realm
of the objective reason, which, through all the wild
phantasmata of the senses, through all the ravings of the
passions, recognizes and loves and treasures what lies
beyond all this, the primal God-implanted inter-relation-
ship of man to man. The complete man, the strong, upright man is he who sacrifices the animal in him for the
sake of the heights to which humanity may aspire. Never
was Christ greater, more objective, grander, more heroic
than at that moment of his Passion when, hanging on the
Cross, he breathed the prayer, " Father, forgive them ;
for they know not what they do " (*Luke* xxiii. 34).

Since Jesus' love for mankind was in the highest
degree objective, it is like neither the love of the visionary
who deifies the purely human, nor that of the fanatic who
regards the purely human as of the devil. It is the love
of one who understands, of a person who knows, as none
other ever has, all the possibilities of humanity from
its loftiest heights to its lowest depths, and nevertheless takes this humanity to his arms with all his soul.
This " nevertheless " made his charity so incomparable,
so unique, so maternal in its tenderness and self-sacrifice,
that it has ever remained graven in the memory of
mankind.

It is a most delightful task to consider in detail this love of mankind as bearing on the spiritual figure of Jesus. This love of his is basically sym-pathy in its original sense, a sharing of the sufferings of men. What differentiates his love from the humanitarianism of sages and philosophers is that it is not mere theory, but a living- and more a suffering and a dying with men. It does not merely regard a man's distress and ponder how it may be relieved. It enters into his distress. It cannot bear merely to know of the trouble but must take it personally on itself. This love bursts the barriers of the heart of Jesus that all men may find shelter in it, or better, that he may pour himself into them, to live and suffer with them to the utmost. Those whom he would thus shelter are above all the poorest of the poor, the publicans and sinners. This is why he so often stayed with them. He not only calls them to him but he gets them to invite him to their houses. This is the bigger thing. " Zacheus, make haste and come down : for this day I must abide in thy house " (*Luke* xix. 5). It is the least among men, the disinherited, those whose lives have suffered shipwreck, whom he calls his " brethren." And so intimately, so personally does he identify their lot with himself, that whatever was done to one of the least of his brethren was done to him (*cf. Matt.* xxv. 40). Blessing the bread and the wine, and uttering the words of mysterious power, " Take ye and eat : This is my body. . . . Drink ye all of this. . . . This is my blood," he expresses his sense of solidarity and brotherhood, his burning desire to take up the whole multitude of mankind with its troubles and its sins into his own pure being, into his own life and death, and therein to sanctify them. With the poor he will be poor, with the outlawed an outlaw, with the tempted tempted, with the dying crucified. He will bear all our infirmities and carry all our sorrows, for he alone can overcome them. Psychologically regarded, this is the point where the redemptive activity of Jesus has its natural roots, where his love of mankind flames up as redemptive love. Here we touch upon the mystery of the Messias. The solidarity, or better the creative motherliness of his love, which takes upon itself all the griefs of humanity and bears them right up to the bitter end, is a thing so new, so unique in the history of mankind, is to all of us so overwhelming, so moving, that we can only say that here if anywhere is man's home, the sanctuary where he may find rest for his soul. If he is to be found anywhere it is in Jesus that the Redeemer must appear.

It was this spirit of pure, self-forgetting, creative love which drove Jesus, that great lonely figure, the man of heroic independence, from the sunlit heights of his luminous thoughts and aims, down into the drab and dingy, all-too-human work-a-day life of mankind. Again and again the evangelists tell us that he "had compassion on the multitude" (*Mark* viii. 2; *Matt.* ix. 36; xiv. 14; xv. 32; *Luke* vii. 13). "He had compassion on them, because they were as sheep not having a shepherd" (*Mark* vi. 34). It is an unheard-of thing that a man whose whole powers are enlisted in the service of one sublime idea, who with all the passion of his ardent will is aspiring above the earth and away from men towards an utterly superhuman, supernatural goal, that such a man should yet take little children in his arms and fondle them and bless them ; that tears should come to his eyes when he looks down upon the doomed city of Jerusalem, or when he stands before the tomb of his friend Lazarus.   And in the wide range of life's realities there was one to which especially his heart went out, when he became as gentle and tender as any mother watching over her sick babe, when there flowed from his lips the tenderest words, the most touching parables, such as those of the prodigal son, the Samaritan or the lost groat.   This reality was the sick and the sinners.   He cannot say no when misery knocks at the door of his heart, not even in the case of a Syrophenician pagan woman (*Mark* vii. 26 *sqq.*).   He cannot help healing the sick, even though he come under suspicion of breaking the Sabbath thereby (*Mark* i. 23 ; iii. 2 ; *Luke* xiii. 14).   He associates with publicans and sinners, even though he thus horrifies the pious and the righteous (*Mark* ii. 26).   He has to say to the repentant thief, though his dying lips can scarce stammer the words : " This day shalt thou be with me in paradise " (*Luke* xxiii. 43).

In view of this we may actually say that the love of Jesus for mankind is in its deepest element love for the suffering and the oppressed.   To him the " neighbour " is he who lies wounded and distressed before him (*cf. Luke* x. 29 *sqq.*).   Here again the close approach to the realities of life of his thought, his will, his feelings is shown. Dedicate as his spirit was to the other-worldly, to the divine, and to the approaching Kingdom of God (we shall have to dwell upon this point later), the need of the moment was never obscured or crowded out by this vision of that kingdom and its joys. He *lives* all the bitterness and wrong which he sees in the life around him so directly, that their redress is an essential element in his evangel. It is from this element that his teaching gets its glowing colours and its joyful light, promising, as it does, redemption not only to sinners but also to the oppressed, to the whole compass of earthly distress. It brings deliverance from all evil. A great part of his life's work consisted in the doing of good, in the healing of the sick, and this without stint. Luke above all the other evangelists has emphasized this profound inspiration in the Gospel of Jesus when, in the beatitudes of the Sermon on the Mount, he brings into special relief the promise of deliverance from earthly sufferings. " Blessed are ye poor : for yours is the kingdom of God. Blessed are ye that hunger now : for you shall be filled. Blessed are ye that weep now : for you shall laugh " (*Luke* vi. 20 *sq.*). It were idle to ignore the proletarian note in these beatitudes and to force an exclusively ethical interpretation on them.

And yet it would be entirely wrong to conclude from them that Jesus was a social reformer in the modern sense. Here as elsewhere he sees too deeply into things to look for salvation in an exterior reorganization of society. In particular no panacea for poverty is to be found in his gospel. "The poor you have always with you" (*John* xii. 8). Salvation, deliverance from all evil, is consummated not in the present but only in the future. It is eschatological. Hence there is no question of ever banishing poverty and suffering from this world. On the contrary : in so far as earthly troubles detach the human heart from earthly lusts and open it to the future glories of the Kingdom of God, in so far, that is, as they awaken or deepen a craving for redemption, they are the right means to the Kingdom of God. Hence, properly speaking, Jesus loves the poor not simply because they are poor but because spiritually they are more capable than the rich of hearkening to the message of the coming kingdom, of hungering and thirsting after justice. Even though they have once been "publicans and harlots" (*cf. Matt.* 28 *sq.*), they are like unto that son of the house to whom his father said, "Son, go work to-day in my vineyard. And he answering, said : I will not. But afterwards, being moved with repentance, he went" (*Matt.* xxi. 28 *sq.*). Contrariwise there is the danger that riches may so satiate the human heart that it will no longer crave for heavenly possessions. "Children, how hard is it for those that trust in riches, to enter into the kingdom of God ! It is easier for a camel to pass through the eye of a needle, than for a rich man to enter into the kingdom of God" (*Mark* x. 24). Jesus here enunciates a fundamental principle. He wants to make it unequivocally clear that poverty by its very nature makes a man incomparably more receptive to the Gospel message than wealth. This judgment will have its application at all times and in all places. But it is equally true that there will always be both rich and poor everywhere, whose actual behaviour will diverge from this. Jesus knows this perfectly well. His fundamental attitude towards the subject is not meant to be a practical judgment on individuals, whether rich or poor. His charity knows no exceptions, nor has it the slightest suggestion of class war. His love embraces the rich. We know of his association with Simon the Pharisee (*Luke* vii. 36 *sqq.*) and with Nicodemus who was of the ruling caste. Joseph of Arimathea, a wealthy man, is explicitly numbered among his disciples (*Matt.* xxvii. 57). On his journeyings he was accompanied by " Joanna the wife of Chusa Herod's steward, and Susanna, and many others, who ministered unto him of their substance " (*Luke* viii. 3). So far as we can see, his apostles, too, came not from the lowest strata of society but, like Jesus himself, from the middle classes. He does not object therefore to rich men as such : but he sees wealth as making difficult the approach to the Kingdom of God. In the majority of the Pharisees and Sadducees, those typical representatives of the property-owning ruling classes of his country, Jesus met with the devastating consequences of the service of Mammon in a terrible form. What separated them from him and from the Kingdom of God was their hard self-seeking and arrogance, which put even their most prized possession, the birthright of the Israelite to be numbered among the people of the Covenant and of the seed of Abraham, in the service of their nationalistic egoism and fanaticism, and which, by a thousand man-made regulations and prohibitions, made religion so exterior a thing and so difficult to follow (*cf. Matt.* xxiii. 4 *sqq.*), that it had become a matter for the rich alone, and all the small fry and the poor, who lacked the money and the time to fulfil all the obligations laid upon them, were summarily discredited as notorious sinners.

Born of wealth and nourishing itself on wealth the religious attitude of the average Pharisee could not be other than that so graphically described by Jesus in his parable of the Pharisee in the temple, bursting with self-satisfaction and scornful of the humble publican standing afar off (*Luke* xviii. 10 *sqq.*). The average Pharisee had no hunger and thirst for justice : he was satisfied. Therefore the fight which Jesus waged against the Pharisees took the form of a fight against riches. " No man can serve two masters . . . you cannot serve God and Mammon " (*Matt.* vi. 24; *Luke* xvi. 13). Hence the apparently " proletarian " colouring in some of his similitudes. This colouring is not a special property of Luke the evangelist, nor does it derive from any sociological ideals. It is a moving expression of the deep love of mankind felt by Jesus, which did not let itself be dazzled by any consideration of class or rank, which was no respecter of persons, and which sought out and found living men just where inherited religious or social prejudices could see nothing but degeneracy and depravity. Whenever we think of the love of Jesus, there will ever come to our minds the story of the prodigal son and how his father ran up to him and fell upon his neck and kissed him (*Luke* xv. 20). Nor can we ever forget the picture of the poor beggar Lazarus, who "was carried by the angels into Abraham's bosom," while the rich man had to suffer torment in hell (*Luke* xvi. 19 *sqq.*). And whether we be rich or poor we shall always remember the great supper, to which the rich did not want to come, and to which the poor and the feeble, the blind and the lame had to be brought in, while at the end even the "highways and hedges" had to be scoured to fill the room (*Luke* xiv. 21, 23).

On the other hand, it is certainly not the case that our Lord's preference for the poor and needy had its source only in the purely rational consideration that they were spiritually more receptive to the Gospel. This preference is something innate in him, a fundamental sentiment, welling up out of that strong impulse of sympathy with the suffering, which cannot bear to have plenty when others are going hungry, or to rejoice while others mourn. And this is why it was his will to have no place to lay his head; this is why he made the same demand of all who would join the band of his disciples. "Go, sell whatsoever thou hast, and give to the poor" (*Mark* x. 21). The love of Jesus for those in distress is not simply a demand of his reason, it is a most intimate need of the very depths of his being. "Be ye therefore merciful, as your heavenly Father also is merciful" (*Luke* vi. 36). Here we have the real Jesus.

If we consider this love from its psychological side,

we again find a heroism such as till then had never been seen on earth. It is, however, not a heroism in the vertical plane but in the horizontal. It is the heroic throwing open of the heart to living men, the tenderest self-dedication to their souls and destinies. How far Jesus is removed from the type of the fanatical zealot, or the visionary prophet, or the mystic who shuts himself off from all the vanities of the world. Their interest is absorbed in and swallowed up by their personal idols. These have sympathy with men only in so far as they share the same dreams. The heart of Jesus belongs to mankind, to every man, to the whole man, to his sorrows—and his joys.

That Jesus did not close his heart to the joys of mankind, that he was not like the Baptist a man of the desert, clothed in a garment of camel's hair, whose meat was locusts and wild honey ; that he went among people in everyday garb, a " coat without seam " (*John* xix. 23) adorned with hems (*Matt.* xiv. 35) ; that he took part quite naturally in their festivities and merrymakings so that his enemies taunted him with being a " glutton and a wine-drinker " (*Matt.* xi. 19) ; that he did not hesitate to work his first miracle to please the guests at a marriage feast ; that he would not have his disciples fast so long as the bridegroom was with them (*Matt.* ii. 19) ; that he held one of his followers very dear and let him lean on his bosom (*John* xiii. 23) ; and lastly that the whole of this exuberant vitality was set in a frame so full of charm and grace and loveliness, that in it alone we cannot fail to recognize a great, a supremely great poet, who with a unique creative touch makes the whole of Nature live for us—the fig-trees and the lilies, the mustard-trees and the vines, the sparrow and the fox, the glad sunshine and the wild tempest; all this betrays such a generosity, openness of heart, breath and responsiveness and tenderness and delicacy of spirit as has no counterpart in any heroic or strictly ascetical nature.

Who is this Jesus? Does not his human nature seem to tend in opposite directions, upward to the heavenly, downward to man and his world. Is his spirituality bi-polar, oscillating not about one but about two foci? Was he internally in a state of unstable equilibrium, of continual restless tension and motion? We see clear lines of his being leading in a definite direction. They take this direction so naturally, so decidedly that we could well take them to be the characteristic, determining lines of his nature. And yet running counter to these are other lines no less plain, no less sharply cut. From the point we have so far reached in our inquiry, it is quite impossible to determine the point where these two sets of lines meet to form a living unity. A dominating nature, a regal figure is Jesus, and yet he washes the feet of his disciples. Impetuous and austere to the point of harshness is his will, yet he can love as tenderly and sweetly as only a mother can. Hallowed by long nights of prayer, he is wholly God's, and yet he gladly foregathers with publicans and sinners. He has dedicated himself to the infinite and the superterrestrial, to the vision of the heavenly spaces, and yet the tiniest things on the earth do not escape his eye and his heart rejoices in the flowers of the field. He is a firebrand blazing in prophetic wrath, and yet he submits to the foulest ignominies in silence. He is a unique, solitary figure, yet he loves men as they have never been loved and dies for them. Who is this Jesus? Where is the point whence these contradictions arise and where they will become intelligible to us?

To discover this point we must abandon the position we have hitherto taken up, whence the spiritual figure of Jesus is visible only in its exterior outlines. We shall have to mount higher, to climb the high summits of his soul, to the region where he cries " Abba, Father." We must attempt to explore the interior life of Jesus, the Jesus of the hours spent apart ; we must watch Jesus at prayer.

V

THE INTERIOR LIFE OF JESUS

" Blessed are they who hear the word of God, and keep it " (*Luke* xi. 28). With these words Jesus reveals his attitude towards the values of our existence. They hold the solution to what constitutes the highest value for man, namely that he should make the word of God his own. In the order of precedence of personal values the religious man takes the highest place.

In this chapter we shall attempt a simple description of the interior religious life of our Lord's human soul. Here we shall again intentionally turn our gaze away from the mystery of his divinity. We want to discover what holy, quickening forces, what impelling religious conceptions were at work in that miraculous human figure, which so far we have considered only in its formal mental and ethical aspects. We want to discover what it was that dominated and animated him.

This can be answered at once ; the ultimate and profoundest motive force, the mainspring of his actions was an unreserved surrender to his Father's will. There is nothing the brush of the evangelists has painted so movingly and strikingly, with such impressive strokes, as the mighty, burning love of Jesus for his heavenly Father. We know of no other man in the whole range of history who has so deeply absorbed and understood

those words of the Old Testament, " Thou shalt love the
Lord thy God with thy whole heart and with thy whole
soul, and with thy whole strength " (*Deut.* vi. 5), and has
made them so absolutely dominant in his life. The first
recorded words of Jesus are a reminder that his home is
with the Father. " Did you not know that I must be
about my Father's business ? " (*Luke* ii. 49), and his last
dying words were breathed to the Father. " Father, into
thy hands I commend my spirit" (*Luke* xxiii. 46).
Again and again the evangelists point out how Jesus
" lived and moved and was " in the Father, and how his
intimate union with the Father overflowed in prayer.
When Jesus was baptized, he prayed and " heaven was
opened " (*Luke* iii. 21). When he set about to choose
his disciples, " he went out into a mountain to pray, and
he passed the whole night in the prayer of God. And
when day was come, he called unto him his disciples "
(*Luke* vi. 12 *sq.*). A great part of his miracles, such as
the healing of the deaf-mute (*Mark* vii. 34), the healing
of the boy possessed by the dumb spirit (*Mark* ix. 28),
the raising of Lazarus from the dead (*John* xi. 41), the
multiplication of the loaves (*Mark* viii. 6 = *Matt.*
xiv. 19; *John* vi. 11) spring up like sweet-smelling
blossoms from his life of prayer. At the height of his
activity when his disciples returned from their successful
mission, " he rejoiced in the Holy Ghost, and said : I
confess to thee, O Father, Lord of heaven and earth "
(*Luke* x. 21). Above all, the whole of his Passion
breathes the spirit and nobility of prayer. In the Upper
Room he dedicates himself and his followers to the

Father, and institutes with thanksgiving and benediction the new covenant in his blood. In Gethsemane " he fell upon his face, praying, and saying : My father, if it be possible, let this cup pass from me. Nevertheless not as I will, but as thou wilt " (*Matt.* xxvi. 39). And his agonizing death on Golgotha was like a struggle to do the will of the Father maintained by ever new supplication to him. If we ask what in all the manifold thoughts and acts of Jesus was the most inward and enduring and immutable, was as it were the abiding golden background to his words and actions, the answer must be his intimate sense of union with the Father. It is the essence of his life. We here draw near to the very centre of his will, and we might already conjecture that here that holy spring has its rise, whence flow both the loneliness of his heroism and his all-embracing, all-compassionate love for mankind, and where they attain unity.

It is of the greatest fascination, and for a knowledge of Jesus indispensable, to listen to him praying and to appreciate his prayers in the light of his disposition. Only thus may we penetrate into the inmost mechanism of his human affections and see Jesus when he is wholly himself, when he is alone with the Father.

What above all characterizes the prayer of Jesus is the virile modesty and seclusion in which it is made. When he exhorts his followers, " When thou shalt pray, enter into thy chamber, and having shut the door, pray to thy Father in secret " (*Matt.* vi. 6), he is telling them to follow his own practice. There is no place he likes better to pray in than solitude, when no other person is by, but only the Father. "And having dismissed the multitude, he went into a mountain alone to pray" (*Matt.* xiv. 23 = *Mark* vi. 46; *John* vi. 15). In the loneliness of the night, when even the sun's rays and the grasses of the field are asleep, wrapt in a vast mysterious silence, was when he found his Father and was alone with him. On the mountain of the Transfiguration his God-possessed state gleamed through his outward appearance and his face shone white like the snow on Hermon. Apart from the Our Father, which Jesus composed not for himself but for the needs of his disciples, and on that account cast it into rhymed form, those of his own prayers which have been preserved still exhale the strong, warm odour of a most personal devotion, of direct living experience. "Father, I give thee thanks that thou hast heard me" (*John* xi. 41); "Father, not as I will, but as thou wilt" (*Matt.* xxvi. 39); "I confess to thee, O Father, . . . because thou hast hid these things from the wise and the prudent, and hast revealed them to little ones. Yea, Father, for so hath it seemed good in thy sight" (*Matt.* xi. 25 *sq.*). It is for this reason that, unlike St. Paul's prayers, they are simple and homely, short and to the point, like little ejaculatory prayers.

But this habit of lonely prayer did not originate in his devotional need to pray with concentration and collectedly. A much greater reason lies behind it; and we again touch on his mystery. Surrounding him there is not only the customary solitude of the devout soul, but there is also the mysterious solitude of the Son. Although his consciousness of his Sonship will have to be discussed in detail later on, reference must be made to it here, for it alone can make his human prayer-life intelligible. When Jesus prays, he steps clean out of the circle of humanity in order to be exclusively in that of his Father.

There is, moreover, the strange fact that Jesus does not need men. He only needs the Father. For close on three years his disciples lived with him ; but for the needs of his interior life he is in no way dependent on them. He never talks over his plans or decisions with them. He never asks for their advice. He never seeks comfort or consolation from them. When he took some of them with him to Mount Olivet and enjoined them : " Stay you here, and watch with me " (*Matt.* xxvi. 38), he did this for their sakes, not for his. They were to steel themselves to meet the approaching danger. " Watch ye, and pray that ye enter not into temptation " (*Matt.* xxvi. 41). The disciples gave him nothing ; he gave them everything. And, considered from this special angle, what was his attitude towards his Mother ? Certainly he loved her as only a child can love its mother. Dying he thinks of her as she stands at the foot of the Cross (*John* xix. 26) ; but one cannot rid oneself of the impression that even the love which as her child he felt for her had always an element of renunciation in it. When he was but twelve years old the question, " Did you not know that I must be about my Father's business ? " (*Luke* ii. 49) came to his lips. Mary and

Joseph had on that occasion lost the Child in Jerusalem
and missed him. The words of the twelve-year-old
boy had their echo later in those of the man at Capharnaum when they wanted to call him out to his mother,
and he refused to go with the words, " Who is my mother
and my brethren ? " And looking round on his disciples
he said, " Behold my mother and my brethren " (*Mark*
iii. 33, 34). There was in Jesus a spiritual recess, a holy
of holies, to which even his mother had no approach,
where only the Father was. In his human soul there was
a point, the deepest, inmost point, wholly free of anything earthly, utterly removed from all worldly relations, which, in a simply unearthly, supernatural vir-
ginity of his whole being, was dedicate to the Father.

The Father was his world, his reality, his life. Only
through the Father does his solitude become a com-
muning, the most fruitful of communings. St. John
repeatedly mentions those remarkable words of his,
" I am not alone " (*John* viii. 16, 29). The last time
Jesus uses them is in anticipation of his death. " Behold
the hour cometh, and it is now come, that you shall be
scattered every man to his own, and shall leave me alone :
and yet I am not alone, because the Father is with me "
(*John* xvi. 32). Here the most intimate association of his
life comes into view, the relation of his being and
life to the Father. His prayer is nothing but an ever-
renewed act of contact with the Father, constrained
by the need to resolve the loneliness of his " I " in the
" Thou " of the Father. It is in prayer that he is
joined to the Father in a oneness which no one, not

even his disciples, can have a share. Whenever Jesus speaks of men and their heavenly Father he deliberately avoids including himself. God is " their " Father, " your " Father; only when Jesus is praying is it " my " Father. The Father to whom he appeals belongs to himself in a quite special sense. His act of prayer is unique in that it is the solitude of the Son with the Father. In this solitude that solitude of his heroism, of which we have spoken, that consciousness of an unqualified superiority, that absorption in the highest aims and labours, that steely, gripping quality of his will find their ultimate roots.

With these are associated still further peculiarities and characteristics of Jesus' attitude in prayer. When a man or even a saint prays, his prayer is above all a *miserere mei*, a cry from the depths of human frailty and moral guilt, a prayer of awe in face of the mystery of God and of his absolute holiness. The purer a man strives to make his life, the more plainly and terrifyingly does the immense hollowness of his whole existence strike him when viewed in the light of the Divine.

It is quite otherwise that Jesus feels and prays. True, in the Our Father he puts into the mouths of men the heartfelt petition, " Forgive us our trespasses, and deliver us from evil " ; but he personally does not use this petition. Never did the cry, " Father, forgive me," pass his lips. Even when the shadows of death encompassed him in darkness and when a sense of utter dereliction weighted down his soul, no one heard him cry thus. They only heard the cry, " Father, forgive them "

(*Luke* xxiii. 34).   He prays as one who knows not sin ; and it is for this reason that his prayers are in great part not petitions but acts of praise and thanksgiving, an exultant outpouring of grateful joy to the Father : "I confess to thee, O Father, . . . because . . . thou hast revealed them to the little ones" (*Matt*. xi. 25) ; "Father, I give thee thanks that thou hast heard me" (*John* xi. 41).   Again, when he does pray for something, it is not so much an anxious, humble petition as the happy and confident request of a child, who is certain that its desire will be granted.   It is like an appeal to his native right, as in the prayer, "Father, I will that where I am, they also whom thou hast given me may be with me" (*John* xvii. 24).   Hence his prayer is almost always a petition on behalf of others.   He prays for Peter that his faith fail not (*Luke* xxii. 32) ; he prays for his disciples that the Father give them another Paraclete to abide with them for ever (*John* xiv. 16).   And even when he seems to be praying for himself, as on the Mount of Olives, it is ultimately the will and the glory of the Father which alone he seeks and to which he submits himself, "Not as I will, but as thou wilt" (*cf. John* xii. 27 *sq.*). Jesus does not stand before his heavenly Father as a beggar, still less as a prodigal son.   He looks up at him with the untroubled, glowing eyes of a child and, as if it were the most natural thing in the world, unites himself with him in the most intimate personal communion.   Never since prayer and sacrifice were offered up on earth has anyone, be he sinner or saint, thus prayed.

*   *   *   *   *

In order to get a clearer insight into all this, we shall
in what follows turn from the subjective act of prayer
to a consideration of the objective religious reality which
in his prayer Jesus confesses and comprehends. It is
ultimately an inquiry into the picture of God which
shone in his human soul and formed his view of the
world.

In the foreground of religious reality Jesus sees the
all-operative, creative God. It is not to the far-off,
wholly transcendental, silent God of contemporary
Hellenism that he prays, nor is it to the God of mysticism,
of the remote abode of the blessed, to which only the
ecstatic soul may ascend. His God is the all-creative,
all-operative God of Moses and the prophets—" My
Father worketh until now, and I work " (*John* v. 17).
His God clothes the lilies and feeds the ravens. And as
he works in the life of Nature so does he in that of
history. All the leading spirits of humanity, the prophets and the Baptist, were sent by him. As the sheep
to its shepherd so does man belong to his God (*Luke*
xv. 6). All upheavals and wars, every world event large
and small is God's act. The entire history of mankind
is for Jesus a revelation of the living God. And since
he finds the creative will of his Father in all things and
in all persons, he sees these things and these persons
not from without in all the deceptiveness of their appearance, but from within in their essential relation to the
will of God, as a revelation of his creative might, as
the embodied will of his Father. Hence he includes
these things and these persons in the love with which

he loves the Father. His love of the world is his love of God applied to it. This makes intelligible to us the paradox that Jesus can embrace the infinite God and finite things, eternity and time, in the same love, and that his heroism in the vertical plane is united with a heroism in the horizontal. Jesus loves all persons and things because to him they are not merely a token, but a manifestation of the Divine will.

But this is not all there is to say. When Jesus speaks of the God who works these words have a deeper and richer sound than in the mouth of ordinary pious folk, especially in these days when rationalism has stunted or destroyed the immediacy of religious experience in them. Jesus does not, like them, contemplate intermediate causes through which the creative God calls all Becoming and Being into existence. Still less do these intermediate causes combine for him into a constant self-sufficient order of Nature looming up between Creator and creature as a rival cosmos of created causal sequences. Such a belief in a rigid order of Nature Jesus never shared. Indeed, it would have seemed to him an idolatry of purely human conceptions and systems. For in the last resort it is man himself who has contrived and gone on contriving such laws and systems, in the hope by their help to master for the moment the colossal, unfathomable, inexhaustible mystery of reality and to repose therein for a little space. Jesus does not need such artificial aids to arrive at things. His approach to them is by way of God not of man. Jesus sees things not where they have already been rigidified for human thought into a fixed significance and being, but where they proceed from the hand of the Creator. He sees them in their inner God-related dynamic, in the living flux of creation, in the creative process of their beginning in God. Hence these things are fundamentally at every moment subject to the Divine call. They cannot take refuge from God behind the armour plates of any kind of order of Nature. Naked and bare they lie in the hand of the creating God, and they have no other surety of existence but that of his almighty will.

In establishing this we touch on an essential feature of Jesus' piety. This is the knowledge of the freedom and absoluteness of the Divine will, the knowledge that behind and beyond all things lies not a dead, soulless piece of mechanism, not any kind of Fate blindly working by natural laws, but absolute life and spirit, absolute mobility and spontaneity, in other words the freedom of God. Jesus lives on this freedom. To him God is absolute free will; absolute power, before which every other will and power are as dust. Whoever has faith in this absolute power " and staggers not . . . shall say to this mountain, Take up and cast thyself into the sea, and it shall be done " (*cf. Matt.* xxi. 21 *sq.*; xvii. 19; *Mark* xi. 22 *sq.*; *Luke* xvii. 5 *sq.*). Jesus can believe his Father capable of such incredible things because he sees everywhere and always the operative God at work. To him God is the immediate tangible reality, the being he meets first in all persons and things, the secret and profoundest meaning of all being, the reality of all realities. He apprehends the creative work of God directly in the here and now of things.   For him it is no longer a belief but direct vision.   Hence there is nothing spasmodic or violent about it.   It is to him so natural and obvious that nothing touches his soul more painfully than the want of faith or the little faith of man. In this visual experience of the all-operative God lies the foundation of the reliance and confidence with which the human consciousness and will of Jesus transcend the possibilities open to created beings, in order to realize the possibilities of God, to work signs and wonders innumerable, not only the casting out of devils and the healing of the sick, but even the raising from the dead.   "Father, I give thee thanks that thou hast heard me.   And I know that thou hearest me always" (*John* xi. 41 *sq.*).   His human will has so penetrated the Divine will and is so absorbed by it that they are as it were a single will. Psychologically regarded, therefore, his miracles are at once the product of and proof of the absolute union of his human will with the omnipotent will of the Father, of a faith that will remove mountains, of a trust which storms the heavens.   Hence, too, the reverent restraint, the straightforwardness, and the discretion of his miracles. Nothing was more alien to his nature than to claim to be a miracle-doctor or a thaumaturge.   The idea of working a miracle, save in absolute surrender to the Divine will, or one which in any way served a selfish purpose, he casts from him as a temptation of the devil.   When the spirit of self-seeking intruded itself, as in the case of his countrymen at Nazareth, " he could not do any miracle there " (*Mark* vi. 5 ; *cf. Matt.* xiii. 58).   He cannot do it since

here the Father has interposed his no, and the will of
the Father is the beginning and the end of his own
human will and potency. The miracles of Jesus are a
unique, unprecedented affirmative response to the operative, creative God, and a prayer which penetrated to the
heart of God as no prayer of man has ever done, and
which laid bare the depths of created nature.

Such then is the piety of Jesus in its first aspect, the
direct vision and experience of the all-operative God.
With it is essentially linked his other certainty, that of
the all-holy God. The absolute will of God for the
being and becoming of things is at the same time the
absolute will of God for the highest values, for the pure
and holy, for the good and perfect, such as he himself
is. So deeply is the spirit of Jesus touched with the awe
of the *Solus sanctus*, that in the light of this infinite
treasury of Divine values its own human work, its own
goodness becomes as nothing. " Why callest thou me
good ? " he said to the man who addressed him as
" Good Master," " None is good but one, that is God "
(*Mark* x. 18).

To us dust-born creatures it is awe-inspiring to see in
what a glory of light this holy God appears in the soul
of Jesus, how he flashes out in his teaching and trans-
figures all his life. His teaching is in great part the
Gospel of the all-holy will of God, and its compelling
power. To attain this one essential thing, the pearl
of great price, the treasure hidden in the field, it is
worth while to give up everything else. Jesus here
shows himself to be in the direct line of the Old Testa-

ment, in particular of the prophets. But he purifies the Old Testament teaching of all that is exterior, formalistic, legalistic, in particular of those ceremonial nonessentials which contemporary Rabbinism, "the tradition of men," had grafted on the law. The tithing of mint and anise and cummin are not the "weightier things of the law," but "judgment, and mercy, and faith" (*Matt.* xxiii. 23). Thus when it is a man's duty to provide for his aged parents no temple offering can relieve him of that duty (*Matt.* xv. 5 *sq.*). The will of God is really the will for the morally good, that which the Lord has elevated to the duty of all duties : "Thou shalt love the Lord thy God with thy whole heart, and with thy whole soul, and with all thy strength, and with all thy mind, and thy neighbour as thyself" (*Luke* x. 27). And just as Jesus here draws out the holy will of God in all its purity, freeing it of all human accretions, just as he thus immensely simplifies the moral law— "On these two commandments depend the whole law and the prophets" (*Matt.* xxii. 40)—so, in deliberate defiance of the merely exterior works of the Rabbis, he deepened and "fulfilled" it, revealing in so doing all its ultimate possibilities and its most interior and delicate demands. The will of the all-holy God goes to the very root of all human affections and thoughts. Where the heart is good, there will a good man be found, and where the heart is evil, there will also the evil man be (*cf. Mark* vii. 15, 20). When man deliberately shuts his eyes to these last depths of the will of God, he no longer belongs to the Kingdom of God, but to the kingdom of the devil. For Jesus there is no half-way house between good and evil. The publicans and sinners, whom he loves, are to him real sinners, really unrighteous, really sick. To him the prodigal son is really a prodigal. Good and evil, good men and bad, Jesus sees in abrupt antithesis, as a Yea and a Nay. The heroic in his nature appears in its full strength in the ethical sphere. Religion is to him utter obedience to the demands of God, obedience to the extreme limit. Hence it involves merit and reward, demerit and punishment, heaven and hell. It is vain to attempt to delete these conceptions from the teaching of Jesus and to water down his message to a kind of autonomous morality. His sermon on the mount and not a few of his parables have as their theme action and reward. It is in the pair of diametrical contrasts—reward and punishment, heaven and hell—that he sees clearly the absolute antithesis of good and evil, the eternal Yea and Nay of the holiness of God. With inexorable force Jesus sets men to face this Yea and Nay. It was not least this austere exclusiveness of his demands, that is to say, the eschatological element in his teaching, which touched the consciences of men. He preached " as one having power," as one who has the judgment, aye, who is the judgment.

And as he preached, so was he—the will of the all-holy God revealed in the human will of the God-Man. As the animal man lives on bread, so he lives on this will. " My meat is to do the will of him that sent me " (*John* iv. 34). Wherever in the Gospels we see or hear Jesus, in the desert, beside the sick-bed, at a marriage feast, on the

Cross, he is ever about his Father's business.   He is for ever by word and deed scattering the seed of the word of God, even if it fall on stony ground.   Even when sitting tired out by the well he drew of the living water for the Samaritan woman.   Even when he is a guest he gives more than he receives.   His road is a continuous road to the heights.   Where it is steepest, there he goes, as if it were a level way.   In the history of man, even of the greatest, such a road to the heights is unknown.   A Jeremias, a Paul, an Augustine, a Buddha, a Muhammad —their lives cannot be told without the telling of vast upheavals and transformations and of spiritual defeats. The life of Jesus alone runs its course without such crises, without any spiritual surrenders.   His first day and his last are lit by the austere clarity of the all-holy Divine will.

This is an exceedingly bold conclusion which we have been obliged to enunciate in the light of the historical tradition.   Yet we shall find the impression of holiness, of absolute sinlessness and purity, powerfully reinforced, if we divert our inquiring glance from his exterior being and works to his interior affections and aims. Look as we may through the Gospels into the inmost crannies of his desires, we shall find nothing anywhere but the will of the Father.   He loves his home and his people ; he weeps when he thinks of Jerusalem and its destruction (*Luke* xix. 41) ; his own teaching is not without a national colouring (*cf. Mark* vii. 27 ; *Matt.* x. 5) ; and yet he leaves his people for the Father's sake, and sees in the destruction of Jerusalem the angry punitive will of his Father. And as from the ties of home and family, so is he free from all other earthly ties. He is the freest of the free because as no other ever has been he is the servant of God. The golden fetters of possessions and wealth do not weigh upon him, for " the Son of man hath not where to lay his head " (*Matt.* viii. 20 = *Luke* ix. 58). Earthly honours and the applause of the multitude have no attraction for him. He forbids that his miracles be spoken about (*Mark* i. 44; iii. 12; v. 43; vii. 36, etc.). Those whom he had healed were not to thank him but the Father (*Luke* xvii. 18). When they wanted to proclaim him king, he hid himself (*John* vi. 15). He has no desire for the pleasures of family life. " There are eunuchs who have made themselves eunuchs for the kingdom of heaven " (*Matt.* xix. 12). He never seeks his own profit. Even the compassion which the weeping women offer him on his way to the Cross, he brushes aside (*Luke* xxiii. 28). He lets himself be betrayed, and for the betrayer he has but one question, put to sting his con- science and to save him (*Matt.* xxvi. 50). He lets himself be denied by Peter, and yet he confidently presses the question upon him, " Simon, son of John, lovest thou me more than these. . . . Feed my lambs " (*John* xxi. 15). Wherever we look into the soul of Jesus we never find purely earthly impulses and desires. Even the strongest impulse man can have, the impulse to live, is overcome by his will to do the Father's will. " He that shall lose his life for me shall find it " (*Matt.* x. 39). Earthly life had nothing to give him, nor could it take anything away from him.

Thus in the human soul of Jesus there was no single point at which temptation could make contact. Evil could only approach him from without; there was nothing within him responsive to it. It is the cool, dispassionate testimony of history that wherever Jesus steps into the light, it is an apparition of the holy. No impression was more deeply graven on the minds of the primitive Christians than this. They call him the " lamb unspotted and undefiled " (*I. Pet.* i. 19), " a high-priest, holy, innocent, undefiled, separated from sinners, and made higher than the heavens " (*Heb.* vii. 26).

Grave and severe, holy and sublime is the picture of Jesus which these words evoke. And yet it is not the whole picture. Clearly as Jesus beholds the all-operative God at work, awed as, in the deepest yearnings of his spirit, he stood before the all-holy God and served him, his soul recognizes and experiences with a corresponding joy and happiness, intimacy and tender love this same God as infinitely gracious, as loving omnipotence, as loving holiness, as the Father in heaven. It is here that new springs break forth in the heart of Jesus, springs which in the Old Testament were rather divined than seen, and which in his own time had been almost blocked up. It is the creative act of Jesus to have moved the Old Testament words on the merciful and gracious God (*cf. Ex.* xxxiv. 6 *sq.* ; *Ps.* ciii. 1 *sq.*) and of the Father in heaven (*cf. Jer.* iii. 4 *sq.*) from the fringes of religion back to its very heart, and thus to have brought home to men the truths and values latent in them with their liberating power and glowing happiness. His teaching culminates in the words: God is our Father. "Thus therefore shall ye pray: Our Father who art in heaven." With this little word Father, Jesus sheds the warmest, sunniest light on the relations of mankind to God and dispels all those gloomy shadows with which the savage demonolatry of the pagans and the cold, rigid belief of the Jews in the *lex talionis* had overcast the image of God. True that God is all-operative and all-holy, true that in his light evil remains evil, the sick sick, the sinner a sinner; for "justice shall be the girdle of his loins" (*Is.* xi. 5), and he who persists in sin will not be released from the prison until he has paid the last farthing. Yet, since the all-mighty, all-holy God is also the all-gracious God, because he is the Father, he will not leave man in his sin. The moment he repents, the moment he calls out from the bottom of his heart, "Father, I have sinned against heaven, and before thee" (*Luke* xv. 18), the Father will bend down to the prodigal son and again put the festal robe on him. Religion is therefore not merely fear and justice; religion is love and mercy. Wherever there is to be found one who, like the publican in the temple, strikes his breast, or, like Mary Magdalen, laments his sins, there close by his side will be the Father and his fatherly forgiveness. But Jesus' vision pierces deeper, and beholds the Father and his love not at the end of the way of redemption but at its beginning. The almighty power of God and of his all-holy will are a power and a will of love. His will does not float isolated in infinite space, but is grounded and rooted in love. The love which is God is at the beginning and the end of all being. The sparrow on the roof-top and the lily in the field are both safely sheltered in it, but above all is this true of man, who may say to his God " Father." Like the pillar of cloud which went before the children of Israel in the wilderness, the awakening graciousness of the Father, his exacting and bestowing love precedes all human accomplishment. " Prevenient grace " is what theologians call this most precious operation which gives to every religious act its content, its consecration, its splendour, and its joy, and which St. John has clothed in the enraptured words : " God first hath loved us " (*I. John* iv. 19). In the knowledge of this prevenient all-merciful love of God the love of Jesus for the sinner has its roots. It was out of his intense recognition of the all-mighty, all-holy God as the God of Graciousness and Mercy that he uttered those final and profoundest words on the mystery of the Divine redemptive purpose, words which up till then had only been heard as from a distance, but which from now on were to ring out clear as a clarion over the whole earth.

It is overwhelming to see with what fervour and warmth, with what trust and confidence, Jesus surrenders himself to the fatherly arms of God. Though the Father's love lead him by way of the Mount of Olives to Golgotha, it is " Father, not as I will, but as thou wilt."

In the abyssal depths of his trust in his Father lie the happiness, the joy, the exultation of his religious life. It is to Jesus unthinkable, absolutely impossible, that the Father could leave disregarded an earnest request, a persistent knocking at his door (*cf. Luke* xviii. 1 *sqq.*; *Matt.* vii. 7 *sqq.*). This is to him a thousand times more impossible than that an earthly father should give a scorpion to his own child when it had asked for an egg (*Luke* xi. 12).

Out of this absolute trust in the Father spring the vital courage and confidence of Jesus. Jesus seldom wonders. But he does wonder that men can fear. "Where is your faith?" he asks of his disciples in the midst of a raging tempest. "Fear not, only believe," is what he says to the father standing before the dead body of his child (*Mark* v. 36). Even the most dreadful thing that can befall a father is for Jesus no cause for fear or concern. To him anxiety is something essentially alien, and it must be foreign to any true disciple of Jesus. True he is under no delusion about the dangers which threaten his followers. "Behold, I send you as sheep in the midst of wolves," he tells them (*Matt.* x. 16). But stronger than any danger is trust in the Father, "and he commanded them that they should take nothing for the way, but a staff only : no scrip, no bread, nor money in their purse" (*Mark* vi. 8 ; *cf. Matt.* x. 9 = *Luke* x. 4 *sq.*). And again : "Be not solicitous therefore, saying : What shall we eat : or what shall we drink, or wherewith shall we be clothed? For after all these things do the heathens seek. For your Father knoweth that you

have need of all these things" (*Matt*. vi. 31 *sq.* =
Luke xii. 29 *sq.*).

I am at my limit; I can go no farther. Who is this
Jesus, who can pray so holily, who can live so confidently and die so guiltless? There is in him a holy folly,
an excess of faith and trust, a lavishness of moral strength,
incredible purity and tenderness. Yes, his life seems
folly; and yet we behold in it a festival of God. When
has there ever appeared on earth a being like unto him?
All human standards fail us here. The religious, like the
intellectual and moral, stature of Jesus, reaches dimensions beyond human measurement. His life is like a
rare poem from a foreign land, and yet it is a living
reality. All that is narrated of him is no external
ornament, no sweet-scented veil of beautiful phrases and
maxims draped about him, such as an Epictetus or a Lao
Tse wore. Indeed, what is told of him is all unpremeditated, inimitable, uninventible, is so graven into
his concrete, work-a-day life, into the reality of the
moment, of the here and now, that only by starting
with the living, working Jesus can we reach to his
interior world. We thus stand on the very bedrock of
history. Once upon a time there was actually a man who
knew himself to be in the most intimate union of life
and love with his Father in heaven, who saw God's
creative power at work as if with the naked eye, and
whose appearance on the scene of history was as an
apparition of sanctity.

Who is this man Jesus? None can answer this
question with full certainty save one—Jesus himself.

Of his innermost relations to existence, of the ultimate roots of his being, of his mystery none save him can know anything with any certainty. So we must go to Jesus himself. No mind is clearer, no heart is purer, no speech is more true than his. Lord Jesus, what hast thou to tell us of thyself?

VI

THE SELF-REVELATION OF JESUS

The figure of Jesus stands before us in its intellectual, ethical, and religious aspects as something entirely new. It has no analogue in the history of mankind, nor can it be explained by a consideration of his antecedents or environment. Indeed, Jesus alone can reveal the ultimate secret of his personality. He alone can know who he really is, what place he occupies in the order of reality, and what the meaning of his life is. What then does Jesus tell us about himself?

If we call up to our minds the picture of Jesus as it is portrayed in the Gospels, we may expect in advance that what he has to tell us about himself will throughout bear the stamp of his personality, the stamp of his veracity, purity, and directness, that, therefore, in dazzling contrast to the noisy, self-advertising apotheoses of the miracle-men, kings, and princes of the Hellenistic period (cf. *Apoc.* xii. 22), it will have nothing violent or strained or unnatural in it, but will well up from out his being like the soft scent of some beautiful flower as something exquisitely obvious. His first trumpet call to men is accordingly by no means one of self-revelation, but the gospel of the approaching kingdom of heaven. The Baptist had called the Jewish people to repentance, "for the kingdom of heaven is at hand" (*Matt.* iii. 2), and the message of Jesus ran, " The time is accomplished, and the kingdom of God is at hand ; repent and believe the gospel " (*Mark* i. 15). The self-revelation of Jesus grows organically out of this teaching. It does not stand by itself as an isolated message in an historical vacuum, but is part and parcel of his gospel of the kingdom of God.

What does Jesus mean by the terms kingdom of God, kingdom of heaven ? Both expressions connote the same thing. If Matthew, writing for the Jews, and the author of the apocryphal gospel of the Hebrews prefer to speak of the kingdom of heaven rather than the kingdom of God (but *cf. Matt.* vi. 33 ; xii. 28 ; xxi. 31, 43), they do so out of the late Jewish shrinking from the direct use of the name of God, and therefore employ in its stead the periphrastic expression " the heavens." Indeed Jesus himself sometimes uses the same word to denote God (*cf. Matt.* xxi. 25 ; *Luke* xv. 7, 18). In any event the same thing is meant by both terms, the kingdom, the dominion of God.

It is significant that Jesus never gives us a closer definition of this " keyword " of his gospel. He not seldom speaks simply of the kingdom (*Matt.* vi. 33 ; viii. 12 ; xii. 38 ; xxv. 34, etc.), supposes in his hearers, that is to say, a knowledge of its meaning. In fact, since the days of the prophets, and particularly of Isaias (*Is.* xl. 1 *sq.* ; lix. 2 *sqq.* ; *cf. Mich.* ii. 12 *sqq.* ; *Zach.* xiv. 9, 16), it was a rooted belief of the Jews that Jahwe at the end of time would set up his dominion over all the ends of the earth. The later Old Testament writers such as

Daniel (ii. 44) and *Tobias* (xiii. 2) specify this dominion more closely as the " kingdom " of God. By this they primarily mean a spiritual dominion in the hearts of men, but from the days of Daniel onwards they conceive of God's dominion in the narrow, concrete sense, as a closely circumscribed, self-contained kingdom of the saints, which will come down from heaven and displace all purely earthly empires.

This kingdom Jesus also has in mind when he comes forward with his announcement that " the time is accomplished, and the kingdom of God is at hand." The purpose of his mission, of which he is fully conscious, is to bring about the establishment of the kingdom of God.

What method will Jesus adopt in preparing this kingdom of God ? His message runs " Repent : and believe the gospel." His primary task is therefore that of a preacher of penance, whose object, like the Baptist's, is to awaken the consciences of men and to make them subject to the Divine will—to the rule of God. For God can only rule where his all-holy will sways the consciences of men. Jesus' call to penance is therefore in its positive aspect the announcement of God's Holy Will. He would engrave on men's minds the words, " Thy will be done on earth as it is in heaven," and " Whosoever shall do the will of my Father, that is in heaven, he is my brother, and sister, and mother " (*Matt.* xii. 50). So far his gospel of the kingdom bears a thoroughly ethical and religious stamp in marked contrast to the conception of the kingdom of God then current among the Jews, who in speaking of it revelled in the representation of the sensible goods and felicities of that kingdom.   Their present was too sad and dismal for them to be able to conceive of the coming kingdom except as a summation and fulfilment of all their earthly longings.   According to the Syriac *Apocalypse of Baruch* (xxix. 5), " The earth shall give of her fruits ten thousand fold.   On each vine there shall be a thousand tendrils, and on each tendril one thousand clusters of grapes, and one cluster shall bear one thousand grapes, and one grape shall yield a cor of wine."   The expectation of the world to come was therefore for the Jewish apocalyptic writers dominated by sensible, selfish interests, by the passionate longing for a happier, richer life.   The ruling passion of Jesus was the will of his heavenly Father, and the religious and moral demands are brought so prominently forward in his teaching that at first sight it seems to announce the gospel not so much of a new and blessed life as of a new and more moral life. His concern is for the " way of justice " (*Matt.* xxi. 32) and indeed for a more " abounding " justice (*Matt.* v. 20), which extending beyond exterior works shall penetrate into the inmost recesses of man's nature.   This in its essence is a perfected love of God and of our neighbour.   Whoever, like the scribe who asked Jesus which was the first commandment of all, is aware of the new moral purpose of the kingdom, is at any rate " not far from the kingdom of God " (*Mark* xii. 34).   Whoever in the new dispensation shall give food to the hungry and drink to the thirsty, the same shall " possess " (*Matt.* xxv.

34) the kingdom. He that shall " do and teach " the least of the commandments shall be " called great " in the kingdom of heaven (*Matt*. v. 19). And whoever shall humble himself as a little child, he is " the greatest in the kingdom of heaven " (*Matt*. xviii. 4). In the preaching of Jesus " justice " and the approaching " kingdom of God " are so intimately entwined that they combine into a single goal of life. " Seek first the kingdom of God and his justice " (*Matt*. vi. 33).

Since, like his forerunner John the Baptist, Jesus, in view of the near approach of the kingdom, issues a call to repentance, his gospel of the kingdom becomes a gospel of the will of God and of the new and better justice. Jesus here takes up the line of the prophets, of Isaias, Jeremias, and Osee, and carries it on to the end. He is their fulfiller and perfecter. Jesus knows this and is therefore conscious that he is the born teacher of Israel, the one teacher whose place none can take. " You call me Master, and Lord : and you say well, for so I am " (*John* xiii. 13). " Neither be ye called masters : for one is your master, Christ " (*Matt*. xxiii. 10).

Earnestly as Jesus emphasizes repentance and justice in his preaching of the kingdom, and certain as it is that an essential part of his teaching is based on this, nevertheless repentance and justice are not the final, or the sublimest words which he has to say to mankind. It is anything but the case that to him justice and the new kingdom were one and the same thing, that his preaching of the kingdom was intended merely to prepare a com-

munity of souls aspiring to the justice of God, that
consequently Jesus was only conscious of a mission to
be the harbinger of a new morality. Those who would
explain his teaching in this moralistic sense fail to perceive
its specifically religious purport, or, more accurately,
the supernatural and eschatological elements of the new
kingdom. Repentance and justice are to Jesus not the
kingdom itself, but rather the way to attain it. They
have the same relation to the kingdom of God as the
human achievement to the hundredfold reward in the
parable (*Matt.* x. 30; *cf. Matt.* xvi. 27). They are
therefore a preparation, a necessary condition for entry
into this kingdom. The kingdom itself, however, the
hundredfold reward is given by God alone. It is an act
of God. It is a kingdom " prepared for the blessed of his
Father from the beginning of the world " (*Matt.* xxv. 34).
It is a plant which the heavenly Father has planted
(*Matt.* xv. 13). Its joys are the " joys of the Lord."
It is to " sit down with Abraham, and Isaac, and Jacob
in the kingdom of heaven " (*Matt.* viii. 11), to drink
anew of the fruit of the vine in the kingdom of the
Father (*Matt.* xxvi. 29). It is a bliss with which God
himself responds to the sincere hunger and thirst after
justice, a blessedness which lies beyond all natural and
human possibilities. In the synoptic Gospels indeed
it is not made clear in detail what good things
the kingdom will bring. Jesus contents himself by
saying that with the kingdom man will receive " life
everlasting " (*Matt.* xix. 29; *Mark* x. 17), and that he
will " go into life " (*Matt.* xviii. 8). But in St. John's

Gospel Jesus declares categorically that "this is eternal life, that they may know thee, the only true God, and Jesus Christ, whom thou hast sent" (*John* xvii. 3), Jesus therefore understands the kingdom of God as unbroken, eternal communion with the Father and himself. Since it is wholly supernatural, a kingdom prepared by the Father, it is also eschatological, that is to say, it is a kingdom whose coming lies in the future and for which we must pray : "Thy kingdom come." What makes the heart of Jesus glow and burn, what makes his speech fiery and eloquent is the fact that the kingdom of God, like a mighty revolutionizing novelty, is breaking in upon mankind from heaven, and is in fact already nigh. "The time is accomplished, and the kingdom of God is at hand" (*Mark* i. 15). The teacher becomes the prophet, before whom the book of the future lies open, and who gives testimony to it with the rapture of an Osee or an Isaias. No one can understand Jesus, his gospel, his consciousness of his mission, if he does not grasp, in all its original force, how Jesus was filled with the sense of this new and tremendous thing, which was actually coming into being, with the knowledge of the imminent intervention of God. What helped to give his gospel and mission their driving, electrifying force was that all this was happening then, that its hour was striking, that the crisis was actually at hand. "Let your loins be girt, and lamps burning in your hands" (*Luke* xii. 35) ; "This generation shall not pass, till all these things be done" (*Matt.* xxiv. 24) ; "There are some of them that stand here, who shall not taste death, till they see the kingdom of God coming in power " (*Mark* viii. 39; *Matt.* xvi. 28). There can be no doubt that Jesus sees the coming of the kingdom in the immediate future, indeed that for him it is already at hand. The burning love he has for his Father and for mankind is concentrated on that near moment when the might of the kingdom of God will become manifest. The living Jesus, as he takes shape before us in act, is the eschatological Jesus, the Jesus whose entire attitude is determined by his orientation to the approaching dominion of God.

How are we to understand this ? Is it that Jesus, like the apocalyptists of his time, was possessed by the illusion that the end of all things, the last day, with the collapse of the old era, with the destruction of the world, with its last judgment, with its heaven and hell was immediately at hand ? Did Jesus, like so many of his contemporaries, couple the end of the world with the approaching destruction of Jerusalem ? Does perhaps this close temporal coupling of the destruction of the world with that of Jerusalem explain the heroic, epic quality of his teaching, the harsh tone of his demands, and the arousing force of his cry to mankind to be prepared ?

* * * * *

It is not so long ago that, under the influence in particular of Albert Schweitzer's alarming book, *Von Reimarus bis Wrede*, this question was unhesitatingly answered in the affirmative, and it was taken as proved that Jesus was nothing but an ecstatic, a prophet of the type of the Baptist, a prophet, moreover, who was mistaken in the very kernel of his teaching. To-day this question is approached more cautiously. If certain cryptic sayings of Jesus, as, for example, that some of the bystanders should not taste death until they saw the Son of man coming in his kingdom (*v. Matt.* xvi. 28), or that the disciples sent out to preach salvation would " not finish all the cities of Israel till the Son of man come" (*Matt.* x. 23) ; if these utterances of Jesus promise the speedy coming of the Son of man, it will not do to explain this speedy coming simply as the coming of the Lord at the end of time to judge the world. It will not do, because Jesus expressly and on principle refuses to make any definite pronouncement as to the " day and hour " of the end of the world. To a question of the disciples he replies, leaving no possibility of misunderstanding : " Of that day and hour no man knoweth, neither the angels in heaven, nor the Son, but the father " (*Mark* xiii. 26). We have here an undoubted saying of Jesus himself. This saying of our Lord cannot possibly derive from the primitive Christian community, disturbed by the failure of the coming of the Lord to take place, if only for the simple reason that the first Christians would never have lent themselves to the notion of crediting their " Lord," the " Son of God," the " Judge of the world " with so striking an imperfection as ignorance of the day of the last judgment. From this it at any rate follows that the precise day and hour of the judgment has no bearing on what Jesus has to teach. For his gospel the question of the day and the hour is of no importance whatever. Whereas the apocalyptic literature of his time, exemplified by the pictorial descriptions of Henoch and the fourth book of Esdras, seeks to arrive at a precise reckoning of the day and hour of the end of the world by means of a system of mystic numbers, to Jesus the chronological aspect of belief in the parousia is a matter of complete indifference. Indeed, we can gather much more from the gospels, for they definitely establish that Jesus not only was silent as to the exact day and hour of the last judgment, but explicitly reckoned on the possibility, indeed it would be truer to say the probability, that the will of the Father might postpone the coming of the last day for a long time yet. In the same eschatological discourse, in which he seems to announce the coming of the day within the lifetime of that generation, he also describes in detail the interior and exterior upheavals which will visit the nations before that day shall come. He refers to the preparatory preaching of the kingdom " for a testimony to all nations " (*Matt*. xxiv. 14), to the hatred which shall be heaped upon the Christian name (*Matt*. xxiv. 9), and to a progressive process of disintegration within Christendom itself, by which " the charity of many shall grow cold " (*Matt*. xxiv. 12). It is quite impossible that the real opinion of Jesus could have been that these events, which from their nature must spread over a long period of time, should all come to pass within the lifetime of a single generation. Not a few of his parables point in the same direction : the bridegroom whom the virgins are awaiting only appears at midnight

(*Matt.* xxv. 6) ; the lord of the house, who had gone into a far country, returns only " after a long time " to demand a reckoning of his servants (*Matt.* xxv. 9) ; and it is only because the lord "is a long time coming" that the unfaithful servant squanders the goods which had been entrusted to him (*Matt.* xxiv. 48).   If we ask what is the dominant note of these eschatological parables, we shall see that they emphasize not the instant, immediate coming of the Son of man, but the suddenness and unexpectedness of this event.   As in the days of Noe, men will lie eating, drinking and enjoying themselves without a thought of his coming, and lo the Son of man shall come (*Matt.* xxiv. 37 *sq.*).   Hence these parables do not culminate in the warning to be prepared since the coming of the Son of man is to be looked for within that generation, but derive their impelling force from the uncertainty of the hour of the parousia : " Watch ye therefore (for you know not when the lord of the house cometh : at even, or at midnight, or at the cock-crowing, or in the morning).   Lest coming on a sudden he find you sleeping " (*Mark* xiii. 35 *sq.*).   Jesus is anxious to leave human life, every human life in the twilight of uncertainty as to the last day with its judgment, that every moment of every human life may be a crisis, since the frightful possibility of immediate judgment must be faced.   But man faces only the possibility.   When the possibility will become actual Jesus deliberately refrains from telling.

We should be forced either to delete or else violently to distort these and kindred passages if we seriously wished to cling to the idea that Jesus himself reckoned on an imminent irruption of the end of time; and that he understood the coming of the Son of man, which he announced, only in this rigidly chronological sense. On the other hand, it is certainly no less true that his vision was directed to the near future and that with the whole strength of his human soul he was expecting an imminent intervention by God, the coming of the Son of man within the lifetime of a generation. He knew that the precise hour of the coming of the Son of man to judge the world was reserved for the determination of the Father; and yet he saw this coming somehow realized within the present generation.

How is this paradox to be explained? It is explained by the consciousness which he has of his mission. Jesus knows that in his person here and now there is spanned the hereafter and the present, the end of time and the generation in which he is living. He knows himself to be the one who, hereafter, surrounded by all his angels, shall sit upon the seat of his majesty and gather together all nations before him, and separate them one from the other as the shepherd separates the sheep from the goats, and shall " set the sheep on his right hand and the goats on his left." Here and now he knows himself to be the Lord of the new kingdom, who shall say to those on his right hand, " Come, ye blessed of my Father, possess you the kingdom prepared for you from the beginning of the world " (*Matt.* xxv. 31 *sqq.*). It is a bold and, in a human mouth, a tremendous thing which Jesus here says of himself. And yet what he says gives us the true key to an understanding of his mission, and explains the apparent paradox of his teaching. Since Jesus knows that he is to be the future judge of this world, the king of the new kingdom—for he himself bears testimony to this—this kingdom appears to his mind as being in some way actually present. In his self-consciousness the present and the future, indeed time and eternity meet. In a prophetic vision incomprehensible to us mortals, he conceives the present judge and the future judgment, the present king and the future kingdom, the present generation and the impending new era as one single actuality. The great thing that is to come is for him somehow already present in his person, and it will manifest itself with power even within his generation. In his person the forces of the new kingdom are already beginning to break out and to work in a truly new and creative way. Because Jesus here and now overcomes demonic forces " by the finger of God " (*Luke* xi. 20), he looks on it as a proof that the kingdom and its powers are already at work. They work invisibly. We cannot determine them by their position in space as we can the stars in the heavens ; we cannot say of them, " behold here, or behold there," for " the kingdom of God is within you " (*Luke* xvii. 20 *sq.*) ; that is to say, he is standing with his invisible powers among the Jews. Unmarked by any, fresh benediction is ever proceeding from him and is ever growing, like the mustard seed (*Matt.* xiii. 31), or the leaven which the woman hid in the meal (*Matt.* xiii. 33). The kingdom of the Father is hus at the same time his kingdom, the " kingdom of

Christ " (*cf. Matt.* xiii. 41 ; xvi. 28 ; xx. 21 ; *Luke*
xxiii. 42). When two or three are gathered in his name,
he is there in the midst of them (*Matt.* xviii. 20). In
him his own are already one, his household, his wedding
guests, who hereafter shall eat and drink at his table
in his kingdom (*Luke* xxii. 29 *sq.*). True, the exterior
majesty and the full ultimate victory, the achievement
of God's dominion are yet to come. His kingdom is
thus essentially becoming, something always to come.
Hence Jesus in his thoughts is ever straining out towards
the future. His orientation is ever eschatological. But,
since he knows himself to be the one in whom this great
thing that is to come will manifest itself in the immediate
future in revelations and wonders, the one whence that
last judgment and that final dominion of God are already
issuing, he can in a true and profound sense announce
the coming of the kingdom for the immediate future.
What he says of the kingdom and of his coming in power
has a double meaning : it applies equally to the end of
time and to the present ; or, rather, it applies to the
present as inwardly related to and received into the end
of time. His prophetic and Messianic purpose of salvation required the revelation not so much of the chronological sequence of the two ages as of their essential
correlation and mutual implication. It is significant that
St. John, who more than any other evangelist has sought
to reveal the interior life of Jesus, should in his writings
have given prominence to this aspect of our Lord's
intuition. In his gospel, much more clearly than in the
synoptics, the present is shown to be actually included in

the eschatological conceptions of Jesus. It is not as if the prince of this world will be judged only at the end of time, for he is "already judged" (*John* xvi. 11). "Now is the judgment of the world: now shall the prince of this world be cast out" (*John* xii. 31).

* * * * *

We cannot get round the fact that the whole of the teaching of Jesus, and in particular its mysterious paradox, has its roots in his consciousness that he, the Galilean, the man of to-day, is at the same time the future judge of the world, the Lord of the kingdom that is to come. From this point of view his figure appears to us in an entirely new light. We no longer see Jesus among the flowers and the children, among the sick and the sinners, but on the judgment seat of God. He is no longer the sublime teacher and the glowing prophet, but the Lord of the approaching end of all time. He is our judgment, the fate of the world.

This consciousness Jesus expressed in close relation to a term by which he designated himself, a term which strikes us of to-day as very singular. He called himself the "Son of man." With this he brings us to the very depths of his personality. What does Jesus mean when he calls himself the Son of man?

The expression Son of man, which originally connoted merely some man or other, had since *Daniel* (vii. 13) spoke of one who "like the Son of man came with the clouds of heaven . . . even to the Ancient of days," acquired for the Jews and especially for their apocalyptic writers, a definitely religious and in fact, Messianic

significance. Though it had never been accepted as
so to speak the official designation of the coming Messias,
it had nevertheless led men's thoughts to that mysterious
figure which, according to the belief of the noblest souls,
would, as Lord of the end of time, one day redeem
Israel. When Jesus deliberately called himself the Son
of man and appropriated the name exclusively to himself, the term acquired from his use of it a strange,
mysterious undertone. It was puzzling and made people
prick up their ears, and it turned their thoughts—
unlike the expression "Son of God," which to the Jew of
that time had purely earthly or at best creaturely asso-
ciations—to the supernatural, divine spheres, to the
clouds of heaven, to the right hand of the Ancient of
days. If Jesus from the outset had appropriated to himself the all-holy name of Jahwe, his countrymen, who had
been nurtured in the strict belief in God's uniqueness and
incomparable majesty, would have summarily stoned
him for blasphemy before he had properly begun his
ministry. If on the other hand he had adopted the
Messianic terminology of his day and called himself
simply the Son of God and nothing else, this term would
have obscured rather than revealed his divine secret.
For the Jews of the period were wont to apply this holy
name to created beings, in particular to the angels of
God, but also to the chosen people themselves, to their
annointed king, even to specially pious individuals;
hence it only meant some created being when they talked
of the expected Messias as the "Son of God." In
order to avoid both dangers Jesus appealed to the

prophecy of Daniel. Whenever he discourses on the last day he always speaks of the Son of man sitting on the right hand of the power of God and coming with the clouds of heaven (*Mark* xiii. 26 ; xiv. 62 ; *Luke* ii. 2 ; *Matt.* xxiv. 30 ; *Mark* viii. 38, etc.). With unparalleled assurance of his mission he knows from the outset that this prophecy is fulfilled in his person. In Daniel's picture of the Son of man he reveals himself as the judge of the world, as the Lord of the new kingdom descending from heaven. The consciousness Jesus had of his mission culminates therefore in the supertemporal and the eternal. His activity in time is accomplished in the closest connection with a mission which, in pure transcendency, is beyond all time, and whose purport is the absolute dominion of God. Thus his earthly life is the prologue, the foreground, or better the space-time transparency of this ultimate and eternal reality. His real and highest field of activity is the realm of the invisible, of the superterrestrial, of the Divine, where is set the throne of the Ancient of days. In his person eternity breaks through into time, the superhistorical into the level of history, the Divine into the human. Thus the claim of Jesus to be the Son of man runs parallel with St. John's phrase : " The Word was made flesh." We have in him an epiphany of the right hand of the power of God, an apparition of the Divine in the garment of the human. Only this epiphany is here seen in its sociological operation within the framework of Daniel's prophecy of the kingdom of God, in reference, that is to say, not to the present but to the future, as a

manifestation of the kingdom of God descended to earth
in the person of the Son of man. Hence it is not an
epiphany of God's Word simply, but of God's Word of
judgment.   In the Son of man the eternal judgment
of God and his eternal kingdom have already appeared.
Therefore he is the judgment of mankind, " set for the
fall, and for the resurrection of many " (*Luke* ii. 34).
He is the stone which the builders rejected and which is
become the head of the corner (*Matt*. xxi. 42).   Our
attitude towards his person in time is decisive for all
eternity.   Therefore he can say, " Every one that shall
confess me before men, I will also confess him before
my Father who is in heaven.   But he that shall deny me
before men, I will also deny him before my Father who
is in heaven " (*Matt*. x. 32 *sq*.) ; and " Blessed shall
you be when men shall hate you . . . for the Son of
man's sake."

*　　*　　*　　*　　*

It is evident that, since Jesus refers Daniel's prophecy
of the Son of man to himself, his consciousness transcends all bounds of human possibilities and his claims
reach up to the clouds of heaven, to the right hand of
God himself.

Indeed, they reach still farther. It is highly significant
that Jesus' conception of himself as the Son of man is by
no means coincident with Daniel's prophecy, nor
exhausted by it.   So exalted, so profound, so rich is the
reality which lives in him that it goes far beyond Daniel's
picture and gives the old phrase Son of man a deepened
sense and a new import.   When, that is to say, Jesus

calls himself the Son of man, he is by no means only looking, as in Daniel's prophecy, to the coming end of time and its glory. He does not limit the term Son of man to its eschatological connotation. Not one half of his declarations about himself as the Son of man have reference to the last judgment. For the most part they apply to his work of redemption in the present, quite in accordance with that fusion of the now and the hereafter, of time and eternity, which characterizes his preaching of the kingdom. When Jesus sets the present with its distress and sin in the clear, dazzling light of his last judgment and in the glory of the new kingdom, he knows himself to be the one who shall take away the distress and the sin, who shall redeem mankind for the new kingdom. As the Son of man he is judge and Saviour in one. Hence his message even as it applies to the present is an evangel. " Blessed are the eyes that see the things which you see. For I say to you that many prophets and kings have desired to see the things that you see, and have not seen them " (*Luke* x. 23 *sq.*). Since he, the Son of man, will hereafter be Lord and King of the kingdom of God, he is already in the present the source of salvation. " Come to me, all you that labour, and are burdened, and I will refresh you " (*Matt.* xi. 28). His eschatological task presupposes the Messianic. Or better they postulate one another. Jesus is therefore fond of using the term Son of man when he is speaking of his redemptive work in the present. " The Son of man is come to seek and save that which was lost " (*Luke* xix. 10). " The Son of man " is he who sows

the good seed, the children of the new kingdom (*Matt.*
xiii. 37). It is the right of the Son of man to liberate
man's ethical and religious endeavour from all extraneous
bonds, even a law so venerable as the law of the Sabbath.
"The Son of man is lord also of the Sabbath" (*Mark* ii.
28). Further, "the Son of man" does even what
God alone does, what to many of the Jewish scribes
exceeded the power of the expected Messias. He forgives
sins. "That you may know that the Son of man hath
power on earth to forgive sins (he saith to the sick of the
palsy), I say to thee, Arise, take up thy bed, and go into
thy house" (*Mark* ii. 48). There is the same claim in his
words to the sinful woman: "Thy sins are forgiven
thee" (*Luke* vii. 48). In the forgiving of sins the
redeemership of the Son of man, which embraces the
present world, reaches its apex, and his Messianic
claims their strongest and most emphatic expression.
Here Jesus attains not only to the right hand of God, but
into his heart. And since he is filled with the consciousness that it is the will of the Father that the redeemership
of the Son of man should be consummated in suffering
and the Cross, that the Lord and king of the new kingdom must win for himself his own by shedding his own
life's blood for them, he always calls himself the Son of
man when he speaks about his Passion. Again and
again, when predicting his Passion, he emphasizes the
fact that "the Son of man must suffer" (*Mark* viii. 31;
ix. 11; *Matt.* xvi. 21; *Luke* ix. 22). "The Son of
man is not come to be ministered unto, but to minister,
and to give his life a redemption for many" (*Matt.* xx.

28 ; *Mark* x. 45). To Jesus when saying this the picture Isaias draws of the suffering servant of God and Daniel's prophecy of the Son of man blend into a single majestic vision. He who, with a self-confidence which has no parallel, sees himself at the end of time as judge of the world and Lord of the new kingdom, at the same time knows himself to be the one whom Isaias foretold, who " hath borne the sins of many, and hath delivered his soul unto death " (*Is.* liii. 11 *sq.*). In the one little phrase, Son of man, the homeliest thing which he could tell us of himself, in the term " man " are concealed the most tremendous contrasts in this consciousness he had of himself. Jesus knows himself to be exalted to the heavens, and he sees himself thrust down into the slime of the earth. He is come to rule ; he is come to minister and to die. King of the kingdom is he, and yet man, indeed the slave of men. We can now understand why Jesus took by preference the name Son of man that by its simple symbolism he might indicate what he intends to be for man : a man among men and yet their king, their judge, and their Saviour, a man from heaven. From this that other term by which his contemporaries expressed their belief in the king of the last age, namely, the Mashiah, that is the annointed, the Christ, took on a new meaning. Whereas the Jews, when in their eighteen-clause petition they prayed for the coming of the Christ, had in mind a restoration of the glories of the kingdom of David, Jesus saw this " Christ " only as the coming Son of man, as the saviour and judge of the world. It was in this sense that he took Peter's con-

fession, " Thou art the Christ " (*Mark* viii. 29 ; *Luke* ix. 21), and because of its mysterious depth he attributed it to an inspiration from on high. " Flesh and blood hath not revealed it to thee, but my Father who is in heaven." It was in this sense that the first Christians took it over from Peter, and since that day there has been no sweeter name in heaven or on earth than " Jesus Christ." If the expression " Christ " had hitherto been cumbered by Jewish conceptions that the expected Messias would be of earthly stock, it henceforth turned men's hearts to the Son of man, to the right hand of the Ancient of days, to the Saviour of the present, the king and judge of the future.

This was the novel and revolutionary element in the claim of Jesus. It stands in the most direct contrast with what the Jews of his time, under the spur of their selfish nationalistic instincts, believed and hoped of their expected Messias. In this too is to be sought the determining cause of the drama of Golgotha. Had Jesus admitted to being a Christ in the Jewish nationalistic sense of the term, he would not have been crucified, even though his claim had been disputed and disallowed. For according to the law applicable to the case, such a claim, even though baseless, was not blasphemy against God, and was therefore not a capital offence. It was only when Jesus in that grave hour not merely gave assent to the high-priest's question, " Art thou the Christ, the Son of the living God ? " but with that serene truth which was of his essence, added the further confession : " And you shall see the Son of man sitting on the right hand of the power of God, and coming with the clouds of heaven "—it was only then that he gave unequivocal meaning and an unequivocal answer to the equivocal question of the high-priest, for this it was when regarded in connection with Jewish Messianic ideas. In his fetters he sees himself at the right hand of the power of God. Arraigned before an earthly judge, he knows himself to be on the judgment seat of God. Could there be a greater paradox, and a more atrocious offence? "Then the high-priest rent his garments, saying: He hath blasphemed, what further need have we of witnesses? Behold now you have heard the blasphemy: What think you? But they answering said: He is guilty of death. Then did they spit in his face, and buffeted him." Jesus died, Jesus had to die, because men were too petty, too narrow, too abject, and too obtuse to comprehend his sublimity and his divinity. He died for these base men because he was the Son of man.

*   *   *   *   *

It is characteristic of the lucidity and depth of his self-consciousness that from the first moment of his public ministry he knew with unfaltering certainty, and with a certainty that admitted of no further growth, that his mission of world-judge in the future and of redeemer in the present were involved in his very nature. Both missions transcended all human dimensions and reached to the clouds of heaven, right into the heart of the Father, and the simple little phrase Son of man expressed both in a way that both veiled and unveiled their secret.

It was not Paul who first brought the heavenly man and
the Saviour of the world into relation. The expression
Son of man, moreover, appears nowhere in St. Paul's
epistles. It was not the early Christians at Jerusalem
who, influenced by their eschatological conceptions,
invented the dogma of the Son of man in order to express
their belief that the risen Lord would return as king at
the last day to judge the world. The term Son of man
has never, even as used by Jesus, had a strictly dogmatic
connotation. It was never a formula of belief. It was
an enigmatic term used to call the attention of the Jews
to the mighty realities hidden in Christ. What these
realities were was shown first by the connection in which
Jesus used the term Son of man. Jesus called Peter
blessed not because he had confessed him to be the Son
of man, but because he had confessed him, the Son of
man, to be the Christ. And Peter's discourses in the
Acts of the Apostles prove that among the early
Christians it was not the Son of man but the " Lord,"
the " Christ," the " Servant of God " which formed the
core of their teaching. Only in the particular circumstances of Jesus himself had the expression Son of man
its comprehensible origin and place. It was a formula to
protect him against the malevolent and a signal call to
those of good will. It was so far a transitional conception
in that it only possessed a meaning and an application
when Jesus in his lonely greatness was alone with his
secret. It grew entirely out of the concrete and unique
situation in which Jesus then was, a situation which
never recurred. This fact guarantees its primitive

genuineness. This, too, is the only explanation of the term Son of man being so soon forgotten in Jewish-Christian circles and still more in the Greek communities, with the result that by the beginning of the second century it was no longer understood.

In all this Jesus does not stand outside his period and its people, but in the midst of them. Hence he took over from them the imagery in which the hopes and ideals of his time were clad, above all the eschatological representation of the king of the last age. But he adopted this to give it a vital content in his own person, and by the strength of his consciousness of his mission to re-mint it in creative works and to enrich it with a new import. Through the flimsy and outworn garb of an ideal conditioned by contemporary circumstances, we are able to see in the timeless distance the world of the supernatural and the Divine and the celestial rays pouring back into his presence, lightning from his eyes and flashing in his words.

Even if we considered Jesus only in the framework of his gospel of the kingdom and of the Son of man, only in his relation to the Messianic movement of his time, we could not efface the claim to the supertemporal and the Divine from his historical image. It will not do to assent only to a Jesus of noble and pure humanity, that is to say, to love in Jesus the incarnation of sinlessness, truth, and graciousness and to leave his supernatural claims to the theorizings of the theologians. The Jesus of history shows himself to have a clear, distinct consciousness of a supratemporal vocation and mission, indeed of a celestial nature and existence. The place where he abides, and where it is his will to be seen, is the throne of the Ancient of days in the clouds of heaven, surrounded by his angels. His whole earthly activity receives from these other-worldly, eschatological elements its consecration and its redeeming power. It is indeed an historical fact that the substance of his teaching is grounded in the message that the kingdom of God with all its power is present in his person. It is certainly not to be looked for primarily in his ethical teaching. To some very important points in this teaching parallels may be found in the Old Testament as well as in contemporary Jewish theology and in Hellenistic philosophy. Jesus certainly rid his precious inheritance of its many purely human wrappings, and by severe reduction and concentration first made its full light visible ; but as far as the principal content of his ethical teaching is concerned, it was all in some measure already in existence. Accordingly it is not here that the really new thing which he wished to deliver and did deliver is to be found. The new thing which was his preponderating interest is the tidings that with his coming eternity enters into time, that redemption is at hand, and that " the acceptable year of the Lord " (*Luke* iv. 19) is now come. Hence we cannot eliminate from the teaching of Jesus his supernatural, Divine claims without destroying the teaching itself. Whoever overlooks this or denies it has no historical right to warm himself at the glow of the philanthropy and sinlessness of Jesus. All his noble human characteristics derive directly from his superterrestrial nature and destiny. Historically they are only intelligible as radiations and revelations of a man who in the heart of his being and consciousness belongs not to humanity but to Deity. Again, how could there have emerged from a world which was falling to ruins—a world of ossified belief in the letter, of a narrowminded caste-spirit and materialistic piety, a world of scepticism, doubt and libertinism— a human nature so incomparably pure, so God-united and holy and gracious, so inwardly detached and free and genuine as his? Whoever gives his consent to the one may not deny the other. We cannot shut our eyes to his Divine mystery.

*   *   *   *   *

In what does this mystery in its deepest aspect consist? When Jesus calls himself the Son of man and thereby declares himself to be the judge and king at the last day, the Redeemer and Saviour of the present, in what is this knowledge of himself grounded? When he claims to be exalted above all prophets and kings, above all angels and men, raised up to the very side of God, in what relation does he stand to this God? Does he know himself to be distinct from him or to be one with him? Is he, the Son of man, a creature of God's, or is he God himself? The question is a tremendous one, indeed it is terrifying. For here we have a man, a man with body and soul, with a human mind, with a human will and emotions, and we ask ourselves, is this man God? Yet this question must be put, for all that we discover in this man cannot be explained by his humanity alone. It all

points in the direction where God is. The historical
figure of Jesus must ever remain an obstinate enigma if
we are forbidden to seek in this direction. All the
pictures of Jesus drawn by the " liberal " school of
theology are incomplete and fragmentary just because
on principle it disregards the Divine in him. It was
only logical that the less cautious successors of this
school could make nothing of their fragments, and
brutally shattered the picture, asserting that this Jesus
had never existed. In saying this they unintentionally
spoke the truth ; for the Jesus they and their masters
meant never had existed. It would in truth be contrary
to all experience and to all historical analogy that that
ineffable purity and grandeur, which even the sharpest
stylus applied to the gospel picture of Jesus has never
been able to efface, should have been found in a mere
man. Such a man has *de facto* never existed. There
has existed only one man, the Man Jesus, who consciously
set himself in his inmost being not with man but with
God. This being the case, the enigma of his historical
appearance can only be finally solved if we take yet
another step and ask ourselves how, if Jesus is from God,
his relation to God is to be defined. Is he a celestial
being sent to us by God or is he God himself, the
apparition of God in human form ?

In order to realize the difficulty of the question in
all its weight, we must keep in mind the fact that Jesus,
as far as his human extraction is concerned, was a member
of the Jewish race, which was very strictly monotheistic
in its thought, whose daily prayer was, " Hear, O

Israel, the Lord thy God is one God," and that he himself in his prayer (*cf. Mark* xii. 29) and teaching bore constant witness to the one God of heaven and earth, to the one Father. Thus seen, our question whether Jesus claimed to possess a Divine nature, can only have a meaning if it neither proceeds from polytheistic premisses nor leads us to a polytheistic conclusion: unless, that is to say, it preserves, in distinction to the polytheistic Hellenistic concept of God, the unity and uniqueness of God in every aspect. The question, therefore, cannot be whether Jesus knows himself to be a divinity equal to Jahwe, whether he sets himself as the Son of the Godhead below or beside Jahwe; it can only relate to a " Son of God " wholly of the same nature as Jahwe, who is Jahwe himself, and has assumed human nature so intimately to himself that this human nature does not belong to itself but is wholly God's, the apparition of God in man. It is clear that this question and this possibility can grow only out of monotheistic soil, that is to say out of Jewish conceptions alone. Hence in our inquiry we need not, in fact we may not, take refuge in the domain of Hellenistic polytheistic thought, unless we are ready to shut our eyes to, or deny the fundamental dogma of, the Jewish people whence Jesus sprang, as well as his fundamental confession to the one living God of heaven and earth. It is an untenable and misleading assertion that our inquiry into the Godhead of Jesus, or our belief in it, can only have any meaning in the soil of the Hellenistic mystery cults, since only here was there any notion of Sons of

God in the natural order of sonship. The point is that Jesus was not such a Son of God according to nature in the Hellenistic sense, and he did not claim to be. He could not have had a consciousness of this kind for the reason that belief in the one living God lay at the root of all his teaching about the approaching kingdom of God, and the whole of Christendom throughout all the centuries of its existence down to the present time has ever remained equally monotheistic. There is no room here for a polytheistic or Hellenistic understanding of the figure of Christ. Whenever, as in the form of Arianism, it tried to become naturalized in the Church, it was the living faith in the one God which overcame and destroyed it.

Thus in view of the strictly monotheistic stamp of Christ's teaching our inquiry can only take the form: What did Jesus think, what did he teach on the subject of the relation of his human nature to the one living God? Did he know that at the apex of his being he was one in nature with this God? Was he a corporeal epiphany of the one living God, or was he not? What do his works tell us, what does he himself say on this point?

If we place the ministry of Jesus in its historical setting, if, that is to say, we connect it with what the prophets had foretold and with the message of the Baptist, we are at once struck by the conscious assurance with which it detaches itself and differentiates itself from them. Its intention is to fulfil and to consummate. To Jesus all that had previously been revealed is but a breaking of the road and its preparation. " Behold a greater than Jonas is here. . . . Behold a greater than Solomon is here " (*Matt*. xii. 41, 42). The most exalted figures among prophets and kings are therefore not so great as Jesus. " Blessed are the eyes," he says to his disciples, " that see the things which you see. For many prophets and kings have desired to see the things that you see, and have not seen them " (*Luke* x. 23 *sq*.). " Abraham rejoiced that he might see his day " (*John* viii. 41). The Baptist is greater than all that are born of woman, greater that is than the prophets and kings of the old Covenant, and yet " he that is least in the kingdom of heaven is greater than he " (*Matt*. xi. 11). Jesus here sets his work higher, and not only relatively but absolutely, than all that had been done previously by the prophets and the kings. He is conscious that his teaching is something wholly incomparable and perfect. When for the first time he revisits Nazareth, " this day is fulfilled the scripture of Isaias which proclaims healing to the poor, deliverance to the oppressed and captives, and sight to the blind " (*Luke* iv. 18 *sqq*.).

This new and absolutely transcendent element in his teaching has its ultimate roots in an unparalleled ascendency, in a boundless authority, in his own person. There is nothing great and holy in the old Covenant, not even its temple, not even its Sabbath-day, indeed not even its law which is not subject to his will and authority. " I tell you that there is here a greater than the temple " (*Matt*. xii. 6). True, God himself had instituted the Sabbath-day (*Ex*. xx. 8 *sq*. ; *Deut*. v. 12, 14) ; yet the

Son of man is " Lord even of the Sabbath " (*Matt.* xii.
8). True, the all-holy God gave the law through his
servant Moses, but here is one who understands the law
more perfectly than Moses did, who, going beyond
Moses and even correcting him, makes it clear and fulfils
it down to its most hidden depths. In the name of the
new inwardness and love Jesus corrects the precepts of
Moses no less than six times. In doing so he does not,
like the prophets of old, appeal to a special Divine commission. He acts of his own right. We never hear from
his lips the words, " thus saith the Lord," with which the
prophets were wont to appeal to the mission they had
received from Jahwe. He speaks only on his own
responsibility, out of his own knowledge, of his own
right : " But I say to you " (*Matt.* v. 18 ; xx. 22, etc.).
If we consider that in the Jewish mind temple and
Sabbath, Moses and the law are inseparably linked with
Jahwe, that in them the will of the all-holy God himself
was expressed, it is difficult to understand the claim of
Jesus to be superior to them, save in the sense that in his
inmost being he knew himself to be wholly one with
Jahwe. He takes his stand precisely where to Jewish
belief only One stands, namely Jahwe himself.

The same impression of essential oneness with God is
aroused by the miracles of Jesus. However much these
wonders may be disputed by extravagant critics, no one
can deny that not only on his disciples but also on his
bitterest antagonists his mighty works made the strongest
impression, and that they are inseparably bound up with
the life of Jesus. The Jewish Talmud itself records

miraculous healings in the name of Jesus. But the spirit in which he wrought his miracles differed from that of other miracle-workers. What distinguishes them is the regal self-certainty with which, according to the unanimous testimony of the gospels, he worked them. Of the prophets also not a few miracles are reported. Elias and Eliseus actually restored the dead to life (*III. Kings* xvii. 19 *sqq.*; *IV. Kings* iv. 32 *sqq.*; *IV. Kings* xiii. 21). The Rabbis also cast out devils. Jesus himself refers to this (*Matt.* xii. 27). But all these mighty works were wrought by appeal to the Almighty and in his name. What strikes us in Jesus is that his miracles do not present themselves as answers to prayer, but as natural operations of his own being. It is not from the Father but from himself that the influence proceeds. "I will. Be thou made clean" (*Mark* i. 41); "Eph-pheta. . . . Be thou opened" (*Mark* vii. 34); "Tabitta cumi . . . damsel (I say to thee) arise" (*Mark* v. 41); "Arise, take up thy bed, and go into thy house" (*Mark* ii. 11). Here is not a Divine commission but omnipotence. It is true that we said above that the human will of Jesus was merged with the Divine will, that Jesus accomplished all he did in virtue of the moral union of his human will with the Divine. This moral union was only the instrument through which he worked; it was not the Source whence this working flowed. His oneness with the will of the Father was taken up and permeated by a higher unity, by his essential union with God. It had its roots in an Ego which was God.

A bright light is thrown on this consciousness of his

oneness with the all-holy God by the absolute self-confidence with which Jesus interprets the prophetical Messianic passages of the Old Testament and, whenever the prophets see God at work, places his own Ego in the place of God. Only because he knows himself to be identical with God can he thus refer to his own action all that the prophets attribute to Jahwe. He is himself that "Lord of Hosts" (*Matt.* xi. 10 *sq.*; *Luke* vii. 27 *sq.*), for whom, according to *Malachias* (iii. 1), a personal forerunner shall prepare the way. He himself is that wonder-working Jahwe (*Matt.* xi. 5) whose acts are foretold by Isaias (xxxv. 4 *sqq.*). He himself is that good shepherd which *Isaias* (xl. 11) and *Eʒechiel* (xxxiv. 11) look for Jahwe to be. To himself (*Matt.* xvi. 16) he applies what was written of the Lord, that out of the mouths of infants and sucklings should proceed power to aid him against his adversaries. He is conscious that Jahwe and his own Ego are one and the same. Hence just as Jahwe is the husband of Israel (*Jer.* iii. 14; *Eʒ.* xvi. 8), so he calls himself the bridegroom of his followers (*Mark* ii. 20).

This conscious identification of himself with Jahwe is prominently brought out in the healing of the man sick of palsy (*Mark* ii. 10 *sqq.*). By explicitly attributing himself to the power to forgive sins, which according to the Jewish belief was reserved to God alone (*cf. Is.* xliii. 25; *Eʒech.* xxxvi. 25), by omitting any mention of God, and by the solemn sanction he gives to this personal claim by the outward acts of the healing of the sick man, he gives unequivocal expression to the fact that he knows himself to be the manifestation of Jahwe, and that his power to redeem and to forgive sins rests on his oneness with Jahwe.

This throws a new light on his intellectual, moral and religious character, and we can for the first time get at its root. This root is none other than the oneness of Jesus with the Divine Word itself. From the Word alone does his human will derive that bold independence and certainty with which he determines his goal, that consistency and finality in all his actions, that perfect openness to the holy and the divine. If the perfection of his humanity finds its unique expression in the fact that there is no trace of gradual development in it, nothing attained by long struggle, but rather the stamp of an innate endowment, so that imperfection and sin are foreign not only to his acts, but also to his very being, so foreign that Jesus has jurisdiction over sin and overthrows it in others and forgives it ; if this be so then the origin of this absolutely new and incomparably pure and holy humanity can only be looked for in substantial holiness, that is to say in God himself. It is only because Jesus is God that the human character of Jesus is a manifestation of the Divine. The Godhead of Jesus is alone able to make intelligible the miracle of his most sacred humanity.

This, too, dispels all the obscurities in his gospel of the kingdom of God. Only on the assumption that Jesus knew that in his inmost being he was a manifestation of the Eternal God is it psychologically intelligible that his teaching should embrace both the present and the end of time, that eternity and time should meet in his consciousness, that he should know himself to be at once the Saviour and the judge of the world, that the kingdom of God should also be his kingdom. His claim to the Son of God has the same basis as his gospel of the kingdom of God. We cannot separate it from this as something alien and exterior, to be explained as a later embellishment. Its origin lies where the teaching on the kingdom of God had its origin, in the knowledge and consciousness of Jesus.

Furthermore, on this oneness with Jahwe is based the insistence and exclusiveness with which he makes his own person the central point of his teaching. True, the kingdom of God is the direct, immediate object of his gospel; but that kingdom is inseparable from his person, for in him it is made manifest. Nowhere in the history of religions do we find anything like this. Whenever in history a religious cult has been founded, the founder was not its object but merely the instrument of its foundation. It was not the person of Buddha or Muhammad or Moses that was the real substance of the new belief or cult, but rather what each taught. We can separate his teaching entirely from any of these men and exhibit it independently of him. Not so in Christianity, for Christianity is Jesus Christ, and the Christian teaching is that Jesus is the Christ. " Whom do you say that I am," was the decisive question put by Jesus on the threshold of the new kingdom. Hence his person alone is the living centre of the new community, the source of all its fruitfulness. " Where there are two or three gathered together in my name, there am I in the midst of them" (*Matt.* xviii. 20). "With desire" (*Luke* xxii. 15) did he desire in that last hour, when he had to leave his disciples, to give to them "for a commemoration" himself, his flesh and blood: "Take ye, and eat: this is my body. . . . Drink ye all of this. For this is my blood of the new testament which shall be shed for many." His last and deepest concern is that his own should be for ever bound to him in the intimate communion of his flesh and blood.

There was from the beginning nothing which Jesus demanded more urgently of his disciples than unconditional attachment to his person, an imitation of him which should have no limit but extend even to the bearing of his Cross. "He that taketh not up his cross, and followeth me, is not worthy of me" (*Matt.* x. 38). He insists just as strongly on this as he does in other places on obedience to the will of God. What he demands for his Father in heaven that also he asks for himself, namely, an unflinching faith in him and a boundless love for him. "Blessed is he that shall not be scandalized in me" (*Matt.* xi. 6). "Blessed art thou, Simon Bar-Jona" (*Matt.* xvi. 17). "You believe in God, believe also in me" (*John* xiv. 1). "He that doth not believe is already judged" (*John* iii. 18). When Jesus lays it down that "the greatest and the first commandment" is to love God with our whole heart and our whole soul, there follows in the same spirit and with the same emphasis his new demand of us : "He that loveth father or mother more than me, is not worthy of me ; and he that loveth son or daughter more than me, is not worthy of me " (*Matt.* x. 37 ; *Luke* xiv. 26). When has a mere man ever laid, or dared to lay, his contemporaries, indeed all humanity, under the obligation of such utter devotion to his person ? There breaks through at this point a consciousness which transcends all created standards. Jesus is not merely with God ; he is God himself. We may inwardly revolt against this fact, we may protest against it, but we can never banish it from the world. The ministry of Jesus, his teaching and actions, are the work of a man who knows himself to be substantially one with God.

* * * * *

We come now to our last question : How does Jesus himself regard this substantial union of his person with God ? From his works we will pass to his words.

When attempting to estimate his prayer-life, we could not but observe how direct and intimate Jesus knew his union with the Father to be, and what a clear line divides his relationship to the Father in prayer from that of all other men. He alone says " my Father." For the disciples God is " your Father," " their Father." This consciousness of being the Son of God is a primary fact, the postulate of his whole life, a blissful, interior motive force, which even in his boyhood made him yearn to be doing something for his Father. In the temple the twelve-year-old lad answered his mother's reproach, " Behold thy father and I have sought thee sorrowing," with the words, " Did you not know that I must be about my Father's business ? " ; thus too making silent allusion to his mother's words " thy father and I." Even at this early age the reality of his unique union with God, his Sonship, is revealed as the most deeply felt reality in his life. The objection that we have here no original self-revelation of the Lord, but a legend of later interpolation, is purely arbitrary. Moreover, it is an intolerable insult to Luke's veracity, who at the very beginning of his gospel explicitly assures us that all that he wrote had been witnessed to " diligently from the beginning " (*Luke* i. 3). And, by no means least, the objection runs counter to the style of the whole narrative, to the simplicity and discrete reserve with which it suggests rather than asserts the mystery of Jesus, a simplicity and a discretion which is wholly foreign to the really legendary accounts of our Lord's childhood, such as, for instance, Thomas's Gospel of the Infancy. Thus the reliability of Luke's narrative cannot reasonably be impugned. Jesus from his childhood up knows himself to be in a special sense the Son of the Father.

At his baptism by John, which marked his first public appearance, this consciousness of his Sonship was confirmed by a voice from heaven saying : " Thou art my beloved Son, in thee I am well pleased " (*Mark* i. 11 ; *Matt.* iii. 17 ; *Luke* iii. 22). All the rich love which, in days of old, Jahwe had manifested in the same words to his chosen people (*cf. Ps.* ii. 7 ; *Is.* xlii. 1), Jesus on receiving his consecration as the Messias sees poured out upon himself in a new and sublime sense. With a fervour unparalleled he had from childhood cried to

heaven his " My Father." " My Son, my well-beloved "
is the answer which rings out to him, as it has never
done among mortals. This full consciousness of Jesus
that he was the beloved Son of the Father is the secret
happiness, the hidden blessedness of his life, which
shines out of his eyes and gives his whole human appearance the lustre of the supernatural, the holy, and the
Divine. St. John in particular beheld this " glory of
God " in his face, " the glory as it were of the only-
begotten Son of the Father " (*John* i. 14; iii. 16; v.
23; xvii. 1). It was this impression of sheer Deity
which made the man with an unclean spirit cry out:
" Thou art the Holy One of God " (*Mark* i. 24; *cf.*
v. 7), which brought to the lips of the centurion at
Capharnaum the confession, " I am not worthy that thou
shouldst enter under my roof " (*Luke* vii. 6), and brought
Peter to his knees with the words, " Depart from me, for
I am a sinful man, O Lord " (*Luke* v. 8). In the bright,
triumphant splendour of this consciousness all the
spectral shadows of the temptation in the desert, all the
doubts suggested by the devil—" If thou be the Son of
God "—are swallowed up, as were all the dark shadows
of his Passion. For, six days after he had begun to
speak to his disciples of the approaching suffering of the
Son of man, there again came to him in the hearing of
some of them on the mountain of the Transfiguration,
the glad words: " This is my most beloved Son:
hear ye him " (*Mark* ix. 6). It was for Jesus the sweetest
and dearest word, which was to throw a golden glow
over his coming Passion.

What does Jesus precisely mean by Son? In what does his consciousness of his Sonship consist? In the light of the fact that he knows himself to be the judge of the world and king of the end of time, it is to begin with beyond all doubt that he must have understood this Sonship in a transcendental sense. As the "sole," "most beloved Son," he stands above the "servants," *i.e.*, above the prophets of the old Covenant (*Matt.* xxi. 33 *sqq.* = *Mark* xii. 1 *sqq.* = *Luke* xx. 9 *sqq.*). When he declares (*Mark* xiii. 32) that of the day and the hour of the last judgment "no man knoweth, neither the angels in heaven, nor the Son, but the Father," he clearly places himself not only above man in the ascending scale, but also above the angels. And Matthew (xxii. 41) reports a dispute between Jesus and the Pharisees in which he expressly rejects the popular Jewish opinion, that the Messias was to be a mere man, a man of the seed of David. It is impossible, as Jesus proves in the form of a Rabbinical demonstration, for the Messias to be of purely earthly descent, if his ancester David, in one of his Psalms, himself calls him "Lord" (*Ps.* cx. 1). Strongly as current Jewish thought in general held to the view that the expected Messias would be of earthly parentage, there was, as the fourth book of Esdras (*cf.* vii. 28 *sq.*) indicates, pious groups to whom the belief in his superterrestrial origin was not alien. Our Lord's testimony that he was himself the Son of the Father in a transcendental, supernatural sense was therefore not altogether without an historical content.

How does Jesus himself explain the character of his

Sonship? An exhaustive and satisfying answer is given in the celebrated discourse, which Matthew (xi. 25) and Luke (x. 21) hand down to us with but slight variations. This discourse breathes the very spirit of St. John's Gospel and must be regarded as the final and most sublime pronouncement of Jesus on his mystery. It is entirely in harmony with our Lord's discreet and reserved manner of teaching, in which he was always careful not " to cast pearls before swine " (*Matt.* vii. 6), that he should accomplish this his profoundest and definitive act of self-revelation not before the Jewish multitude, but in the circle of his intimate followers. .

Jesus had sent out the seventy-two disciples to preach the gospel of the kingdom all over the country. They returned rejoicing with the news that evil spirits had been subject to them. And Jesus tells them that they should rather rejoice because their names were written in heaven. And " in that same hour he rejoiced in the Holy Ghost, and said : I confess to thee, O Father, Lord of heaven and earth, because thou hast hidden these things from the wise and prudent, and hast revealed them to the little ones. Yea, Father, for so it hath seemed good in thy sight. All things are delivered to me by my Father, and no one knoweth who the Son is but the Father ; and who the Father is but the Son, and to whom the Son will reveal him. And turning to his disciples, he said : Blessed are the eyes that see the things which you see. For I say to you that many prophets and kings have desired to see the things that you see, and have not seen them ; and to hear the things that you

hear, and have not heard them " (*Luke* x. 21 *sqq.*;
cf. Matt. xi. 25 *sqq.*; xiii. 16 *sq.*).

Jesus speaks here with a joy and a triumph past
measure. The success of the seventy-two has proved to
him that the Messianic seed is germinating, that belief in
his mystery is awakening. Precisely in the fact that it is
the "little ones" who believe in his name he sees a
special sign of God's graciousness and compassion. And
so, overcome by this love, he draws from the welling
riches of his own nature, where this love has proved itself
more creative than it has anywhere else. There are
three glories with which the Father has invested him.
" All things are delivered to me by my Father "—all
things, all honour and greatness, all authority and power,
mankind and all the angels. There is literally nothing
which is held by the Father alone, nothing which does
not belong also to Jesus. These are words which span
infinities upon infinities. St. John explains and supple-
ments them by other sayings of Jesus. " All things
whatsoever the Father hath are mine " (*John* xvi. 15).
" All my things are thine and thine mine " (*John* xvii.
10). " As the Father raiseth up the dead, and giveth
life ; so the Son also giveth life to whom he will. For
neither doth the Father judge any man : but hath given
all judgment to the Son. That all may honour the Son,
as they honour the Father " (*John* v. 21 *sqq.*). " Thou
hast given him power over all flesh, that he may give
eternal life to all whom thou hast given him " (*John*
xvii. 2).

And the second glory lies yet deeper. It is properly

the source of the first. " No one knoweth who the Son is but the Father ; and who the Father is but the Son." The Son is a reality to which, in its ultimate depths, no one has access save the Father alone. Conversely, the reality of the Father is revealed to the Son alone. Thus Father and Son stand in a wholly unique, exclusive communion, in which no one else has any part. And the uniqueness of their communion lies in the fact that they are Father and Son. Jesus here paraphrases his essential relation to the Father, making use of conceptions native to the Jewish people and to Hellenistic mysticism beyond their borders. According to them no perfect knowledge of God is possible to man. Only God can have such knowledge of himself. Man can only be known by God (cf. I. Cor. viii. 1 sqq. ; Gal. iv. 9). Quite otherwise, as Jesus here emphasizes, is his own relation to God. He and he alone has the same perfect knowledge of the Father as the Father has of him. And this knowledge is his because he and he alone is the Son. On the other hand, to men the reality of the Son is no less mysterious than that of the Father. So hidden and so inaccessible is it, that only One knows it, and this because he is the Father. If we strip this self-revelation of Jesus of its mystical covering, we find the kernel to be nothing but a clear, unequivocal attestation to the unique, essential relation of his person to the Father and of the Father to him. They alone know and possess and permeate one another down to the very depths of their being, because they alone stand in the relation of Father and Son to one another. What Jesus here reveals with sublime simplicity is congruent with those self-revelations of Jesus which St. John, the evangelist of the interior life, relates. "Do you not believe, that I am in the Father and the Father in me?" (*John* xiv. 10). "Philip, he that seeth me, seeth the Father also" (*John* xiv. 9). "Neither me do you know, nor my Father: If you did know me, you would know my Father also" (*John* viii. 19). "I know mine, and mine know me, and I know the Father" (*John* x. 14 *sq.*). "Believe the works: that you may know and believe that the Father is in me, and I in the Father" (*John* x. 38).

The third glory follows directly from this oneness of being which united the Father and the Son. It was given definitive expression in the same discourse in which Jesus bore witness to himself, when he said, "No one knoweth who the Father is but the Son, and to whom the Son will reveal him." In its deepest sense his teaching and that of the Christian religion is therefore summed up in the words, "through the Son to the Father." There is no other way to the Father but by the Son. Here, too, we catch in the synoptic account the voice of the Johannine Christ, a clear proof that St. John, the beloved disciple, has faithfully preserved and handed down to us the inmost thoughts of Jesus and of the manner in which these were communicated to his disciples. To the question of Thomas, "Lord, how can we know the way?" Jesus answered, "I am the way, and the truth, and the life. No man cometh to the Father but by me" (*John* xiv. 6). "Just Father, the world hath not known thee: but I have known thee:

and these have known that thou hast sent me " (*John* xvii. 25*).

With this the last veils have fallen from the mystery of Jesus. Proceeding from his purely human, mental and moral nature, through his religious interior life, we have found our way to his supernatural mystery; to the Divinity of his nature, to the Son of man as the judge and Lord of the future and the Saviour of the present. We have seen that what was earthly in him was based upon the superterrestrial, and that only from this standpoint could his human life be made historically intelligible. His superterrestrial nature is in turn revealed to us as the mystery of his Sonship, as the direct sharing in the nature of the Father, as a oneness with him. The enigma of his historical appearance has been resolved in his own words : " No one knows the Father but the Son " ; " I and the Father are one."

At these words thought fails and our tongue stumbles. The conception they express is staggering. Once upon a time, within historical memory, there lived a man, thoroughly sound in mind and body, who was gifted with an unusually lucid insight into the facts of existence, into the greatest as well as the least, and with extraordinarily keen understanding. He was a man who was more selfless and unself-seeking than anyone who has ever lived, and whose life was devoted to the service of the poor and the oppressed. And this healthy, clearsighted, selfless man, from beginning to end of his life, knew himself to be the unique well-beloved Son of the Father, to be one who knew the Father as no other man could. More than this, there was once a man, within historical times, who, as a child of the Jewish people, knew only of one God of heaven and earth, of a unique Father in heaven, and stood in reverential awe before this heavenly Father : a man whose meat was to do the will of this Father, who from his earliest youth in good days and bad had sought and loved this will alone, whose whole life was one prayer ; a man, further, whose whole being was so firmly united with this Divine will, that by its omnipotence he healed the sick and restored the dead to life ; a man, finally, who was so intimately and exclusively dedicate to this will, that he never swerved from it, so that not even the slightest consciousness of sin ever oppressed him, so that never a cry for penance and forgiveness passed his lips, so that even in dying he begged pardon not for himself but for others. And this man from the intimacy of his union with God could say to afflicted mortals, " Thy sins are forgiven thee ? " And it was this holy man, utterly subject as he was to God throughout his whole life, absorbed as he was in God, awestruck as he stood before him, who asserted, as if it were the most natural and obvious thing in the world, that he was to be the judge of the world at the last day, that he was the suffering servant of God, nay more, that he was the only begotten Son of God and consubstantial with him, and could say of himself, " I and the Father are one."

Can we, may we, dare we give credence to this man ? We are asked to believe in the Incarnation of God, that is to say, we are asked to accept the fact that God so humbled himself as to "empty" himself, to use St. Paul's words, of his Divine majesty (*Phil.* ii. 7). Is it not our duty to conclude that a man was mistaken, though he were the holiest who ever lived, rather than to believe that God would humble himself so immeasurably? Is not a man here rising up against God? Is it not in the last resort unbelief, if we believe? Does not our alert, reverential sense of God's uniqueness and eternal majesty actually oblige us to refuse our assent and either, like Caiaphas, to rend our garments and to cry out: "He hath blasphemed," or with his kindred to lament his madness? Must we not, with Chesterton, rather "expect the grass to wither and the birds to drop dead out of the air, when a strolling carpenter's apprentice says calmly and almost carelessly, like one looking over his shoulder: 'Before Abraham was I am,' 'I and the Father are one'"?

We can only say that a man who at this point, when confronted with the paradox of God the all-perfect, all-holy, eternal, becoming a man, a carpenter, a Jew haled before the court and crucified, shrinks away, can go no further, and breaks down, may be actually less remote from a living piety than one who coolly accepts all this and glibly repeats his Credo, or indeed than one who does homage to the noble humanity of Jesus yet has the temerity to pooh-pooh what Jesus said of himself as harmless rhetoric, the innocent exaggerations of a pious eccentric.

And yet, in this question of all questions, has man, for all his faith and his conception of God, really the last word? What does "conception of God" mean? Is it not itself man-created? Is not God greater than man's conception of God? Is not the wisdom of man folly in God's sight? How if God willed to prove himself God and to reveal the infinity of his omnipotence and the measurelessness of his love by becoming for our sakes a creature, a man who allowed himself to be crucified? In the infinite possibilities of God all conceivable possibilities are included, even the possibility of a Bethlehem and a Golgotha. What if God demands of man precisely this belief in the unbelievable? Suppose it was in this unbelievable way, and in no other, that it was his will to break down our human pride, to shatter all our human standards of what is possible, and to bring our minds and being into subjection to himself, and to himself alone? We cannot ignore Jesus. He is a possibility of God's. And given the possibility that God appeared on earth, we can see clearly that the humanity of Jesus was the right, true, unique place for his theophany. For nowhere else do there appear all the attributes of God, his majesty and omnipotence, his holiness and justice, his compassion and grace, so purely and continuously as here. If God appeared on earth in the form of man, he can only have appeared in Jesus. Nor is this all. The Divine is shown in Jesus with such overflowing richness, such impressive force, such evident clarity that we should have to close our eyes to the evidence and impugn the possibility of a fact attested by history, if we would deny the Divinity of Jesus. We are faced with a reality so evidently credible that our mind and conscience are bound by it.

But dare we believe, even if we should like to ? In the last resort does not our judgment of its credibility still rest only on the witness, the self-revelation, of one single man, who, holy and exalted as was his nature, and plainly as he spoke of his oneness with the Father, yet appeared to us in purely human form, in the dubious condition of all that is transitory and temporal.

In fact when something so prodigious, so staggering, so sublimely holy, so Divine, aye, when God himself is in question, the final decisive word can only be said by God himself. O God, where is thy amen, thy testimony ? Like the sinning woman of old we kneel at the feet of Jesus, we clasp his hands to stay him from leaving us, and in ardent faith and yearning we call out to the Lord : " God, O God, where is thy testimony ? Where is thy amen, thy categorical affirmative ? O God, ' Glorify thy Son, that thy Son may glorify thee ' " (*John* xvii. 1).

VII

THE RESURRECTION OF CHRIST

It is no small proof of the fidelity and trustworthiness of the Gospel accounts, that they do not merely relate in general terms the dull stupidity and want of real understanding with which the large majority of the disciples received the gospel of Jesus, but in their detailed narrative do not hide the fact that, although actual eye- and ear-witnesses of Jesus, they nevertheless never succeeded during his life on earth in penetrating into the inmost depths of his mystery. Of course they had heard Jesus call himself the " Son " and speak of his Passion and Resurrection, but they only heard with half an ear. " They understood not the word, and it was hid from them, so that they perceived it not. And they were afraid to ask him concerning this word " (*Luke* ix. 45, *cf. Mark* ix. 32 *sqq.*). Only Peter, James, and John listened with keener attention. Illumined by a special Revelation of God, Peter saw into the inmost sanctuary of the soul of Jesus, when at Cæsarea Philippi he confessed him to be the Christ. But even his receptiveness was limited. The thought that the Christ would have to suffer was intolerable to him. " And Peter taxing him, began to rebuke him, saying : Lord, be it far from thee, this shall not be unto thee " (*Matt.* xvi. 22). What held the thoughts and aspirations of the disciples was the traditional ideal of a Christ of majesty and power, of a Messias who in the near future should ascend the throne of his father David and rule all peoples in justice and wisdom. It was an ideal which fell in with their own selfish instincts for power and glory, a man-conceived ideal, a human possibility. It had taken such firm and complete hold of their minds that there was no room for the possibilities of God, those possibilities of a suffering Christ of which Jesus was ever speaking. These were felt by them to be burdensome, disagreeable, cramping possibilities, and they pushed them into the background of their minds. "Their heart was blinded," are the words used by the evangelist to convey their failure to grasp the divine intentions (*Mark* vi. 52). Only just before his Passion, the mother of James and John came with her sons to Jesus to secure for them in good time places of honour on the right hand and on the left of the Messias (*Matt.* xx. 20 *sq.*). And when at the Last Supper Jesus spoke of the imminent crisis and told them that they would now have need to carry a sword, they eagerly said, "Behold, here are two swords" (*Luke* xxii. 38). So little had they understood his words. We cannot keep before our minds too clearly the difficulties imposed on the disciples by their Jewish Messianic conceptions and, indeed, by their whole Jewish outlook, which hindered them from penetrating into the profoundest reality of Jesus, into the reality of a suffering and crucified Son of God. Brought up in the inflexible Jewish belief in the one God and, as true Galileans, having their thoughts set on warlike offensive and political success, they had no doubt a longer road to travel to reach the idea of a *Deus crucifixus* than we have. Another reason why their road was longer and more difficult than ours is that they felt the purely human in Jesus, the impression he gave of a created being, with the limitations imposed by that state, immeasurably more strongly than we can do, who are separated from him by many centuries, more even than St. Paul, who knew not the Jesus who endured hunger and thirst, who wept and suffered, but only the transfigured Christ. It was therefore only at moments when God's grace was especially active in them that they penetrated the divine mystery of their Master (*cf. Matt.* xvi. 16). In general the highest point to which his wise and loving guidance could bring them was a perception of the power of God at work in his humanity, a knowledge of his uniquely holy life, a sense of his special relation to God and of his election by God, and a reverence which made them apply to him the highest names known to them, those of Prophet and Messias. He "was a prophet, mighty in work and word before all the people . . . we hoped that it was he that should have redeemed Israel." Thus simply did the disciples of Emmaus themselves indicate what Jesus had meant to them during his lifetime (*Luke* xxiv. 19, 21).

When on that terrible Friday Jesus was raised not to the throne of David but on to the Cross, it meant for the disciples in the then state of their minds the sudden shipwreck of the greater part of their hopes. The last thing they had was the spiritual power even to think of

Christ's promises concerning his resurrection, let alone to rely upon them. Nevertheless, it was not the collapse of their whole belief in Jesus. They had seen the finger of God in his life and work too plainly, and he had revealed himself to them too intimately, for the events of a few hours to suffice to lead their minds wholly astray about him. That after the arrest of Jesus the disciples still remained together in Jerusalem, and that the women sought out his tomb in the early hours of that Easter morning, are proof that in their secret souls they remained bound to Jesus and that if their faith was shaken, it was not destroyed. What, however, was utterly and for ever shattered was the earthly human mould into which their wilful and selfish Messianic conceptions had forced their belief in him. Their hope of a Messias of exterior might and majesty, who should in the near future ascend the throne of David, vanished utterly in face of the Cross and of the closed sepulchre, and with it vanished all the self-seeking dream and expectations of a kingdom of human possibilities which they had secretly cherished, and with which they had brightened their own present and immediate future. What Jesus when alive had been unable to do he effected in his death, namely the final cure of their naïvely childish belief that the way of God must be man's way, a path of roses full of glorious sunshine and not rather a way of suffering and the Cross. Faced with the Cross, they breathed for the first time the air of eternity, were conscious of something wholly strange, a touch of that wisdom which to man is folly. A space was cleared in

their souls giving free access to the possibilities of God.
It was the death of Jesus which first opened their souls
to the infinite depths and incalculable ways of God's
decrees and cleared the road for a spiritual understanding
of Christ.

What, as a matter of fact, led up to this spiritual understanding of Christ and implanted it unshakably in the
minds of the disciples, were the events of Easter and
Pentecost : for we are bound to name Easter and Pentecost, the Resurrection and the sending of the Holy
Ghost, together.

We have, apart from apocryphal accounts, six biblical
narratives of the Resurrection of our Lord, those of
Matthew, Mark, Luke, and John, a few short but revealing references in the Acts of the Apostles (i. 3 *sqq.* ;
x. 41, etc.), and lastly St. Paul's account in his first
Epistle to the Corinthians (xv. 3 *sqq.*). This account by
the Apostle of the Gentiles is, from the historical point
of view, the most valuable. Firstly, because it is the
oldest to be reduced to writing. It was written between
A.D. 53 and 55, more than ten years before the accounts
of the Resurrection in the synoptic Gospels and more
than twenty years before the narrative in St. John's
Gospel. Further, it is expressly given as an element of
primary importance in the apostolic tradition, and Paul
stresses the point that the account which he had delivered
to the Corinthians first of all was what he himself had
received (ὃ καὶ παρελαβον). This is the same turn of
speech with which the Rabbis of his time were wont to
characterize their narratives as traditional. In St. Paul's

account we have, therefore, not merely something individual to him, but the tradition which was common property to the Twelve and to the primitive Christian communities. The peculiar style of his whole narrative points, too, in the same direction. The similar construction of his clauses in the description of the events and his repeated appeal to the Scriptures (κατὰ τας γραφὰς) give it the air of a liturgical formulary. Most scholars agree in thinking that St. Paul's account, at any rate in its main introductory clause, is taken directly from the apostolic catechesis, perhaps even from the baptismal profession of faith of the early Christians. Hence we have here the witness to the Resurrection of the whole primitive Church. With great solemnity St. Paul testifies to this at the beginning of his account. " Now I make known unto you, brethren, the gospel which I preached to you, which also you have received, and wherein you stand " (*I. Cor.* xv. 1). And at the end of his narrative he repeats : " For whether I, or they [*i.e.*, the apostles], so we preach, and so you have believed " (xv. 11). Paul is therefore fully aware that he is here delivering a fundamental dogma of the faith which the apostles and he himself have preached to the Christian communities in practically the same terms. His account, however, affords us a yet deeper glimpse into the matter. When he tells us that he has taken his Easter gospel from tradition, he likewise reveals the particular source whence he derived it. For we know from the Epistle to the Galatians (i. 15 *sqq.*) that St. Paul immediately after his experience on the road to

Damascus went into Arabia, partly to escape for the moment the hatred and machinations of the Jews, partly to be able in strict seclusion to bring order into the tremendous new impressions which he had received at Damascus and to complete the transformation of his entire inner life. In this no one could help him, not even the Twelve, but only the Holy Ghost. After three years he returned to Damascus and went thence to Jerusalem " to see Peter " and " tarried with him fifteen days." But other of the apostles he " saw none ; saving James the brother of the Lord." This can only be the apostle St. James the Less. We must therefore conclude that St. Paul derived his Easter tradition, so far as it was not contained in the vision leading to his own conversion, primarily from Peter, the head of the apostles, and from James the brother of the Lord. These two apostles with St. John were accounted the most important eye-and ear-witnesses to the whole life of Jesus. In the same Epistle (ii. 9) St. Paul describes them as " pillars " of the new community. Another circumstance proves the dependence of his account on the information he received from Peter and James, namely that he is the first to tell of those appearances of the risen Lord with which Peter and James had been personally blessed. Only Luke mentions, and that quite cursorily, the meeting of the risen Lord with Peter (*Luke* xxiv. 34). And it is only in the apocryphal gospel of the Hebrews that reference is made to the appearance of Jesus vouchsafed to James. Paul alone, and decades before this was written, mentions explicitly that the

Lord appeared after his resurrection to Peter and James. Obviously he had learnt of the fact directly from them. Hence we have not only the general witness of the primitive Christian community in Jerusalem to the Resurrection, but also, in the accounts of Peter and James, the testimony of immediate eye-witnesses. If, reckoning from the Epistle to the Galatians (ii. 1), we assign St. Paul's conversion to the year 33, the earliest testimony to the Easter events, namely Paul's, must date back to at least the year 36, at which time its immediate sponsors, the original witnesses, Peter and James, were at the peak of their powers and activity. A more primitive and reliable testimony is historically impossible. Paul's account of the first Easter derives therefore from what Peter and James had experienced and from whatever had been revealed to himself on the road to Damascus. There is nothing in it which Paul could have got from purely literary sources.

How does St. Paul's account run? "For I delivered unto you first of all, which I also received: How that Christ died for our sins according to the scriptures: And that he was buried, and that he rose again the third day according to the scriptures: And that he was seen by Cephas; and after that by the eleven. Then was he seen by more than five hundred brethren at once: of whom many remain until this present, and some are fallen asleep. After that, he was seen by James, then by all the apostles. And last of all, he was seen also by me, as by one born out of due time. For I am the least of the apostles, who am not worthy to be called an apostle, because I persecuted the church of God. But by the grace of God, I am what I am ; and his grace in me hath not been void, but I have laboured more abundantly than all they : yet not I, but the grace of God with me : For whether I, or they, so we preach, and so have you believed."

What led the Apostle of the Gentiles to give this detailed enumeration of the appearances of Jesus ? In Corinth doubts as to the resurrection of the body had become clamorous, though no difficulty was felt about the continued existence of the soul after death.   To Greek or Hellenistic thought the immortality of the soul presented no real problem. The resurrection of the body was the stumbling-block ; for to the Greek mind, dominated as it was by the dualism of Plato, the body, the sensibly material, earthly element, stood in the sharpest contrast to the spirit. The body was accounted an evil, the fetters, the prison-house of the soul. Hence the mere possibility that this body, the enemy which cramped the spirit, should rise again and in union with the spirit have eternal life, was resisted as repugnant. It is therefore quite intelligible that ideas derogatory to the body should have insinuated themselves into the minds of the Greek and Hellenist converts to Christianity and have aroused serious doubts as to the resurrection of the body. The keen mind of St. Paul saw at once that the very foundations of Christianity were being shaken by such views. Accordingly he writes : " If there be no resurrection of the dead, then Christ is not risen again. And if Christ be not risen again, then is our preaching vain, and your faith is also vain. Yea, and we are found false witnesses of God, because we have given testimony against God, that he hath raised up Christ; whom he hath not raised up if the dead rise not again. For if the dead rise not again, neither is Christ risen again " (*I. Cor.* xv. 13 *sqq.*). So Paul made it his care to prove the bodily resurrection of Christ from the dead to have been an historical fact, and he advisedly lays emphasis on the point that Christ really was one risen from the dead, one who really rose from the tomb, that he did not merely live on as a disembodied spirit, like all other departed souls.

Of what kind of body is the Apostle thinking? Is he picturing the transfigured body of the crucified and buried Lord, and, consequently, an essential identity of the buried with the transfigured body of Jesus? Or does he think of the body of the risen Christ as something entirely new, as a spiritual and divine reality which revealed itself to the apostles, as a kind of luminous body by which the departed spirit is materialized, in the way, perhaps, in which according to current belief the angels appear in a glory of light?

The question is one of capital importance, since some scholars have sought to explain the appearances of Jesus recorded by St. Paul in a definitely pneumatic and visionary sense and to set them in irreconcilable antithesis to the realistic Gospel narratives of the first Easter. Their views may be summarized as follows. Paul cannot possibly have identified the transfigured, celestial Christ who had appeared to him and to the apostles with the Christ of flesh and blood who hung upon the Cross. Does he not quite definitely and clearly say to the Corinthians in the same Epistle (xv. 50) " that flesh and blood cannot possess the kingdom of heaven "? In the same Epistle, too, he answers the question, " How do the dead rise again ? or with what manner of body shall they come ? " (xv. 35) by a reference to the fate of a grain of wheat, which is laid naked in the ground and there wastes away and perishes, the bodily form which it afterwards receives being something entirely new and owing its existence only to the will of God. For this reason the " body " of the transfigured Christ, which according to Paul appeared to the disciples, must be understood as a wholly new being, so utterly different, so celestial and spiritualized that the Apostle can actually call the Lord a " spirit " (*II. Cor.* iii. 17). This new corporeality cannot be identified in any way with the buried and risen body. The empty tomb had therefore no place in St. Paul's Easter gospel. It is significant that he never speaks of it. Since then St. Paul's account is the oldest and rests on the witness of the apostles, in it alone is to be found the primitive understanding of the Easter gospel. What the synoptists tell of the empty tomb and what they have to say in this connection about the identity of the crucified with the risen Lord, for instance about his strange challenge : " Handle, and see : for a spirit hath not flesh and bones, as you see me to have " (*Luke* xxiv. 39), or about the transfigured wounds of the risen Lord which they so graphically describe, about his talking to them and breathing on them, about his eating and drinking with them—all these synoptic traditions are not primitive but secondary. They owe their rise to the apologetic interest of the first Christians and to the concern of the primitive Christian missioners to make the resurrection of Christ as tangible and impressive a thing as possible. And since the synoptic narratives centre in Jerusalem, the whole " Jerusalem tradition," which tells only of appearances of Christ in the city, is secondary and suspect. It is much more true to say that Christ's appearances to the apostles took place without exception in Galilee, in accord with the injunction which the angel at the sepulchre, as Matthew tells us, and afterwards the risen Lord himself gave to the women : " Go, tell my brethren that they go into Galilee, there they shall see me " (*Matt.* xxviii. 10 ; *cf. Matt.* xxvi. 32 ; *Mark* xvi. 7). Thus the oldest tradition knows only of appearances in Galilee. Hence we must also transfer to Galilee the scene of the appearances recorded by St. Paul. It was only later on that the legend that Christ had first appeared to his disciples in Jerusalem itself was put together by the early Christians in order to meet the needs of their apologetic. This legend was popularized by Luke in particular, who puts in the mouth of the risen Lord the command, " Stay you in the city [*i.e.,* in Jerusalem] till you be endued with power from on high " (*Luke* xxiv. 49), which runs directly counter to his injunction to the disciples to go before him into Galilee. Accordingly, since the primitive Easter narratives tell nothing of the empty tomb, indeed have nothing to do with Jerusalem and are cognizant only of the apparition of a shining, celestial figure among the lonely mountains of Galilee, the modern mind, familiar with the phenomena of normal and abnormal psychology, is able to explain this celestial figure as a mere vision and hallucination. It may be that these visions were sent by God and to this extent have an objective, metaphysical basis ; but they were purely subjective experiences, psychogenetically induced images and concepts, mere phantoms of the senses. It was no objective, celestial reality which met the eyes of the apostles. And this is St. Paul's own explanation of the phenomenon, for he describes his experience as a "vision," that is to say, as a visual impression. In his account he four times repeats the phrase, "he was seen by" (*I. Cor.* xv. 5 *sqq.*). To King Agrippa he himself describes his experience as a "vision" (ὀπτασία, Acts xxvi. 19), and with this vision he summarily aligns the Easter experiences of the apostles (*I. Cor.* xv. 8). So in our interpretation of the miracle of Easter we need not be more apostolic than the apostles themselves. What they report are subjective experiences—creations, revelations of their touching faith in the victorious Jesus, or at best experiences permitted by the benign providence of God, who is able to turn even human self-deception to good account.

This is nothing but the old vision theory of Renan and Strauss, which in our day is again raising its head, now that Reimarus' hypothesis of deliberate deception, and the trance theory fathered by Gottlob Paulus, have once and for all been discredited. But the old vision

theory is this time being bolstered up with much greater
care than heretofore, not only by philosophical considerations, but also by arguments drawn from the Bible.
Can it really be the case that the Bible contradicts itself
at this point?

All the objections to the biblical accounts of the
Resurrection lead back to two fundamental questions.
The first is this: Does St. Paul, whose account is the
oldest, consciously identify the transfigured, risen body
of Christ with his earthly body which had been placed
in the sepulchre? Or are the appearances of Christ in
his view only apparitions from heaven? The importance
of this question is of course obvious. If it can be shown
that to the Apostle, the buried body of Christ and his
transfigured body are identical, then the empty tomb
also has a place in his Easter gospel. And in this case it
is purely arbitrary to class as secondary the Jerusalem
tradition, in which the identity of the two bodies and
therewith the empty sepulchre are capital points. Then,
too, it is more than ever arbitrary, in fact it is perverse,
to attribute conscious deception to the Jerusalem tradition and to its evangelist Luke. The second question
is: Can the Easter experiences of the apostles and of St.
Paul really be fully explained as subjective visions, as
hallucinations? Were the apostles really naïve enough
to regard their subjective experiences as objective
appearances of the risen Lord? Were they, in fact, on
that nrst Easter morning psychologically receptive to
hallucinations? By examining these two fundamental
questions we shall at the same time be put in a position

to unfold the Easter gospel of the apostles in all its breadth and depth.

An unprejudiced examination of the Pauline account must at once establish the fact that St. Paul sets the resurrection of Jesus in the closest relation to his death and burial. In the same breath and with the same solemn formality with which he gives prominence to the resurrection on the third day, he tells " how that Christ died for our sins according to the scriptures : And that he was buried " (*I. Cor.* xv. 3 *sq.*). Paul was therefore fully aware of the burial of Jesus as well as of his death, and it is in direct reference to this death and to this burial that he speaks of how he " he rose again (ἐγήγερται) on the third day." In view of this connection it is simply incomprehensible that this rising again can have any other meaning than a resurrection from the dead and from the grave. In other words, Paul must have regarded the risen body as identical with the dead and buried body. It is true that this risen body is, according to the Apostle, no longer " flesh and blood " —carnal (σάρξ), that is to say, in the Pauline sense of the proper seat and instrument of sin (*cf. Rom.* vii. 14, 18)— but it does remain a body (σῶμα), that is, an organic structure. It is essentially the same body that was laid in the sepulchre, save that its mode of existence differs and has become transfigured and celestial. Paul therefore in the same connection speaks of its being " changed " (πάντες δὲ ἀλλαγησόμεθα, *I. Cor.* xv. 51). And the subject of this change is not in any way the transfigured spirit, but the body which had been laid in the ground. " For this corruptible must put on incorruption ; and this mortal must put on immortality" (xv. 53). Thus, as Paul in verse 37 of the same chapter pictures, there arises from the seed which was sown in the ground and has perished the new germinating life. True, it is not the seed itself which arises (xv. 36), but the new body springing by the will of God naturally from the seed which perishes (xv. 38). But in the Apostle's conception the new body proceeds from the seed which was sown and the possibility that the life thus newly brought into existence has no longer any relation to its old state is explicitly excluded. It is, rather, the will of God that it should actually be quickened into new life by its death. And Paul goes on to say : " So also is the resurrection of the dead. It is sown in corruption, it shall rise in incorruption. . . . It is sown a natural body, it shall rise a spiritual body " (xv. 42, 44). It is this constant juxtaposition of the ideas " sowing " and " rising again " which proves how deliberately he links the conception of the Resurrection with that of sowing and burial, how to him there is no other resurrection save from the dead and from the grave. It is true that the body risen from the grave is no longer flesh in bondage to sin, but is now under the dominion of the spirit. It is wholly transfigured and spiritualized by the divine power. But this spiritual, celestial state does not exclude a bodily form, and precisely that form of body which Jesus had in the grave and on which the change is worked. Clearly and unequivocally is this essential relation of the earthly to the celestial body brought out by St. Paul in his Epistle to the Philippians (iii. 21), where he speaks of Christ as one " who will reform the body of our lowness, made like to the body of his glory, according to the operation whereby also he is able to subdue all things unto himself."

This being so, since, that is to say, to Paul the trans-figured body is essentially identical with the mortal, buried body, his belief in the Resurrection presupposes a knowledge of the empty sepulchre. If the Apostle does not explicitly mention the empty tomb he tells us that Christ was buried and rose again from this tomb. Belief in the empty tomb was, as it was with the synop-tists, a definite part of his faith.

Paul, however, further agrees with the evangelists in the fact that his tradition includes appearances of the risen Lord not merely in Galilee but also in Jerusalem. This follows clearly enough from the introductory section of his account when he says that " according to the scriptures " Christ " rose again the third day." The point the Apostle accordingly has to prove in what follows is not that Jesus did appear at some time or other, but that he actually rose again on the third day. If his argument is not to break down at an important point, some at least of the appearances which he records must have taken place on the third day. This being so, they could not have occurred in Galilee, but only in Judæa and Jerusalem; for it would have been impossible for the disciples to get to Galilee within the short time from the Friday evening to the Sunday morning. Moreover, the message of the angel at the sepulchre, that the risen Lord had gone before them into Galilee, presupposes that the disciples on that Easter morning were still in Jerusalem. If therefore Paul wished to testify to appearances of Christ on the third day, he could only have had in mind appearances which took place in Jerusalem.

What Paul here only suggests is explicitly affirmed by the evangelists' accounts. According to Matthew (xxviii. 9) Jesus actually appeared to the women at no distance from the empty sepulchre. According to the canonical closing passage of St. Mark's Gospel (xvi. 9) and to St. John (xx. 14 *sqq.*), he appeared to. Mary Magdalen in the garden. According to Mark (xvi. 11) and to Luke (xxiv. 13 *sqq.*), he appeared to two disciples on the road to Emmaus. According to Luke (xxiv. 36 *sqq.*) and to John (xx. 19 *sqq.*), he appeared to all the apostles in a house at Jerusalem. We have every reason to accept this last-named appearance of Jesus to his disciples as being coincident with the appearance to the " eleven " which St. Paul records (*I. Cor*. xv. 5). When St. John speaks of a second appearance of the risen Lord to the apostles and expressly mentions that on the previous occasion Thomas had not been present (*John* xx. 24), this again has a striking correspondence with St. Paul's account, which also speaks of two such appearances to the apostles. Christ appeared to the " eleven " and afterwards was seen by " all the apostles " (*I. Cor*. xv. 5, 7). Unless we are to assume the improbable, namely that by " all the apostles " as distinct from " the eleven " is meant the seventy-two disciples whom Jesus had gathered to him during his public ministry, we have in this deliberately drawn distinction between the two appearances of Christ to the apostles a striking agreement between Paul and John. Evidence of the close connection between the Pauline and Gospel accounts of the Resurrection, and especially of the fact that at least some of the appearances mentioned by Paul must have taken place in Jerusalem, is furnished by Luke's report that the two disciples on their return to Jerusalem from Emmaus were greeted with the joyful news : " The Lord is risen indeed, and hath appeared to Simon " (*Luke* xxiv. 34). There are very few passages in the New Testament which give so great an impression of being unpremeditated, spontaneous, and primitive as does this remark of Luke's. But St. Paul also tells of an appearance of the risen Lord to Simon, the only difference being that he calls him Cephas, and it is the first of all the appearances which he records. Since then the Apostle wishes his narrative to be understood as being set out in chronological order, the appearance to Peter must be at any rate one of the first of which Paul had any knowledge. We have therefore every reason to assume that this appearance coincides with that to Peter recorded by St. Luke, and that therefore it occurred in Jerusalem and in fact on the first Easter day itself. This does not preclude a later individual appearance of the risen Lord to Peter in Galilee, as Mark seems to imply (xvi. 7). Thus of the five appearances which Paul records, three, or at least two, are a part of the Jerusalem tradition. They did not take place in Galilee

but in Jerusalem and on that very third day when Jesus
rose again.

It cannot, therefore, be maintained that St. Paul's
narrative proves the Gospel accounts of the Resurrection
to be secondary. On the contrary we have a unanimous,
consistent tradition. The fact of the matter is that some
of the appearances took place in Jerusalem, though the
greater number, especially those in which the risen
Lord spoke to his disciples " of the kingdom of God "
(*Acts* i. 3), occurred in their own Galilee, where, far
from the noisy bustle of the metropolis and unmolested
by the machinations of their mortal enemies, he gave
them their commission to go forth and teach all nations
(*Matt.* xxviii. 17 *sqq.*). The message of the angel at the
sepulchre that Jesus would go before his disciples into
Galilee doubtless had these latter appearances in view.
And this is in no way contradicted by the words of Our
Lord quoted by Luke : " Stay you in the city, till you
be endued with power from on high " (*Luke* xxiv. 49).
For the injunction to remain in Jerusalem does not refer
to a waiting for their risen Lord, but to the coming of the
Holy Ghost, with which their world mission was to
commence. It was precisely because our Lord had commanded the disciples to go into Galilee and there await
his appearance, that it was necessary for him to impress
upon them that they must await the descent of the Holy
Ghost not in Galilee, but in Jerusalem. Jerusalem was to
be the germ-cell of the new kingdom of God. From all
this it is evident that the accounts of St. Paul and of the
evangelists are complementary down to the last detail.

If we examine the gospel testimonies to the Resurrection by themselves, we may at first sight find it odd that they do not seem to be wholly free of contradictions and discrepancies, and that in comparison with St. Paul's account they are very meagre. Remembering, however, what has been said above, if we turn our eyes from the certainly striking divergencies in the various accounts— Matthew (xxviii. 7, 16) tells of only one appearance to the disciples upon a mountain in Galilee, and Luke (xxiv. 36; *cf. John* xx. 19) tells only of appearances of the Lord in Jerusalem on the Easter day itself, and, in contrast to his own testimony in the Acts of the Apostles (i. 3), almost gives the impression that Jesus had ascended into heaven on the same Easter day—we shall find that all the other discrepancies between the evangelists are of but secondary importance, in fact for the most part are of no significance whatever. It does not really affect the reliability of the evangelists at all, whether the risen Lord first appeared to Mary Magdalen alone (*Mark* xvi. 9; *John* xx. 14 *sqq.*) or also " to the other Mary " (*Matt.* xxviii. 1, 9 *sq.*) and to the other women (*Luke* xxiv. 10). Nor is it of any real importance whether the women returning from the empty tomb kept their experience a secret " and said nothing to any man, for they were afraid " (*Mark* xvi. 8), or whether, as Luke (xxiv. 9) reports, they at least told " the eleven and all the rest." Nor again does it really matter whether the apostles' circle, on being told by the disciples from Emmaus that they had seen the Lord, received the news sceptically (*Mark* xvi. 13) or with exultation (*Luke*

xxiv. 34). We are here concerned with accounts which are only apparently divergent. Everything points to their referring not to the same but to different stages of one and the same event. They have all their proper place in the piecing together of the story of what happened on that Easter day. Only the Gospel accounts are too meagre for us now to fix their place with any certainty. At any rate, their apparent inconsistency mirrors the confusion and excitement of those first hours of the day of the Resurrection, when nerve-racking events crowded one after the other and the most contradictory reports were in the air. Moreover, it is actually these very discrepancies that give us assurance of the primitiveness and reliability of the Gospel accounts. For in them there is no artificial editing of the news, nor the slightest attempt to bring the various reports into harmony with one another. The writers are concerned only to give simply and faithfully the immediate impressions of eye witnesses. The same primitiveness and the same reliability is shown by the meagreness, indeed, the baldness, of these reports. Had the evangelists wanted to spin fables, the extraordinary phenomena of the Resurrection would have supplied them with suitable matter a-plenty. To be satisfied on this point, we have only to compare them with the apocryphal gospel of the Hebrews and especially with the gospel of Peter or with the account of the Resurrection given in the Old Slavonic translation of Josephus's *Jewish War*, where the Resurrection is depicted as a cosmic, world-shaking event taking place before the eyes of the Jews and

Romans, and where the authors embellish every detail to the point of sheer grotesqueness. Again, in the Ethiopian and Coptic " Conversations of Jesus with his disciples," a series of maxims and adages are put in the mouth of the risen Lord which obviously derive from the promous verbosity of the author himself. There is nothing like this in the Gospels. It is characteristic of the cleanness of their reporting that they are quite silent about the actual incident of the Resurrection. They tell nothing about the Resurrection itself, but only about the risen Lord. And what they report the risen Lord to have said conforms to his usual style of teaching in being concise, reserved and authoritative, steeped in the solemnity and sanctity of the occasion. In view of the thoroughness with which the evangelists describe the rest of our Lord's life, we may actually conclude that it was not the concern of the evangelists, as it was of St. Paul, to give an exhaustive account of the Resurrection. Their aim was, rather, only to say enough about the Resurrection to show it as the glorious conclusion to a truly divine life, the amen of God to all that Jesus had accomplished on earth. The fact of the Resurrection as such and not so much the facts of the different appearances of Jesus was what chiefly concerned them. This one fact of the Resurrection of Jesus was the new reality which occupied their present, the sublimely obvious thing on which they lived, and which, just because they did live on it, had not to be expressly proved. It is therefore perverse to apply the standards of the modern historian to the evangelists' accounts of the Resurrection. Their aims are not historical but dogmatic and missionary. As we learn from the Acts of the Apostles (*cf.* ii. 24, 32 ; iii. 15, etc.), the apostles in their preaching were concerned only to give prominence over and over again to the sublime event of the Resurrection, to the blessed fact that God had indeed raised this Jesus from the dead, without going into any descriptive details. Similarly it was the evangelists' wish to preserve and hand on only this essential core of the apostles' preaching.

But little weight as the apostolic witnesses and the evangelists attached to historical knowledge of individual events in the modern sense, they did take very seriously the historicity of the fact of the Resurrection as such. For they knew that their whole Easter gospel rested wholly and solely on the certainty that Christ had really and truly risen from the dead. In this witness to the Resurrection of Jesus they saw the true essence of their apostolic office. When a new apostle has to be elected to take the place of Judas, Peter expressly lays it down that the choice must lie only among those " men who have companied with us, all the time that the Lord Jesus came in and went out among us " (*Acts* i. 21). The dogmatic interest of the apostles, therefore, in no way destroyed their historical interest, though the latter was not and could not be the interest of the professional historian. They were fully conscious that by the will of God and of the Lord Jesus Christ the faith of all future generations would be based on the uniqueness of their Easter experience and on the reliability of their memories, their sense-perceptions, and of their judgment. For the men of future generations would not be able to see and judge the evidence for themselves, but must rely upon their vision and their judgment as eye-witnesses. Their apostolic enthusiasm and their devout pride in being apostles of Jesus Christ, were rooted in the fact that their individual witness to the unique event they had seen and their judgment on it would actually have by Christ's will a superhistorical and timeless validity. For they knew themselves to be not mere chance witnesses but authentic witnesses, called by God and chosen by Christ, accredited by ever fresh signs and wonders. They were conscious, too, that, as the " witnesses preordained by God " (*Acts* x. 41) for all generations to come, they were laying the foundations of the new world era and the new faith as surely and effectively as Moses and the prophets had done for the old era and the old faith. We cannot appreciate the apostolic witness to the Resurrection in its full sincerity and cogency, in the absoluteness of its claim to truth, if we fail to take into consideration this distinctive consciousness of their apostolic call and mission. It would almost seem as if secular historians, simply because they are in general concerned only with secular things, are in danger of giving a false interpretation to the events of the Resurrection, since their eyes are not always sufficiently keen to appreciate the purity, sensitiveness, and power of a conscience touched by God and possessed by a sense of God's demands. The apostles preach the Resurrection because they must. A " necessity " lies upon them, for " wo is unto them if they preach not the gospel " (*cf. I. Cor.* ix. 16). In their witness to the Resurrection there lies more than the conviction of the eye-witness ; there is the awful knowledge of their mission, the heavy responsibility resting on one called by God, on a prophet, a confessor, a martyr. We should have to regard what is most intimate, most pure, most powerful in man, his religious conscience, as illusion and deception, if we had to suppose that the apostles were victims of a pitiful delusion on the very point which possessed their conscience, namely their own intimate relation to the Easter gospel. This delusion would needs have its origin in the all-holy, all-truthful God himself, and we should no longer have any reason to believe in him.

*   *   *   *   *

This throws some light on that question to which we are still seeking the answer. It is the question whether the disciples, even if subjectively they were of good faith, might not have been the victims of self-deception, of subjective visions and auditions. This is the second prop on which the vision theory is erected. Is it thinkable that what the original apostles and Paul had to tell was only their visionary experiences in Galilee and that they were naïve enough to take these hallucinations of theirs for realities ? It is unthinkable that the living God should permit such a thing. It is unthinkable that all the moral power, all the enthusiasm of sacrifice, all the earnest purity of intention, all the love for God, which entered the hearts of men with the Easter miracle and are ever descending on them, should be born of the sombre womb of a dreadful self-deception. It is literally the fact that such self-deception would have to be laid to the charge of God himself, and all belief in an all-wise, all-good, creative Will would be at an end. Not spirit but non-spirit, not sense but non-sense, something alogical, indeed meaningless, something demonic and satanic would be at the back of all reality. We, however, believe in an ultimate, supreme meaning in all history, in the ultimate connection and consonance of the celestial and the terrestrial, of the human mind and God. And this applies also to what happened at that first Easter. In the last resort we believe in this with all the force of our affirmation of our own Ego. We believe in it because the most elementary instinct of our mind forbids us to believe that the true sense of the realities of the world is non-sense and nihilism, indeed devilry. Our belief in the Resurrection is certainly to some extent a biological function, a manifestation of our own healthy will to live : contrariwise unbelief is and always has been the expression of a broken, disintegrating vitality, the effect of degeneration and decay. Our Easter belief is thus not only insight but also will and act. In this respect it is founded on the requirement of our very existence that our world should have a meaning, this world whose beginning was the Word, the Word that was with God, the Word that is God.

Yet in our controversy with the vision theory we may not content ourselves with this argument *a priori*, nor are we tempted to do so, deeply as it is rooted in the very depths of our being. We therefore pass on to a critical examination of its arguments. If we keep before our minds that, according to this theory, the suggested basis for the experiences of the apostles after the Resurrection lies in the mere subjective visions of Jews and of Jews in the days of Christ, the primary error in the whole vision theory will at once be recognized. It is the error of forcibly reading into the mentality of ancient Eastern Judaism our modern conceptions and ideas, or more accurately the conceptions and ideas of our Western, rationalistic culture. In essential contrast to the Greek thought of the West, Judaism in the time of Christ viewed the relation of soul to body not dualistically but monistically. The Jews always saw body and spirit as one. The living spirit was to them at the same time the living body. In their view the spirit could only *effectively* reveal itself in and through the body. The idea that a departed spirit could maintain real life and activity independently of the body would have been incomprehensible to the Jewish mind. The spirits in Sheol lead a being-less, action-less, shadow-existence. Thus Christ's disciples could never have got the impression that he really was risen from the dead and a living being unless they had direct perception both of his bodily appearance and of his bodily functions. The spirit of Jesus without the body of Jesus would have been to the Jewish sentiment of the apostles something wholly abnormal. To them it would have been a ghost. And, indeed, at the first appearance of Jesus to them they " supposed that they saw a spirit," until he ate and drank with them (*cf. Luke* xxiv. 37).

From this it follows that the apostles, as true sons of Israel, could only believe in the real appearance of the risen Lord and hold fast to this belief if they could be quite sure that the body no longer lay in the tomb, in other words that the sepulchre in Jerusalem was empty. It was a psychological necessity to their belief in the Resurrection, if this was to have any stability, that it should also include the knowledge of the empty tomb. If, as the vision theory would have it, the disciples had only seen apparitions of Jesus in Galilee, without having heard of the empty tomb at Jerusalem, these appearances could never have had permanent significance for them. They would have regarded them as nothing more than remarkable apparitions of a ghost, as they had once before done on the waters of the Lake of Genesareth. The Easter experience of the disciples certainly included, therefore, an objective, outwardly visible, perceptible, wholly demonstrable, verifiable element, namely the fact of the empty tomb. Without this fact the apostles' enduring, living belief in the Resurrection would have been incomprehensible in the light of their own mental predisposition. And every theory which, disregarding this, talks of purely subjective experiences in Galilee without at the same time accepting the empty tomb, stands self-convicted of being the creation of a rationalism divorced from history and inimical to it.

There are not a few modern scholars who recognize this issue and therefore proceed to build the fact of the empty tomb into their vision theory, or rather to make the empty tomb itself the actual origin and source of the

disciples' visionary experiences. They say something
like this: the disciples did in fact find the tomb of
Jesus at Jerusalem empty. The body had possibly been
stolen by some unknown persons; or it had perhaps
been thrown into some common grave, so that it was no
longer recognizable. At all events the disciples could
not find the body. This fact then kindled their conviction that Jesus must have risen from the dead, and from
this conviction proceeded their hallucinations.

It is scarcely necessary to point out the multitude of
difficulties, in fact impossibilities, which beset the fiction
that the body of Jesus was somehow or other removed
from the sepulchre by alien hands without the knowledge
of the disciples. Who should have made away with the
body? The Jewish authorities, the Sanhedrin? In
order perhaps to prevent a possible institution of a
cultus of his body by the disciples? But such a cult of
relics was utterly alien to Jewish sentiment and therefore was not to be feared from the disciples. The later
Christian veneration of relics does not derive from
Jewish but from specifically Christian conceptions, in
particular from the living belief in the resurrection of the
body. It therefore postulates the very fact this theory
denies, the Resurrection of Christ. Moreover, if the
Jewish authorities really removed the body of Jesus
from the sepulchre, why did they not produce it when the
apostles were stirring up the whole Jewish land with
their cry of " He is risen, He is no more here "?
There could not have been a more convenient and
convincing way of discrediting the whole Christian

movement than by coolly exhuming the body of Jesus and exhibiting it.

If we accept the suggestion that the body of Jesus was thrown into a felons' grave and that this was why the disciples could not find it, we must take the hazardous course of setting down all the biblical sources, which, Paul not excepted, are unanimous in speaking of a "burial" of Jesus, as untrustworthy and mendacious, without being able to assign the slightest proof to this effect. We should also be forgetting that Jesus was convicted and put to death according to Roman law; and Roman law knew of no common felons' grave, but left the judges to dispose of the corpse at their discretion. Moreover, even in this case the body of Jesus would still have been discoverable. Why did not the Jews draw if out from the felons' grave or at least point to it as being there, in order to nip the belief in the Resurrection in the bud? Why instead of this did the Jewish authorities throw the witnesses to the Resurrection into prison and scourge them with rods?

Riddle upon riddle, indeed a maze of impossibilities, faces us if we are to suppose that it was really alien hands which removed the body of Jesus without the knowledge of the disciples. The only course left is to make the disciples themselves responsible for the removal of the body, as the Jewish authorities actually tried to do by spreading the report that his own disciples had stolen the body (*Matt.* xxviii. 13), as may to this day be read in the Talmud. But this is to abandon the whole vision hypothesis. For it is psychologically impossible that impostors of such a kind should be so intoxicated and fascinated by their own deception as to take the illusion they had themselves created to be a truth and to suffer death for it. Moreover, we know the souls of these so-called impostors better. We know from the Gospels how simple and straightforward and genuine they were, and we learn from the Acts of the Apostles and from the Epistles how from the very first day of their mission they were faced with opposition and ignominy and death, and that, nevertheless, they never ceased proclaiming to the world their gospel of the Resurrection of Jesus. Impostors who deceive in the full consciousness that their deception will bring them not the slightest advantage but only outrage, poverty, misery, and death; impostors who, on the ground of their deceit, go on living a life of renunciation and heroic sacrifice; impostors such as these the world in all its history has never seen. To-day, therefore, the deception theory of the Wolfenbüttler fragmentists has been universally abandoned.

To return to the vision theory. We have made it clear that a visionary experience alone, one which had not been attended by knowledge of the empty tomb, could never have given to the Jewish minds of the disciples the conviction that Jesus really was risen from the dead. It would have left with them at most the impression that they had seen a ghost. We have further established that the possibility of the body having been removed by alien hands or by the apostles themselves must be rejected. So that the empty tomb, the very thing which in the experiences of the apostles at that Easter was visibly and perceptibly a fact, remains an obstinate enigma, so long as we keep to a purely natural, psychological explanation of the primitive Christian belief in the Resurrection.

The position becomes still more embarrassing for the vision theory if the attempt be made to see in this obstinate enigma the actual origin of the Easter experiences, if, that is to say, the alleged hallucinations of the disciples are referred to the empty tomb and are explained by the hypothesis that the disciples had been misled by it into imagining that Jesus must have risen from the dead.

Here one question in particular forces itself on us : How should the disciples have hit upon this possibility ? For we know that the Jews of Christ's day did not believe in a particular resurrection of each individual just man immediately after death. They believed only in a general resurrection at the last day. How could the disciples with their Jewish ideas have come to expect an immediate resurrection precisely in the case of Jesus ? This question is a particularly awkward one for the unbelieving investigator, since he refuses to admit that Jesus in his lifetime had clearly spoken of his coming resurrection.

If, further, we carefully examine the Gospel accounts in the endeavour to discover this alleged connection between the empty tomb and the awakening belief in the Resurrection, we are driven to the sobering conclusion that the sight of the empty tomb by itself was very far indeed from kindling the disciples' hopes. On the contrary, the biblical sources actually prove that the first impression left by the empty tomb on the women and on the disciples was one of depression and discouragement. Luke (xxiv. 4) as well as Mark (xvi. 8) and John (xx. 2) report that the empty tomb dismayed and frightened the women, and that the first thought forced upon their minds was not that Jesus must be risen from the dead, but that the body had been taken away (*Luke* xx. 2, 13). To the apostles the news of the empty tomb and of the angel at the sepulchre seemed to be " idle tales " (*Luke* xxiv. 11), and they did not believe what the women had told them until Peter himself (*Luke* xxiv. 12, 24) and John (*John* xx. 3 *sqq.*) had personally convinced themselves of its truth. It can, therefore, certainly not be maintained that the empty tomb alone aroused in the disciples any passionate hopes of a Resurrection. Indeed, they would certainly have abandoned themselves to torturing uncertainty, if the exciting news, " He is not here," had not at once been followed by, " He is risen."

Thus the whole foundation of the vision theory is laid in a morass. Fiction is strung on fiction. It is a mere fiction that the body of Jesus was removed from the sepulchre by alien hands, and it is again a mere fiction that the disciples' belief in the Resurrection was kindled by the empty tomb alone.

* * * * *

We now come to our third and last point. If we take the Easter experience of the apostles by itself and examine its origin and content, does it offer any loophole for a visionary explanation? Even if the fact of the empty tomb were to remain for ever inexplicable, do not these experiences of the disciples in themselves betray a visionary character? The answer to these questions will disclose the peculiar character of the testimony to the Resurrection.

The first question which obtrudes itself is this: Do the disciples show signs of a visionary disposition? If we limit this question to the two chief apostles and the two most important sponsors of the tradition of the Resurrection, namely Peter and Paul, then it is indubitable that both had at other times visionary experiences. According to the Acts of the Apostles (x. 10 *sqq.*), there came over Peter, when at the sixth hour he went up to the house-top to pray, a rapture, " an ecstasy of mind." He saw the heavens open and a vessel like a large sheet descend, in which were unclean beasts; and a voice called to him, " Arise, Peter, kill, and eat." And Paul also had not only " visions in the night " (*Acts* xvi. 9), but, like Peter, ecstatic experiences. In his second Epistle to the Corinthians (xii. 2 *sqq.*) he tells them explicitly : " I knew a man in Christ above fourteen years ago (whether in the body, I know not, or out of the body, I know not, God knoweth), such an one rapt even to the third heaven." To neither of the chief apostles, therefore, was the visionary, ecstatic state foreign. But because they knew this state, they were also in the position to differentiate mere visions having to do with imaginary ideas from genuine experience of objective reality. As a matter of fact, both kept visionary and real experiences consciously apart. Thus on his release from Herod's prison by an angel, Peter asks himself whether what had happened to him was "true" (ἀληθές) or only imagined, a "vision" (ὅραμα). To him the "vision" is therefore something untrue, is the antithesis of the real. For this reason Peter did not base his belief in the risen Lord on suchlike visions. Well as he knew and proclaimed that with the coming of the Holy Ghost, according to Joel's prophecy, a superabundance of inner experiences and mystical occurrences would be showered on the new community of God, he never dreamt of basing his message of the Resurrection on these uncontrollable, ecstatic happenings. He rests it exclusively on what could be historically established and proved to all. Thus in his first sermon after Pentecost Peter goes straight to the point : " Ye men of Israel, hear these words : Jesus of Nazareth, a man approved of God among you, by miracles and wonders and signs, which God did by him, in the midst of you, as you also know. . . . Whom God hath raised up, having loosed the sorrows of hell" (*Acts* ii. 22, 24). And as here so every other sermon of the Apostle culminates in the concise statement : " God hath raised him from the dead, of which we are witnesses " (*Acts* iii. 15 ; *cf.* ii. 32 ; x. 41).

Like Peter, Paul, too, never dreams of using " the visions and revelations of the Lord," which he has experienced (*II. Cor.* xii. 1), to support his belief in the Resurrection. It is only with some hesitation and because the attacks of his opponents force him to it, that he tells of the rapture which had seized him fourteen years before. And he deliberately abstains from pronouncing any judgment on its exact character. Whether it was " in the body " or " out of the body," that is, whether it was a purely subjective or also an objective experience he does not know. " God alone knoweth." All the more definite is his judgment on what happened at Damascus. He has not the slightest doubt whatever that he had really " seen Christ Jesus our Lord " (*I. Cor.* ix. 1), that on the road to Damascus " there shone round about him a great light," and that he had heard a voice saying, " I am Jesus of Nazareth, whom thou persecutest." It is significant that in his account of the Resurrection he uses the dative with the verb " see " ($\ddot{\omega}\phi\theta\eta$). The " seeing " of this new reality, Jesus the risen, was absolutely forced upon him against his will. There was nothing subjective about it. No fewer than six times Paul tells in more or less detail of his meeting with the glorified Christ (*I. Cor.* ix. 1; xv. 8; *Gal.* i. 12, 16; *Acts* ix. 1 *sqq.*; xxii. 4 *sqq.*; xxvi. 9 *sqq.*). To him this is on a par with the apostles' experience after the Resurrection. And for this very reason it qualifies him to be not less of a witness to the Resurrection, nor less of an apostle than the other disciples. It is with positive passion that St. Paul stresses this one essential foundation of his apostolate. " Am I not an apostle ? Have not I seen Christ Jesus our Lord ? " (*I. Cor.* ix. 1).

In the light of our sources it is then indubitable that both Peter and Paul had knowledge of the ecstatic state.

But both Peter and Paul draw a sharp dividing-line between these visions and their experiences of the Resurrection.

What these apostles say of their own attitude is borne out in its entirety by the other sources, which mention three facts that rule out any subjective origin of the Easter experiences, any possibility that their belief in the Resurrection might have forced its way up from the depths of their subconscious minds. First, they declare that never during the Lord's lifetime had the disciples taken seriously his prophecy that he would be crucified and buried and would rise again on the third day. True, there was talk of his resurrection on the third day not only in their own circle, but also among his enemies (*cf. Matt.* xxvii. 63) ; but the disciples neither understood it, nor did they wish to, for they were unable to grasp the idea of the suffering and death of Jesus, which his resurrection involved. Did not Peter go so far as to " rebuke " Jesus for speaking of the sufferings of the Christ (*Matt.* xvi. 22 = *Mark* viii. 32) ? Second, the sources testify that the disciples did not eagerly seize on our Lord's promise that he would rise again on the third day after his death, and anchor their hopes in it. They did not behave at all like people who in spite of everything are sure of final victory. On the contrary, they fled and hid themselves (*cf. John* xx. 19), they mourned and wept (*Mark* xvi. 19) ; and it would not have occurred to them at all to go and look at the sepulchre on the third day, had not the women brought news of the empty tomb and the angel's message. And even this report they regarded as an "idle tale" and refused to believe it (*Luke* xxiv. 11 ; *cf. Matt.* xvi. 11). This behaviour of the apostles would be simply unintelligible if, even in the remotest corner of their subconsciousness, there had been the faintest expectation of the Resurrection. The sources (*Matt.* xxviii. 17 ; *Luke* xxiv. 37, 41 ; *John* xx. 19) testify also to the third and decisive fact. The disciples still doubted, even when the risen Lord appeared to them. They "supposed that they saw a spirit" (*Luke* xxiv. 37). Their scepticism was shaken only when our Lord showed them his pierced hands and feet and the wound in his side, and it was not till he actually ate and drank with them that it was finally dispelled (*Luke* xxiv. 41 ; *John* xxi. 10 ; *Acts* x. 41). From the point of view of the vision theory, such doubt at the very moment of being faced with this experience is wholly unintelligible. For according to it the appearances of Jesus or, if you will, the visions of the risen Lord, must actually have originated in the sure belief in and absolute certainty of the Resurrection. They could have been nothing but realizations of their belief, inspired by the certainty of their expectation. They would not have led to doubt and scepticism, but to extravagant enthusiasm.

There can be still less question of a psychological origin of the appearance of the glorified Christ in St. Paul's case than in that of the Eleven. For before the occurrence there was in St. Paul's soul not only doubt and mistrust and anxiety but a deep-seated hatred. Again and again Paul emphasizes the fact that before his conversion he "beyond measure persecuted the church of God, and wasted it" (*Gal.* i. 13; *cf. Acts* xxii. 4 *sqq.*; xxvi. 9 *sqq.*). There was in him no secret belief in Jesus, no secret love for him, which might have prepared the way for his conversion. The words of our Lord, "It is hard for thee to kick against the goad," do not allude to any antecedent, interior struggle of the Apostle, but his painful, present situation, as he vainly sought to ward off the grace of Christ which was invading his soul. Throughout his whole remaining life this was his great secret grief, as it was also an ever renewed source of joy and gratitude—that at the eleventh hour he, as one born out of due time, had been snatched from his hatred of Christ by the incredible mercy of God. The whole of the Apostle's theory of justification and grace is based on his sure knowledge of the one fact, that it was God, and God alone, who had come to him on the outskirts of Damascus, and that there had been nothing, literally nothing, in him which might have been a preparation for this conversion, or could have induced it.

From whatever side we seek to probe the genesis of the apostles' belief in the Resurrection, we shall never find the slightest fact that might justify a purely psychological explanation of it. Their whole attitude when faced with the event was so cautious, so hesitating and sceptical, and, in St. Paul's case, so definitely hostile, that the new belief could have been awakened in them only by the influence of an exterior event, a well-established, incontestable fact breaking in upon them and convincing them that it was a reality which could be objectively verified.

This conclusion is definitely confirmed when we come to examine the true nature and object of the disciples' Easter experience. According to the hypotheses of the vision theory, the image of the risen Lord which the disciples saw must have coincided in essentials with the ideal picture of the Messias which they had hitherto borne in their hearts. For on that hypothesis the risen Lord was simply the disciples' ideal picture of the Messias, which, embedded in the depths of their subconscious minds, forced its way up to the surface of their consciousness. But we know what that ideal was. It was that of a Messias-king, as the prophets had seemed to draw him, seated on the throne of his father David, and making all his enemies his footstool. This was the Messias of the apostles' dreams; it was also St. Paul's dream. As late as the day of the Last Supper, the disciples brought two swords in order to make their dream a reality by force. Then there dawned that first Easter morning, and at a stroke the old dream-picture was obliterated and a wholly new figure, a wholly new Messias, a wholly new faith entered the consciousness of the disciples.

The first and most immediate reaction which the appearance of the risen Lord produced in the disciples was a new and overwhelming realization that he was really the Lord. "The Lord is risen indeed, and hath appeared to Simon," was the cry of the Eleven which greeted the two disciples on their return from Emmaus

(*Luke* xxiv. 34). " It is the Lord," cried out St. John
when he saw the risen Christ standing on the shore of
the lake (*John* xxi. 7). " My Lord and my God," was
Thomas's confession when he saw the marks of the
wounds in the risen Christ (*John* xx. 28). And Paul's
question on the road to Damascus was, " Who art
thou, Lord ? " (*Acts* ix. 5). This " Kyrie " was the first
response of their new faith to the Easter message.
" Therefore let all the house of Israel know most certainly that God hath made both Lord, and Christ, this
same Jesus, whom you have crucified," was Peter's
solemn peroration to his first sermon on the day of
Pentecost (*Acts* ii. 36). In Jewish and Hellenistic
phraseology " the Lord " ($\kappa\acute{\upsilon}\rho\iota\sigma\varsigma$) is the God as he
manifests himself in power to the faithful. If prior to
their Easter experiences the disciples had primarily seen
the humanity of Jesus, and his divinity only as it were in
broken flashes, when by sign or word it broke through
its human veil ; from henceforth, since they know that
the Risen Master is in their midst, it is this divinity which
is at the centre of their faith, and their conception of his
humanity is now regulated by that of his divinity.
Their Easter experiences brought, therefore, to their
idea of Christ a significant deepening and clarifying.
Their old impression of the human nature of Jesus was
now absorbed in and permeated by the new impression
of his Godhead. For the first time it had become an
evident certainty to them that Jesus, the man, was in his
essence " their Lord and their God."

Further, since it was the Lord himself who in his

human form had appeared to them, their other conceptions were clarified by the clear conviction that his true place, his original dwelling-place, could be nowhere but in heaven at the right hand of the Father. To this the risen Lord himself had testified when he said, " I ascend to my Father and to your Father, to my God and your God" (*John* xx. 17). Henceforth, therefore, the apostles preach with jubilation the tidings that Jesus " was exalted by the right hand of God " (*Acts* ii. 33 ; v. 31 ; vii. 55). From that day to this the *Sedit ad dexteram Patris* has never been absent from the creed of Christendom.

To this there was automatically linked the further certainty that from this risen Lord, all life and all spirit, all grace and forgiveness, all authority and power would henceforth pour down on mankind. They had heard this in many different forms from the risen Lord himself : " Behold I am with you all days, even to the consummation of the world " (*Matt.* xxviii. 20) ; " I send the promise of my Father upon you " (*Luke* xxiv. 49) ; " Receive ye the Holy Ghost : Whose sins you shall forgive, they are forgiven them : and whose sins you shall retain, they are retained " (*John* xx. 22 *sqq.*) ; " All power is given me in heaven and in earth. Going therefore teach ye all nations : baptizing them in the name of the Father, and of the Son, and of the Holy Ghost " (*Matt.* xxviii. 18 *sqq.*) ; " Simon son of John, lovest thou me more than these ? . . . Feed my lambs " (*John* xxi. 15 *sqq.*).

And as the power of the risen Lord reached up to the

heights and summits of spirit, so too did it penetrate down to the very depths, down to the ultimate roots of all being, where life wells up from a thousand springs and where death lurks. The most far-reaching and revealing fact graven on the minds of the disciples by their meeting with the risen Lord, was that in his new life they now found the assurance of their own eternal life. For them, too, the Resurrection of the Lord was a truly cosmic event, since it guaranteed the resurrection from the dead not only of themselves, but of all the dead from the beginning of time until the end. For the realization that " he whom God hath raised from the dead, saw no corruption " (*Acts* xiii. 37), implied the recognition that in the risen Lord the resurrection of all mankind is involved. " For by a man came death, and by a man also the resurrection of the dead " (*I. Cor.* xv. 21). Hence St. Paul has no more passionate wish than that he " may know him, and the power of his resurrection, and the fellowship of his sufferings " (*Phil.* iii. 10). And Peter knows himself to be " regenerated unto a lively hope, by the resurrection of Jesus Christ from the dead " (*I. Pet.* i. 3). It is by the Easter experiences of the apostles more than by anything else that the traditional Jewish conceptions of the Messias were exploded. Jesus Christ is not only the redeemer from sin and guilt, but also the redeemer of the dead to life. He " hath raised us up together, and hath made us sit together in the heavenly places through Christ Jesus " (*Eph.* ii. 6). Only by this light could the disciples penetrate the deeper meaning of those words which,

shortly before his departure, he spoke at the tomb of
Lazarus : " I am the resurrection and the life : he that
believeth in me although he be dead, shall live " (*John*
xi. 25). " Martha, thy brother shall rise again " (*John*
xi. 23).

If we compare what the disciples learnt from their
Easter experiences with the belief about Jesus to which
they had previously clung, it will be obvious that
spiritual distances had been opened up to them of which
hitherto they may have caught fugitive glimpses, but
which they had never embraced with any lively faith.
The new fabric of ideas so far transcends the old picture
of their dreams that the former cannot possibly be
explained by the latter. This new insight could not
have come from within, but only from without, from the
realization of a new and wholly unexpected truth, which
rushed in on them with overwhelming, catastrophic
force and overthrew the old Adam in them. Wherever
we look : on the empty tomb, on the mentality of the
disciples, on the peculiar genesis and nature of their
Easter experiences, there flashes upon us the supernatural, something not to be deduced from its antecedents, wholly inexplicable. If the transcendental, the
supernatural, a divine revelation, a true act of God can
be discovered anywhere in history, it is here.

What also contributed to the iron tenacity of the
apostles' faith in Jesus was something to which they
gave emphatic prominence in their preaching, namely
that God in the miracle of the Resurrection had himself
set his unbreakable seal on the life of Jesus. Again and

again there rings out in their early sermons the confession: "This Jesus hath God raised again" (*Acts* ii. 32; iii. 15; iv. 10; x. 40; xiii. 30, 37; *I. Cor.* xv. 15); "The God of Abraham, and the God of Isaac, and the God of Jacob, the God of our fathers, hath glorified his Son Jesus" (*Acts* iii. 13); "Him hath God exalted with his right hand to be prince and saviour" (*Acts* v. 31); "Giving faith to all by raising him up from the dead" (*Acts* xvii. 31). It is true that the heavenly Father himself had announced that he was "well pleased" with his "beloved Son," when Jesus entered upon his public ministry (*Matt.* iii. 16 *sq.*), and again when Jesus was at the height of his activity (*Matt.* xvii. 5); but that had been only "a voice from heaven," a clear sign of God's presence, but in outward form not differing essentially from the utterances made to many other men of the Old Testament, such as Elias and Jonas, indeed even to the fratricide Cain. In the risen Lord, however, had been revealed in unique majesty and power he who is the God of miracles. Here he no longer speaks by signs and symbols, nor through created media. He is no longer speaking through the living word and work of Jesus. Here he speaks in the overwhelming immediacy of his action through the dead Jesus. By it he tells us that he has raised this dead man to life, nay more, that he has raised him in glory to the celestial and divine life, that he has exalted the crucified to his right hand. What we are dealing with is not the raising up of a mere man, but the Resurrection of the Christ, not the mere flaming up of an extinct natural life, but the creative breaking through of that divine life, which Jesus from the very beginning knew to be his own in the perishable frame of his mortal body, and which now on the third day after his death, reuniting soul and body, clothed and glorified his whole human nature with the majesty of God. During the forty days that the risen Lord appeared to the disciples (*Acts* i. 3) and actually ate and drank with them in some mysterious fashion utterly beyond our range of experience (*cf. Luke* xxiv. 30, 43 ; *John* xxi. 12 *sq.* ; *Acts* x. 41), the reality of God appeared again and again before the eyes of the disciples as something entirely transcendent, a *mysterium tremendum*. By the compelling force of a reality directly perceptible and overwhelmingly impressive, their minds were directed from the earth and its powers to the celestial Christ and the " power of his resurrection " (*Phil.* iii. 10). The world of time and space is no longer taken for granted as the final truth of reality. The things of earth no longer press their importunate claims. The world has sunk to a reality of the third and subordinate rank. The kingdom of God, once present in the simple figure of the Son of man, shyly and almost unnoticeably putting out its roots in the soil of Palestine, is now revealed in the glorified Lord as the kingdom of God in that original exalted sense in which the seers of the Old Testament saw it, as a kingdom come down from heaven, a dazzling miracle, an overwhelming revelation of the divine power. Its centre of gravity has shifted from earth to heaven. If the death of Jesus had shattered the sensual, egoistic hopes of the disciples for an approaching earthly and political Messianic kingdom, the repeated appearances of the risen Lord engraved ineradicably on their minds the supernatural character of this kingdom. While our Lord in those forty days was " speaking of the kingdom of God " to them (*Acts* i. 3), his evangel was losing more and more in their eyes all its earthly wrappings, all its temporal attachments, all its Jewish limitations. It was no longer a question of discussions with the Pharisees, a more abounding justice, or the testimony of the Son of man, but with the Resurrection and eternal life, the coming of the Holy Ghost, forgiveness of sins, baptism, truth and grace. No longer now was their gaze kept fixed on Israel, on its temple, its rites, and its high-priest. What now stood out in their minds was the new Messianic flock which Peter, as the vicar of the Shepherd-Messias, would henceforth have to shepherd, the company of the faithful, the Church which embraces all peoples. We have reached the great and glorious moment when the apostles hear and understand the old evangel of the Lord in a new manner, translated, that is to say, into the spiritual and the supernatural as a gospel of life for all peoples. All that the Lord had once said about the " Son of man " and the " Son," about his judging the world, about his suffering and death, was now first seen by them in its clear context and its ultimate significance. Out of this understanding St. John wrote his life of the Lord. It was the hour when true Christianity was born, when the risen Lord fully unveiled to them the spiritual nature of the truths, ordinances, and powers, of which he had planted the germ in the days of his earthly ministry. Christianity was now revealed to them as the religion of the spirit. Now was the time, too, of the coming of the Holy Spirit, to which the risen Saviour referred explicitly when he said to them, " You shall be baptized with the Holy Ghost not many days yet " (*Acts* i. 5 ; *cf. Luke* xxiv. 29). It will be the Holy Ghost who will within a very short space testify to this his Easter gospel, the *evangelium quadraginta dierum*, and make it a living reality to them.

It is psychologically readily intelligible that, faced with this wealth of new conceptions which the glory of the risen Lord forced upon them, the disciples were, as it were, blinded and instinctively sought for some point at which they could relate their newly won impressions and knowledge to their old mental attitude. So they harked back to the hopes and expectations on which, as true children of the Jewish people, they had from youth up been nourished. And they asked Jesus, " Lord, wilt thou at this time restore again the kingdom of Israel ? " (*Acts* i. 6). It was once more a human possibility which allured them, a temptation to which their human natures and the Jewish blood in their veins made them susceptible. Jesus freed them from these last earthly shackles by diverting them, with the authority of one to whom all things were given by the Father, from the way of man to the way of God. " It is not for you to know the times and moments, which the Father hath put in his own power : But you shall receive the power of the Holy Ghost coming upon you, and you shall be witnesses unto me in Jerusalem, and in all Judea and Samaria, and even to the uttermost part of the earth" (*Acts* i. 7 *sq.*). With these words Jesus delivered the disciples from the last tangled web of their earthly selves and ordered their future, their lives and works solely to the *magnalia Dei*, which with his Resurrection were to spread over the whole world. When Jesus ascended into heaven, he left the disciples with their thoughts and wishes, with their whole being rooted in the miracle of his Resurrection, and with the knowledge that they were chosen to stand where two world eras met and to bear witness to those powers of the Resurrection and of eternal life which were henceforth to pervade mankind.

Thus they saw in the Ascension of our Lord not so much the end of his earthly history as the beginning of a new life and activity at the right hand of the Father, the solemn confirmation and fulfilment of all that had been manifested in the risen Lord, namely that he, and he alone, is the Lord, the King of Glory, in whom and through whom all mankind, indeed every created thing, has its being and its destiny. The Ascension was to the disciples the dawn of a new day which should have no night and in which they must work until the Lord should come again (*cf. Acts* i. 11). In their confession of the Lord who is to come again lay also the heart of their new faith, the source of their new hope and their new joy. "And they adoring went back into Jerusalem with great joy. And they were always in the temple praising and blessing God" (*Luke* xxiv. 52 *sq.*). In the profession of this their first martyr gave his life. "Behold!" said

Stephen, " I see the heavens opened, and the Son of man standing on the right hand of God " (*Acts* vii. 55). It was in confessing this that the apostles henceforth exulted. " Blessed be the God and Father of our Lord Jesus Christ, who according to his great mercy hath regenerated us unto a lively hope, by the resurrection of Jesus Christ from the dead " (*I. Pet.* i. 3). " Who is on the right hand of God, swallowing down death, that we might be made heirs of life everlasting " (*I. Pet.* iii. 22). " God also hath exalted him, and hath given him a name which is above all names ; that in the name of Jesus every knee should bow, of those that are in heaven, on earth, and under the earth : And that every tongue should confess that the Lord Jesus Christ is in the glory of God the Father " (*Phil.* ii. 9–11).

The exultant testimony of the Apostles to the glorified Christ " who is on the right hand of God " was at bottom a testimony to the victorious powers of the risen Lord, which from his place on the right hand of the Father were to penetrate and renovate the world. Their joy in the Resurrection comprised at the same time their expectation of Pentecost, since Jesus himself had, in the last days of his life, promised that in the hour of persecution the Spirit of their Father (*Matt.* x. 20), " the Holy Ghost " (*Luke* xii. 12), the " Spirit of truth " (*John* xv. 26), " another Paraclete " (*John* xiv. 16, 26), should be with them. And after his Resurrection he had commanded them to remain in Jerusalem until they " be endued with power from on high " (*Luke* xxiv. 49).

Thus the miracle of Easter was consummated in the

miracle of Pentecost. In the rushing of the mighty wind which shook the whole house and in the tongues of fire which descended on each one of the disciples (*Acts* ii. 2 *sq.*), there appeared the " power from on high." And the disciples " were all filled with the Holy Ghost, and they began to speak with divers tongues, according as the Holy Ghost gave them to speak " (*Acts* ii. 4). He came upon them like a new and mighty kindling power which snatched them out of themselves into that transcendent and divine world, where the Spirit of God alone lives his mighty and holy life and carries on his sublime and incomprehensible working, like the wind of which " thou knowest not whence it cometh and whither it goeth " (*John* iii. 8). All the ideas which they had gained from the earthly life of Jesus and from the glorified Christ now lost, in the mighty agitation of their souls, their characteristic earthly centre of gravity, and they were raised to such heights of experience, to such a power of will, to such a clarity of thought that all pettinesses, trifles, all human limitations, all nervous hesitation and anxiety were swallowed up. The very depths of their souls were torn open and filled with the " power " of the glorified Lord, so that they saw and comprehended the mighty acts of God of which they were the subject in all their power, in the absoluteness of their demand, in their timeless application to the men of all tongues and of all countries. The moment was come when " the Paraclete " should teach them and bring back to their minds whatsoever Jesus had said to them (*cf. John* xiv. 26). The supernatural had obtained dominion

over them, had stirred their hearts and forced its way
to their lips, thence to pour itself out on mankind in
ever new and strange utterances and tongues. They
were no longer merely receivers, as once they were,
when Jesus rose again and ascended into heaven. They
were now themselves mighty givers, creative witnesses
who, out of the fullness of the Spirit bestowed upon
them, were bringing to mankind the new gospel of the
glorified Lord. " Do penance, and be baptized every one
of you in the name of Jesus Christ, for the remission of
your sins : and you shall receive the gift of the Holy
Ghost " (*Acts* ii. 38). Now, too, was gone all nervous-
ness and fear of men. They no longer hid in Mark's
house. They stood openly before the whole of Jerusalem, before the very Council, and cried out the most
dreadful of all charges : " The author of life you killed,
whom God hath raised from the dead, of which we are
witnesses " (*Acts* iii. 15). When they were forbidden
to speak, they replied in holy defiance, " We cannot but
speak the things which we have seen and heard " (*Acts*
iv. 20), and " We ought to obey God rather than men "
(*Acts* v. 29). After being scourged " they went from the
presence of the Council, rejoicing that they were
accounted worthy to suffer reproach for the name of
Jesus " (*Acts* v. 41). A new man was risen to dominion
in them, the man of strong faith and burning love, the
supernatural man, the man of self-surrender and sacrifice, the μάρτυς, the " witness."

There could be no more complete confirmation of the
Resurrection and Ascension than the miracle of Pentecost,

when the Lord " being exalted to the right hand of God,
and having received of the Father the promise of the
Holy Ghost, poured it forth on the disciples " (*Acts* ii.
33). And the same power of the Holy Spirit worked on
the thousands converted and baptized by the disciples,
just as it had done on them. From out of the midst of
a crumbling world there arose the infant Church of
Christ in its entire being, with the disposition of its
ordinances and offices, with its word and sacraments,
and with its holy life, a unique confession to the glorified Lord supported by the power of the Spirit, a unique
act of faith and love and prayer in the Holy Ghost.
Although at its very beginning this holy life of the
Church seemed to be perishing in a sea of blood,
although later it looked to be withering in the rank
undergrowth of human error and human illusion and
stifling under the veneer of a materialistic culture,
the Holy Ghost of Pentecost came again and again to
" blow upon those slain, and make them live again " (*cf.*
Ez. xxxvii. 9). In its life and being the Church is nothing
but the permanent epiphany of the powers of the risen
Lord, the permanent creation and revelation of the
Holy Ghost (*I. Cor.* xii. 7 *sqq.*), the ever-present miracle
of Pentecost. In her and through her we are brought
into a connection with the Resurrection, the Ascension,
and the sending of the Holy Ghost, in which there is no
historical break. For through the unbroken line of her
popes and bishops we are, as it were, transported across
time and space into the presence of the apostles and can
listen directly to their testimony. And in that the Church

is the communion of the Holy Ghost we come through her into religious connection, indeed into personal companionship with the glorified Lord. For it is the Holy Spirit that opens our inmost being, the core of our personality, to his grace-bringing presence and makes us sensible of the " power of his resurrection." Thus it comes to pass that when we pray in his name we avail ourselves not only of his words and works, but also of himself : we possess him. " For where there are two or three gathered together in my name, there am I in the midst of them " (*Matt.* xviii. 20). It is his precious and loving legacy, bequeathed by him at the Last Supper, that " the chalice of benediction, which we bless, is the communion of the blood of Christ. And the bread, which we break, is the partaking of the body of the Lord " (*cf. I. Cor.* x. 16). Whenever the Church does for a " commemoration " of him what he then did, there is accomplished that mystery of his uttermost love by which we are drawn up into a real communion with his death and sacrifice, and thus into the communion of his Resurrection and of his life. Again, it is the Holy Ghost who deepens this sacramental communion into a living union of heart and spirit, so that our inmost selves are surrendered to his death and to his life. When we eat his flesh and drink his blood, we abide in him and he in us (*cf. John* vi. 55). Moved by the breath of the Holy Spirit we touch and experience Jesus in the worthy reception of the Blessed Sacrament as directly and as personally as did once the disciples in that Upper Room. If to-day he were to step into our midst as we were breaking his bread, if his

Easter greeting were to sound in our ears as we were setting forth his death, we should know him better than we do our fathers and mothers, indeed better than we know ourselves. He who centuries ago was slain as a felon in an out-of-the-way corner of the world, to-day lives the same sublime life among us, in us, with us. He is more alive than all the living. Above all the needs of the present, above all the cramping limitations of human existence, above all the quarrels of states and nations, above the graves of our loves there still floats his figure in its gleaming whiteness. And we know that he alone is the real union of the living and the dead, that he alone is our eternal life. We see him more plainly than we do visible things. We love him more than we do any human being. We confess him no less sincerely than did the disciples in days gone by. For the truth is that every genuine Christian life proclaims, with an ever new voice in ringing tones, the fact to which the apostles once testified with their blood : " He is risen from the dead, of which we are witnesses."

VIII

THE ATONEMENT

The glad tidings of the Resurrection are also the glad tidings of the Atonement. The Easter light throws its clarifying rays on Golgotha and on the Cross. It is only by this light that we can unveil and interpret that mystery which to the Jews was a stumbling-block and to the Gentiles a foolishness (*I. Cor.* i. 23). We are not merely fronted by the heroic act of a holy person obedient unto death to the heavenly Father, but by the death of a man who is God, by the death of our Lord, by the death of one who is the judge of the world. It is an event so dreadful, so past all conception, that the sun pales in the heavens, the earth quakes, and the veil of the temple is rent from top to bottom (*Matt.* xxvii. 45, 51). Something cosmic is happening here, a world catastrophe. The God-Man is dying.

We know very well that God, in himself, cannot die. But it is not God as such, who is dying : it is a man substantially united to the Word of God, a man who *is* God. And for this very reason we know also how unintelligible it is that anyone should pass casually over the mystery of the Cross, on the pretext that it was merely a primitive conception of expiation by blood taken over from other cults—the conception, namely, of a god slaying his own son as an act of reparation to himself.

For in this case it is not the Father who accomplishes the sacrifice but the Son, and he accomplishes it by an act of supreme moral freedom, a spiritual act of heroism past all conception, for the honour of the Father and for the salvation of mankind. No act has ever been performed so freely and so deliberately, so wholly of the agent's choice as this act. " I lay down my life that I may take it again. No man taketh it away from me : but I lay it down of myself, and I have power to lay it down ; and I have power to take it up again " (*John* x. 17 *sq.*). On the other hand, it is not his own divine nature, which the Son of God dedicates in free surrender to the Father, but a created nature which he had made his own, which in his incomprehensible mercy he took upon himself, namely the nature of man. This is that nature which once in blasphemous self-idolatry was wrenched by Adam, who as the parent of the human race first bore it, from its supernatural orientation towards and union with God. And this nature had ever since borne the stain of deprivation of the divine, of remoteness from God, of what we call original sin, and had as from a poisoned soil put forth sin after sin and crime after crime. This human nature, as handed down from Adam, which had become corrupted in its manner, feeling, thinking, and willing, was the proper seat of all evil concupiscence on earth and the cunning instrument of all that is done which is repulsive to God. It was therefore the immediate object of the divine wrath, the true culprit in the case. Hence it was fitting and just that the judgment of God should fall precisely on a human nature, and that the Son of God should take it upon himself with all its frailty, weakness, sin excepted, and mortality, as a victim for sacrifice, in order in it and by it to offer reparation.

Certain as it assuredly is that on the day when the Son of God died, it was not his divinity but his humanity—his created human nature—which suffered and died, so is it equally certain that it was indeed the very Person of the Son of God who offered himself on Golgotha. It was not a mere man who had been *adopted* as son of God; nor yet a mere man to whom the Word of God had become linked solely by some permanent bond of affection. It is a man who *is* God: God incarnate. He had made the human nature so intimately, so indissolubly, so utterly part of himself, that it had no separate existence independently of the Word of God. Its human consciousness, its human freedom, its human resignation were assumed into unity of person, together with his divine nature with its divine knowledge and its divine will. Being in the " form of God," he had nevertheless " emptied himself " in order to assume the " form of a servant " (*cf. Phil.* ii. 6, 7). In that he thus " emptied himself " of his own power and glory in order to become as one of us, he manifests his own unconditioned, absolute freedom—the freedom of God.

Hence the drama of Golgotha has its ultimate, eternal background in heaven, where the Son proceeds from the Father. Because he is the Son who has received all things from the Father—his divine nature, its omnipotence, its wisdom and love, all its hidden mysteries, above all, too, the free, divine decree of self-oblation for mankind—his mission is to be the subject and accomplisher of the decree. Therefore is he " sent " by the Father. The free, divine assent which the Son gives to his " sending " by the Father, he also gives to his Incarnation and to the expiatory sufferings involved in it. " Wherefore when he cometh into the world, he saith : Sacrifice and oblation thou wouldest not : but a body thou hast fitted to me. . . . Behold I come . . . that I should do thy will, O God " (*Heb.* x. 5 *sqq.* ; *cf. Ps.* xxxix. 7 *sqq.*). Thus the free, deliberate self-oblation of Jesus on earth is the realization in time of the eternal decree of redemption in heaven which springs from the inmost sources of divine love. Hence the drama of Golgotha is no mere chance event of history, no mere episode of yesterday. Its ultimate *raison d'être* is to be found in a free, deliberate act in the utmost depths of the divine life. It is the will and work of the triune God accomplished by the only-begotten Son. It will already be clear from this that its primal and most sublime explanation is nothing less than God himself, his own honour, the unveiling of the majesty of his being. When God's creative word called worlds into existence out of nothing, when he clothed the earth in splendour and beauty and drew a myriad forms of life from its womb, he showed himself to be the all-mighty, all-wise, all-majestic God. When he formed man after his own image and likeness and set the nobility of a divine sonship in his soul, he showed himself the God of fatherliness and love, the magnanimous and holy God, who is lavish with the fullness of his own riches and gives to man a gracious portion in his own life. But another kind of omnipotence and wisdom and love shines forth on the Cross, an omnipotence which divests itself of itself, a wisdom which humbles itself to foolishness, a love which is all self-donation. God's perfection is so incomprehensible and so utterly beyond all human possibilities, that it not only works creatively from its eternity by free acts and bestows on creation a well of created blessings, but also of its charity bestows itself, humbles itself, sacrifices itself. Just as, therefore, the triune God is from all eternity free, creative act, so also is he, in the same infinite power of his free will, uttermost self-donation. The free self-sacrifice of the Son has its foundation in that mysterious, essential donation of the Father to the Son and of the Son to the Father which from all eternity proceeds in the Holy Ghost, and from which the Holy Ghost derives his eternal life. For it is in the person of the Holy Ghost that there is expressed in substantial individuality the incomprehensible, ecstatic quality of the divine will, a property of the divine nature transcending the bounds of personality and all imaginable limits and standards. When the consubstantial Son of the Father assumed human nature, his human consciousness and his human will derived their profoundest and decisive motives from the infinite riches of his divine self-devotion. His human life was a life of perfect surrender to the Father, of entire obedience to his will. Since he offered himself for the guilt of fallen humanity, this obedience culminated in a sacrifice of utter renunciation and intense suffering.   But in its essence it remained the reflection of that infinite self-donation accomplished in perfect purity from all eternity in the divine life of God.   The mystery of the Cross of Christ is therefore intimately related to the mystery of the most Holy Trinity and in particular to the mystery of the Holy Ghost.   We are standing before the ultimate abysses of the divine being and life and the free, divine decrees mysteriously arising from them.   No created intellect can penetrate them.   We can only know that it is some-where in God that their ultimate meaning and purpose are alone to be sought.   For God, the all-perfect, cannot strive after something extra-divine, that is to say infra-divine, as his ultimate goal, without debasing his own absolute value.   It would be, so to speak, a " fall " in God.   Hence the ultimate and profoundest meaning of Christ's death on the Cross can only be God himself, the revelation of the glory of his love.   The self-donation of the Son of God is in itself the sublimest praise of the divine essence and the loftiest possible act of veneration of God, whether men believe in it or not, whether they are redeemed by it or not.

Actually they are redeemed by this oblation.   Actually the eternal self-oblation of the consubstantial Son of God, precisely because it is the supreme revelation of the glory of the divine love, produces at the same time the highest imaginable source of happiness for men. Entering into time and manifested in history in the bloody offering on Golgotha, it is become the sacrifice of our redemption.   In it culminates the redemptive ministry of Jesus for " sinners," for the " sick," for " the many." It is the definitive act of Christ, the act in which above all others he proves himself the Saviour of mankind.

Jesus was careful to lay the utmost stress upon this distinctive character of his act of sacrifice. For it is quite untrue that belief in the Atonement arose at a later date as the product of Hellenistic Christianity. From the moment when Peter in the name of the disciples made his solemn confession, " Thou art the Christ," Jesus " began to show his disciples that he must go to Jerusalem . . . and be put to death " (*Matt.* xvi. 16 *sqq.*). It is now his concern to perfect the confession of his apostles by bringing home to them the fact that the Christ in whom they believed, was a Christ who must suffer and die, and that it would be actually by his suffering and death that the God-appointed mission of Christ would be accomplished. So strong is his desire to bring this home to them that when Peter, whom a moment before he had appointed to be the rock of his Church, opposed the idea of a suffering and dying Christ, he repulsed him with the same indignant severity as that with which he had on another occasion driven the devil from him (*Matt.* iv. 10). " Go behind me, Satan, thou art a scandal unto me : because thou savourest not the things that are of God, but the things that are of men " (*Matt.* xvi. 23). To Jesus it is therefore something devilish to fail to understand or to deny the necessity of the Passion. Suffering he regards as an essential part of his mission. Hence the three great

prophecies in which he spoke of his death (*cf. Matt.*
xvi. 21 ; xvii. 21 *sqq.* ; xx. 17 *sqq.*). In the parable of the
vineyard, in which the husbandmen first kill the " servants " sent by the lord of the vineyard and, last of all,
his own well-beloved son, Jesus explicitly brings out the
relation of his own death to salvation (*cf. Matt.* xxi.
33 *sqq.*). It is a sacred obligation which cannot be
ignored. " The Son of man shall be betrayed into the
hands of men " (*Matt.* xvii. 21). " As Moses lifted up
the serpent in the desert, so must the Son of man be lifted
up " (*John* iii. 14). " I have a baptism, wherewith I am
to be baptized : and how am I straitened until it be
accomplished " (*Luke* xii. 50 ; *cf. Mark* x. 38). This
obligation is not simply the tragic result of the historical
situation, nor is it a cruel natural doom : it is an obligation imposed on him by the Father, in the economy of
redemption, " as it was written of him " (*Mark* ix. 12 ;
Matt. xxvi. 24, 54). According to Luke (xxii. 37),
Jesus expressly applies to himself the words of Isaias
about the suffering servant of God who " was reputed
with the wicked " (*Isa.* liii. 12), and indeed he was fond
of quoting from this part of Isaias (*cf. Matt.* viii. 11
with *Isa.* xlix. 12 ; *Matt.* xi. 5 with *Isa.* lxi. 1 ; *Matt.*
xxi. 13 with *Isa.* lvi. 7). Hence it is not arbitrarily, but
out of his intimate knowledge of the necessity of his
suffering imposed by God's decree, that Jesus applies
to himself feature by feature the picture of the suffering
servant drawn by Isaias, in order to bring home to his
disciples his own mission as redeemer. " The Son of
man is not come to be ministered unto, but to minister,

and to give his life a redemption for many " (*Matt.* xx.
28 ; *Mark* x. 45). If this expression of a " price paid "
(כמר, *kopher*, λύτρον, *redemptio*) does not derive from
Isaias himself, it is of current Old Testament usage (*cf.
Ex.* xxi. 30 ; *Num.* xxxv. 31). It signifies the sum of
money with which one who had incurred the death
penalty might buy back his life. In declaring it to be his
will to pay by his own life the " redemption of many,"
he proves unequivocally that he ascribed to his death a
redemptive value, indeed an expiatory, atoning, vicarious
value. It is waste labour to impugn this significant self-
revelation of Jesus and to see in it merely the intrusion of
Pauline or, ultimately, Hellenistic conceptions. If the
expression " redemption " is an isolated one in the
treasury of Christ's sayings handed down to us, it is,
nevertheless, in complete harmony with what, after
Peter's confession, Jesus again and again said concerning
the suffering of the Christ and its necessity for salvation.
The term " redemption " merely sums up concisely in
one universally intelligible concept what had always lain
at the back of his consciousness of his mission and of his
statements about his suffering. Historically it goes back
to a tradition attested alike by Matthew and Mark. It
may seem at first sight strange that Luke is silent about
" redemption " and the giving of his life by Jesus " for
many," though he is well aware of and quotes the
parallel saying of Jesus about " ministering." But this
silence of his is not deliberate in the sense that he consciously intended to deny the redemptive significance of
Christ's death as emphasized by Matthew and Mark.

For, a few verses earlier, his account of the Last Supper makes explicit reference, quite in St. Paul's manner, to this redemptive value. Moreover, as already pointed out, Luke hands down a literal quotation of our Lord's from Isaias (*Luke* xxii. 37) and thus, independently of the other evangelists, proves clearly how deliberately Jesus identified himself with the expiating servant of God in Isaias' prophecy. If the third evangelist does not himself hand down the expression " redemption," but only mentions that of " ministering," this is sufficiently explained by the intimate way, peculiar to himself, in which, unlike the other evangelists, he couples the doctrine of redemption with his account of the Last Supper. It was repugnant to his feeling for style to allude twice over to a special expression of Jesus about the redemptive significance of his death, in his account of one single incident, which after all culminated in the offering of the body and blood of Christ.

Thus Luke's silence can in no respect detract from the value of the testimony of Matthew and Mark. Both evangelists witness to the fact that it was Jesus himself who first described his death as an atonement, and not Paul nor anyone else. Later on Paul more than any other over and over again witnesses to the expiatory, redemptive power of Christ's death on the Cross and explicitly speaks of the " great price " with which Christians had been " bought " (*I. Cor.* vi. 20; *cf. I. Cor.* vii. 23). But closely as these and similar formulæ approximate to the statement of Jesus, they are in no place identical with it. They differ from it not only in wording,

but also in their polemical accent, due to the time
when they were written. Moreover, other apostles,
such as Paul and John, speak of the expiatory power of
Christ's sufferings in general, and of the " redemption "
by the blood of Christ in particular (*I. Pet.* i. 18; *Ap.* v.
9), and in their sermons there actually often recurs the
leitmotif of Christ's gospel of redemption, namely the
suffering servant of God (*Acts* iv. 13, 26; iv. 27, 30).
Thus the line of tradition goes back through Paul and
the apostles to Jesus himself. And Paul expressly attests
the continuity of the tradition when, in his first Epistle
to the Corinthians, he counts the doctrine of the redemptive death of Jesus among those parts of the gospel which
he himself had " first of all received " and " delivered "
to them (*cf. I. Cor.* xv. 3). In talking of having " received " the message he is " delivering ", the former Rabbinical student deliberately uses the technical expression
($\ddot{o}$ $\kappa a\grave{\iota}$ $\pi a \rho \acute{\epsilon} \lambda a \beta o \nu$) by which in the language of the
Palestinian schools the faithful transmission of the Torah
was spoken of. He thus assures his readers in emphatic
terms of the reliability of his tradition and forestalls any
suspicion that he might have derived it from some anonymous source such as, say, some Hellenistic mystery cult.
Anyhow, is it conceivable that Paul and the other apostles,
reared as they had been from childhood up in hatred
and enmity to all things pagan, should have actually
borrowed one of the tenderest and most pregnant
mysteries of their new faith from the pagan world surrounding them, and that despite this borrowing they
should throughout their lives have been conscious

of standing in sharpest antagonism to the pagan religions, an antagonism which in their day and in subsequent centuries had to be paid for by the most terrible martyrdoms. Moreover, the history of comparative religion has not found a single convincing non-Christian parallel to the Christian belief in the Redemption. Having their origin in the misty shadows of the prehistoric past, the legends of the Hellenistic mystery cults had, as their themes, earthly, sensual needs, struggles and murders, or passionate love adventures. And we have already emphasized in another connection how fundamentally different was the spiritual atmosphere in which they had their roots. To the pagan Hellenistic way of thinking the deity was only a part of nature itself, or at most the expression and index of the creative forces of nature. The gods, therefore, in their lives and activities, were, like men, amenable to the blind laws of nature and in the last resort to the power of fate, to which all being is subject. The Hellenistic redemption-deities in particular were originally nothing but fertility gods, and were therefore as changeable and fluid as the nature of which they were a part. Hence they experienced suffering, death, and resurrection fatalistically as an unwelcome tragic destiny imposed upon them from without, against which they struggled. In all the mystery legends of antiquity we shall seek in vain for any figure of a redeemer who, like Jesus, of his own free intention takes it upon himself to die a death of expiation for mankind. Hence in the mystery cults the redemption of the initiate ($\mu\acute{\upsilon}\sigma\tau\eta\varsigma$) does not come through these deities, but rather in company with them : the believer, in the course of his initiation, copies, in a purely exterior manner, by magic rites and ceremonies, the experiences of the god of the cult. The redemption achieved is therefore exclusively in the ritual, ceremonial sphere. Hence its effective result is not any rebirth of the soul of man, any oneness with the mystery god achieved and maintained by penance, faith, and love, but is a direct apotheosis, a divinization contrived by magic. The μύστης himself becomes Isis, Osiris, or Mithras. In this world of ideas, grounded in pantheism, performing savage ritual and theatrical mummery, steeped in sensuality, self-divinization was the object. In such a world there could be no place for the belief in a mediator or for the sacrificial suffering of an incarnate God through whom man is reconciled to God. If we look up from these swampy lowlands to the Cross of Christ, to that awful and sublime mystery of God's sacrifice of himself for mankind ; if we listen to the untold voices of devotion and love which, in surrender to this mystery, echo the words of the Apostle, " For me to live is Christ : and to die is gain " (*Phil.* i. 21) ; if we think of the new reality inspired by faith, absolute purity, and self-surrendering love which with that sacrifice of all sacrifices has come to us men, we shall realize more clearly than in any other way the infinite abyss which separates the ideas of redemption embodied in the Hellenistic and Christian cults. We find here the essential contrast of body and spirit, of earth and heaven, of the world and God. It argues an uncommonly false conception of the whole nature of the Christian faith to ascribe to pagan influences its noblest and most precious mystery, that of the Atonement.

No! It is clear that nothing Jesus ever said sprang so truly from the very heart of his consciousness of his mission, from his very soul, than the words with which he tells us that he, the Son of man, the judge of the world, the only-begotten Son of the Father, was come only to minister and give his life for the redemption of many. His ultimate object in coming was not to heal the sick nor to work miracles nor to preach the kingdom of God. These were all only the externals of his Messianic activity. The true essence of his redeemership lay in the purchase of our life by his death. In that farewell hour at the Last Supper, when he revealed his tenderest and most intimate longings and desires and his sublimest intentions, this will to sacrifice himself for mankind is visibly demonstrated and made actual in that mysterious act, absolutely unique in the whole spiritual history of mankind, which transcends all human standards and leads us to the truly divine reality from which springs the redemptive act of Jesus. " Whilst they were eating, Jesus took bread : and blessing broke, and gave to them, and said : Take ye, this is my body. And having taken the chalice, giving thanks he gave it to them. . . . And he said to them : This is my blood of the new testament, which shall be shed for many " (*Mark* xiv. 22 *sqq.*). In the simple forms of bread and wine Jesus, with creative omnipotence, anticipates his self-oblation, his sacrifice on the Cross, his mangled body and flowing blood ; he sets it before him ; gives it to his disciples to be their own, in order that they may share in his sacrifice and its benefits. By so doing and bidding them do the same for evermore for a commemoration of him (*Luke* xxii. 19 ; *I. Cor.* xi. 24 *sq.*), Jesus brings the bloody sacrifice of the Cross into the present, into the here and now of the moment, in a bloodless form, and makes it the true and only source of all redemption and all benediction. It does not follow, however, that we are only enabled to understand his bloodless sacrifice in the Upper Room by the bloody sacrifice on the Cross. Precisely the reverse is true. From the Upper Room proceed the final illuminating rays which throw light on the Cross. Jesus, in anticipating the sacrifice of the Cross and its benediction by the gift of his body and blood in the form of bread and wine, utters his last, definitive word on the redemptive significance of his death on Golgotha. Thus seen, Christianity is nothing else than the gospel of our redemption by the Cross of Christ, by the death of Jesus for our salvation, by Christ's expiating blood. And the first confession to Christ of which we know, that which the Old Testament, in the mouth of John the Baptist, delivered to the world, runs : " Behold the Lamb of God, behold him who taketh away the sin of the world " (*John* i. 29). Thus too did St. Peter preach : " Knowing that you were not redeemed with corruptible things as gold and silver, from your vain conversation . . . but with the precious blood of Christ, as of a lamb unspotted and undefiled " (*I. Pet.* i. 19 *sq.*). And St. Paul also testifies that " in him we have our redemption through his blood " (*I. Eph.* i. 7). Similarly St. John proclaims that " the blood of Jesus Christ cleanseth us from all sin " (*I. John* i. 7). And the song of songs of the blessed in heaven shall for ever be : " Salvation to our God, who sitteth upon the throne, and to the Lamb " (*Apoc.* vii. 10).

* * * * *

But why had Christ's sacrifice for us to be accomplished ? How could it ever happen ? Was the spiritual state of mankind really of a kind to make such a sacrifice of Christ necessary ? Could mankind not in some way have redeemed itself ? What was the deepest meaning and the ultimate reason of the vicarious expiation, the *satisfactio vicaria* by the God-man ? In asking these questions, we turn our gaze to those obscure heights where the mystery of man and the mystery of God meet. Only the light of revelation can penetrate these dark places. Only to consecrated souls, to believers, to true initiates, is the mystery world of Christianity disclosed.

* * * * *

What is man, man in himself, the purely natural man ? A mere " drop in the bucket " on a little planet set in the vortex of myriads of star systems, he and he alone of all visible beings is the eye of creation. He alone sees things in their broad relationships and masters them. As a conscious spirit he is in the universe and yet above it. Without him it would be little more than a dumb play of forces, an eternal rise and fall of invisible waves, a mazy dance of electrons. Only the thinking mind of man can lift the curtain on its drama and interpret its flow. He supplies what is lacking to the visible universe; that is to say, only through him does the universe receive a meaning. In him it steps out of night into day, from chaos becomes cosmos. Thus man is the ordained interpreter and exponent of visible things, their born king and master, their lord and their subduer. And yet, to look at the other side of the picture, what a slave is this same man, bound as he is to these same things, his bodily and spiritual being in bondage to them. Yes, he is a part of them, or better, they are in him in the hierarchy of their powers. He is the universe in little, the microcosm. The forces of this earth, their blind and monstrous pressure, their passions and lusts, their instability and impotence, are in him in all their ambiguity. Indeed, inasmuch as he has fallen from grace into bondage to sin, he is himself their ambiguity incarnate. So much are these forces his portion that they claim dominion over his regal dignity, over the sovereignty of his spirit. They seek to force him into their service and to despiritualize him. Man is nothing but nature unchained, in so far as his pure earthliness is concerned, that which he receives from the earth and shares with it.

But is this the whole man? It is not. Greedily as he puts forth a thousand roots into the earth, he yet cannot live by its bread alone. For even his earth-bound spirit remains spirit. The true locus, the primal world of this spirit of his will ever lie beyond all phenomena in the region where the essence of things becomes sensible. He will ever grasp at the invisible and the imperceptible in individual things and beyond them, and he will ever hanker after the supra-sensual. In his mind man possesses an organ susceptible to the being that transcends material things, to that metaphysical background from which the phantasmata of sensible phenomena emerge. And with this organ he is able to investigate the reason and meaning of visible things taken individually and as a whole, of the entire visible universe. The impulse to get to the very bottom of all being is innate in the mind of man. The apex of his spirit strives to reach beyond the transitory to the intransitory, beyond all that is conditioned in time to the unconditioned and eternal, beyond all that is frail and broken to that which is perfect. It strives after God. And only in thus striving, does the human soul find that last and highest centre of reference which shall direct his powers upwards and bridle and counteract his instinct for the earthly. In his purely natural state he can only see God as from an infinite distance; he can never hope to attain to him by his unaided natural powers alone. But even so, God remains his highest goal, the motive of action of his being, that which guards him from the danger of becoming a " misbegotten animal." A longing for God is the natural dowry of the human soul, its immortal jewel, the most illuminating of the sparks of the divine love which are shed on human nature.

The purely natural man is thus a two-fold entity,

earth and spirit. He cannot realize and perfect himself in the lap of mother earth, but only by reaching out towards God. Even the natural man needs this orientation to God to be wholly himself. Of himself he is unfinished and fragmentary, never self-sufficient, never autonomous. The forces of the earth are ever threatening and entangling him. He is continually lapsing into chaos, if he tries to stand alone. Man is an enigma. Set at the meeting point of two worlds he needs both to be man. Time and eternity, earth and heaven meet in him. He is that point in the reality of the universe where the created thing becomes conscious of its ambiguity and insecurity, where it becomes conscious of the fact of God, and where it is ready for the call of the divine love.

Is the man of to-day this purely natural man? The Book of books teaches us that Adam, the first man, the father of the human race, that one unique being who by God's disposition bore within himself the whole race of men with all its possibilities, all its dispositions, all its powers, and whose choice in its hour of trial was, by the will of God, to be decisive for its whole bodily and spiritual existence, had been raised from the beginning to be of an order transcending all human and, indeed, all created needs, to a purely supernatural order of being, to a nearness to God which by nature falls to the lot of no creature, not even the highest seraph, and which is pure, gratuitous overflowing grace, namely divine life. God, the all-powerful and the all-good, was from the beginning more than Adam's sublime, transcendent goal which gave to his natural strivings their right direction and consecration ; he was by him and in him, ever pouring out fresh grace and love upon him, revealing himself to him as the benign Father and ennobling him by making him his child.   From the beginning Adam was by God's grace raised from the close and narrow prison-house of his nature into the wide spaces of the divine life.   And because of this there fell away from him all natural limitations, all natural imperfections, all that is problematical in human nature.   Concupiscence, suffering and death were removed from his existence.   It was as a perfect man that Adam came into the world, as a man of complete interior harmony and stability, as a man of absolute beauty and happiness, as a superman in the best sense, as the child of God.   So glorious was this age of first faith and first love, and so deep a mark has it left on mankind, that legends of the golden age are still current among men.

By Adam's fall this humanity was for ever thrown into disorder, and a new humanity, that of sin and concupiscence and death, took its place.   The nature to which man is born is the fallen nature of our first parent, a nature estranged from God and antagonistic to him, a nature stained by that lust, to which Adam and Eve yielded, to " be as God," to make itself absolute, born of the dust though it is, and to deprive God of his divine attributes.   A secret instinct against God is in our nature, a lurking impulse to idolize itself, the stealthy defiance of a slave who feels God to be a cumbrance and puts himself on guard against him.   This instinct corrupts the inner purpose of the acts of man's nature, its primitive God-ward disposition, its straight growth, so that even its most brilliant works are " rather vices than virtues." And wherever man panders to this distorted nature and yields to its perverse tendencies, the guilt which is of his nature becomes personal guilt. Sin after sin springs up in this poisoned soil and smears humanity with its foul slime of egoism and self-seeking, of falsehood and lying, of adultery and murder. It is Adam's first sin which now as original sin for ever puts forth its rank growth in man, and like some unclean germ cell penetrates and devastates the inmost fibres of his psycho-physical nature.

Hence this fallen nature must needs be hated by God, because antipathy to him and lust after its own self-deification are of its essence. God reacts against it with the whole force of his will, with that infinite force which finds expression in those words of his, " I am who am." And his answer to revolting nature is, " Thou shalt die the death." If before the fall of our first parents our nature was raised into the fullness of God's personal life and " made partaker of the divine nature " (cf. II. Pet. i. 4), it was thenceforth thrust back into its own dust, into its own nothingness. It had lost God, the life of its life. And therewith it lost also those supernatural privileges which before had protected its bodily and spiritual existence from the demands and forces of nature. There awakened in it unordered, passionate concupiscence, blind irrational impulse. No longer controlled by looking up to God, the flesh mutinied against the spirit. The logos died under the greedy embrace of eros. From then on the forces of nature play their terrible *rôle*, bringing forth from earth's dismal womb sickness and suffering and engendering life only to destroy it. At one stroke death came upon us, and like a vampire sucked from our existence all hope and all confidence. Man was now alone with himself. His kingdom was himself, a kingdom of defectiveness, of decay, and of death. By seeking himself in wanton alienation from God, his own existence became the brand of his guilt. He became liable to judgment and everlasting punishment. St. Paul sets out with terrible emphasis how sin, judgment and death work their sad work in fallen man, and how their ravaging forces are in the service of satanic powers, " the princes of this world " (*cf. I. Cor.* ii. 6, 8). He knew better than anyone from his own experience what this unredeemed state means. " Unhappy that I am, who shall deliver me from the body of this death ? " (*Rom.* vii. 24).

A terrible thing is original sin and its consequences. How was it possible for this terrible thing to come about, for the first sin of one man to become the original sin of all ? This question leads us to the abysses of the divine decrees. " Who hath known the mind of the Lord ? " asks St. Paul (*I. Cor.* ii. 16). Does the eye of the all-wise God see the bodily and spiritual connections between the generations of men as being closer and more intimate than we can divine ? We cannot tell. This much only is certain, that we men do not stand in God's scheme of redemption as isolated, individual beings, but in essential solidarity with the entire human race; or rather, that it is in this essential unity of the race that God sees us, and in which he leads and directs us, rewards and punishes us. When God created Adam he at the same time created us all in his seed. He created us as in a natural and supernatural common destiny with him. Mankind is nothing but the expansion in history of this first man. Humanity is, therefore, not a fortuitous concatenation of successive individuals, but an organic unity and totality, a single " we." It is precisely this primary fact of the solidarity of our bodily and spiritual unity which God's redemptive decree presupposes, and on which not only the communion of our guilt but also that of our redemption is based. " As by the offence of one, unto all men to condemnation : so also by the justice of one, unto all men to justification of life " (*Rom.* v. 18).

If that original sin shattered the supernatural union of man with God's life and love, it also wounded his natural being by deflecting that innate orientation towards God which had given to his natural efforts order and shape, and by thus surrendering his body and spirit to the wild tumult of the senses. Thus fallen nature is broken and sick in itself, and hence cannot redeem itself. It cannot do so because, since it turns its powers away from God to itself, it can only reaffirm itself and therefore can create only what is imperfect, deficient, and diseased. And this is true for the primary reason that the roots of its disease lie in the transcendent sphere, where, in its servile revolt against God, it tore itself away from its true life-goal. It suffers from an infinite guilt, from its guilt towards God. Its ailment is the judgment and chastisement of an outraged God. Hence its redemption must depend upon God, upon his merciful word of forgiveness.

* * * * *

We know that God spoke this word. He spoke it through his incarnate Son. It is " the revelation of the mystery, which was kept secret from eternity " (*Rom.* xvi. 25), " the mystery of his will," that it was " his good pleasure . . . in the dispensation of the fulness of times, to re-establish all things in Christ, that are in heaven and on earth, in him " (*Eph.* i. 9 *sq.*). Christ came to free fallen humanity from its bondage to Adam's guilt and to place it in a new solidarity and communion with himself. Thus Christ is he " who of God is made unto us wisdom, and justice, and sanctification, and redemption " (*I. Cor.* i. 30). In him, " the clemency and love of God is revealed to us " (*cf. Rom.* viii. 39 ; *cf. Eph.* ii. 7).

But why in Christ ? Why in the incarnate and crucified Son ? Why does God not forgive us of his own overflowing mercy and love by a mere word of his creative omnipotence ? And why on the basis of this forgiveness does he not endue us with new supernatural powers, so that like our first parents we may serve and love him and him alone ? This is the question of what our redemption through Christ means. We know, indeed, that Christ's redemptive act is based on the Son's eternal, self-surrender to the Father, and that its ultimate and profoundest meaning is God himself, the revelation on earth of the glory of his love. But since this revelation took place in time and to us men, we may examine it not only from the point of view of God and his majesty, but also from that of mankind and its need of redemption. And our question will be : Why did God redeem us in this particular way ?

It is a bold thing to inquire into the motives of God, for we run the danger of reading our own human thoughts into God's thoughts. When St. Paul comes to speak of the ordinances of the Eternal God for our salvation, he bursts out into a hymn of wonder and of praise : " O the depth of the riches of the wisdom and of the knowledge of God ! How incomprehensible are his judgments, and how unsearchable his ways ! For who hath known the mind of the Lord ? or who hath been his counsellor ? " (*Rom.* xi. 33 *sq.*). God of his essence transcends all created possibilities ; he is the human impossibility, the incomprehensible, the *mysterium*. How differently would man have plotted the road which should lead to the Redemption. It was as a gracious, smiling Messias, as a wise teacher, as a benevolent philanthropist, as an exalted and glorious personality, before whom all error and all sense of guilt crumbles to dust, that the Redeemer was described by the many who in human fashion had created a dream picture of the Christ. And for centuries the Jews had put away from them the figure of that suffering servant of God which their prophet had contemplated, and had set their thoughts on a Messias of earthly might and majesty. And how many times did not

the disciples of the Lord succumb to the temptation
to see the life of Jesus in the mirror of their purely
human expectations ? We can therefore only listen in
humility and reverence to what God has said, and trace
what with his own fingers he has indelibly inscribed on
the history of mankind.

It is the majesty and terror of his justice, the awe of
the *tremendum mysterium*, which overshadows the way of
the Redemption and gives to it its particular form.
Through the whole of the Old Testament there runs the
note of the *ira Dei*, of the incomprehensible and incalculable wrath of God. And even in the New Testament
this note is not mute. In not a few of the parables of
Jesus, and especially in his descriptions of the judgment,
it sounds in undiminished intensity. God is indeed our
loving Father, but his love is quite unlike natural,
human love. God loves like a father whose loins are
girt with justice. His love is urgent for the essence of
men and things, for the restoration and preservation and
safeguarding of those primal relations which obtained
between the creature and the Creator, and from which
alone joy and happiness and the fulness of life and power
arise. It is a holy love, a love charged with values,
indeed creating values. Even when it meets affliction and
sin in fallen man, where it is revealed as a merciful, forgiving love, there is no empty pardoning, no mere over-
looking and ignoring of our guilt ; it is always a creative pardoning, that is to say, a pardoning which removes
and wholly and strictly makes good the destruction of
value attaching to sin—namely conscious denial of the

primal worth of God and rebellious idolization of a created, personal value—in the whole compass of its endless effects and the eternal punishment which is its due. Not a shadow of the old negation, not a speck of the old disorder, not a thing which should not be, may any longer cling to that primal relation of man to God, once he has mercifully blessed it. In other words : if God is to redeem fallen human nature in the full sense of the word, his redemptive act will include not only the forgiveness of the guilt and not only the creative renovation of the old man, but also full reparation and expiation, the complete fulfilment of that obligation to make full compensation, with which man by his sin had weighted his relation to God.

This being so and since it is in harmony with the perfection of God that his love should be a love *secundum rigorem justitiæ*, the way of redemption could not be purely a way of God's mercy, if it lay in his free decree to give an outward reflection of this perfection of his nature, namely the unity of his love with justice. Somehow or other the way of redemption had to be a way of justice, of the creature's reparation and expiation.

But how could a mere man with his thousand limitations and frailties and imperfections have made reparation to the infinite and perfect God ? Even if God had prepared a sinless, saintly soul, a man full of grace, and had called him to be an expiatory sacrifice for his brother-creatures, this act of expiation, however heroic in dimensions, would have been confined within the bounds of the human, could never have been anything but imperfect and limited, on this side the chasm which man's sin towards God had opened up. Moreover, if God by some invisible creative act had transformed the whole of the human race to its inmost depths and had awakened it to do penance in sackcloth and ashes, its fundamental relation to God would still have been weighted with infinite arrears of unexpiated, unpaid-for guilt, which had mounted up as a consequence of Adam's sin running through all the generations of the human race. Certainly God could graciously remit these arrears and forgo the expiation, but then there would remain for all eternity the fact of a guilt towards God which had been left unexpiated. The dark shadows of something that should not exist would rise out of the depths of being, and would appear as a stain on the garb of him who will not let his honour be smirched, who through the mouth of the prophet uttered the threat: "If then I be a father, where is my honour? and if I be a master, where is my fear?" (*Mal.* i. 6).

God's justice thus rules out every possibility that a mere man might make full reparation. But because it does not admit this human possibility, God's love seizes on a possibility beyond all human reach, belonging to him alone, which only he, the all-wise and all-mighty, can conceive and realize, the possibility of one, "who being in the form of God," emptied himself, taking the form of a servant, being made in the likeness of men, and in habit formed as a man" (*Phil.* ii. 6 *sq.*). If justice demands an infinite expiation, love gives an infinite expiation. Justice and love meet in the Incarnation of the Son of God. God is so utterly different from all else, so incomprehensible, so truly God, that when he empties himself of his glory, he preserves it ; when he surrenders his honour, he guards it ; when he dies for us, he wins life for us.

Thus did the eternal sacrifice of the only-begotten Son take form in time and in the likeness of man. The consubstantial Son of God entered the finite, conditioned existence of a created being, the cramping limitations of human nature, of human will and thought and affections. One who dared say to the heavenly Father, " I am as thou art," became as one of us, and we became his " brethren." Certainly his human nature is as pure and unspotted and perfect as anything created can possibly be, but it is nevertheless a human nature in its entirety. Thus Christ is at once truly God and complete man, uniting in himself the extreme limits of all being, this world and the next, heaven and earth. He is the true mediator between God and the world, between heaven and earth. Because he is man, he can make his own and take upon himself all the needs and responsibilities and obligations of man ; and he can overcome them and liquidate them in infinite completeness, because he is God. Hence our redemption has its foundation and its preparation in the mystery of the Incarnation of God.

And how was it consummated ? In weighty and pregnant words the apostles answer the question. " He humbled himself, becoming obedient unto death, even to the death of the cross " (*Phil.* ii. 8). " Who his own self bore our sins in his body upon the tree; that we being dead to sins, should live to justice: by whose stripes you were healed " (*I. Pet.* ii. 24).

St. Paul has described step by step the way of vicarious expiation which Jesus trod. As " the first-born among many brethren " (*Rom.* viii. 29), " one tempted in all things like as we are, without sin " (*Heb.* iv. 15), who of his infinite love for mankind felt all human suffering as his own and bore it within himself, the Redeemer of his free volition entered that vale of misery to which the equitable chastisement of God's justice had consigned the human race. He was exposed to every one of those evil forces which work for the destruction of man. He, who was without sin, took on sinful flesh (*cf. Rom.* viii. 3). " Him, that knew no sin, for us God hath made sin " (*II. Cor.* v. 21). And because he took upon himself sinful flesh he was also " made under the law " (*cf. Gal.* iv. 4) and under its " curse " (*cf. Gal.* iii. 10, 13). He had to die. He was plunged into the desolation of human existence, down into the uttermost depths of human misery, down to the point where soul separates from body. And in his death the powers of hell triumphed; for it was they who in the true sense nailed the Redeemer to the Cross (*cf. I. Cor.* ii. 8). The Apostle is anxious to direct the eyes of Christians to these grave and bitter consequences which for Christ were attached to the Incarnation. Nothing that could be called human misery was spared him. All that the evangelists have to tell of the poor, tempted, weeping, suffering, dying Saviour is seen by St. Paul in the light of Christ's act of redemption. As the second Adam the Redeemer makes all this suffering his own in its bitterest form, in order, in freely given obedience to the heavenly Father, to offer it as an infinite sacrifice of praise and thanksgiving and reparation for mankind.

Two things give a special stamp to this suffering of Christ, and it is only when we keep them in mind that we approach its ultimate meaning. Above all, there is its character of solitariness, loneliness and dereliction. Certainly it is the divine Word who suffers, and the human will of Jesus is certainly rooted in that act of free and divine surrender which made the Son say, " Behold, I come to do thy will, O God " (*Heb*. x. 9) ; but it is nevertheless his human nature alone in which and through which the Redeemer suffers. There is therefore all the frailty and obscurity of the purely human in this suffering. It is a Passion of sinister loneliness and dereliction. The human mind of Jesus is certainly conscious of its personal union with God from the beginning of its existence, and it experiences again and again moments when this union with the Godhead manifests itself even externally in a radiant glory. But the true essence of his self-emptying, of his $\kappa\epsilon\nu\omega\sigma\iota\varsigma$ (*Phil*. ii. 7), is that his entire sacrifice is set in the narrow confines of the purely human. It is shrouded in the night of affliction, a striving and struggle in tears and anguish, the suffering of one " in the days of his flesh with a strong cry and tears offering up prayers and supplications to him that was able to save him from death " (*Heb*. v. 7). So great was this distress, that in

the hour of his death his soul felt in anguish for the
hand of the Father and his lips uttered the words, " My
God, my God, why hast thou forsaken me ? " (*Matt.*
xxvii. 46 = *Mark* xv. 34). This marked the extremest
depth of his self-humbling. Assuredly, even from this
depth, there glowed in his consciousness the fact that he
was the Redeemer, the Christ. For the cry of agony,
which was forced from him, is an echo of a prayer in the
very psalm in which the suffering of the coming Messias
is foretold (*Ps.* xxi. 2). But certain as it is that Jesus
intended this cry of agony as a Messianic prayer, it is
nevertheless the cry of a measureless sense of dereliction, quivering with the horror and dread of one cast
out and execrated, of one " struck by God " (*cf. Is.*
liii. 4). The sense of God's remoteness, which belongs
to fallen human nature, was laid on him, and his soul
experienced its horror all the more intensely for his
consciousness of oneness with his Father. Solitary in
his nearness to God, he was not less solitary in his remoteness from him, when he was " led as a sheep to the
slaughter " (*cf. Is.* liii. 7).

And just as loneliness and dereliction are marks of his
suffering as our Redeemer, so too is the terrible form in
which it came to him characteristic of it. It was not to
the power of some moral intelligence and legitimate,
responsible authority that he was delivered up, but to
the cruel play of human passions. " They have opened
their mouths against me, as a lion ravening and roaring "
(*Ps.* xxi. 14). The motive forces of the drama of his
passion are envy and covetousness, stupidity and narrow-

mindedness, pride and hatred, cowardice and meanness, blood-thirstiness and cruelty. From Judas, who betrayed him to the raging, howling mob, to the blasphemous thief crucified with him, the most bestial human passions were let loose on him. In the whole course of this terrible event there was not a crevice through which the tiniest gleam of new hope might flicker. Certainly he had only to ask his Father and he would have given him " presently more than twelve legions of angels," but " how then shall the scriptures be fulfilled, that so it must be done ? " (*Matt.* xxvi. 53 *sq.*). Thus even in his extreme misery the help of his Father is denied him. The way of the Crucified is strewn with *débris* and his end is catastrophe. Jesus dies a felon's death and even over his grave the waves of hatred and calumniation and meanness continue to break.

If we appreciate the death of Jesus in the light of these two facts, that is to say, that it is a death in loneliness and dereliction by God and a death under the lash of the vilest human passions, the unique character of his sacrifice stands out with harsh clarity. This uniqueness consists in the fact that Jesus was wholly thrown back upon himself, that God's help whether within him or without was denied, that he was delivered over to the dreadful consequences of sacrilegious, original sin, to all the frightfulness of the merely natural and the merely human, both in his interior distress and his exterior suffering. Since the guilt of humanity culminates in the fact that man wishes to be nothing more than himself, nothing but what is purely human and natural, the Redeemer, since he will surrender himself as a redemption for mankind, now faces the whole, unrestrained power of the merely human. Like wild beasts the powers of earth tear at his body, and fear and dread penetrate to the lower regions of his spirit and seek to reduce his natural appetite (*voluntas ut natura*) to confusion and despair. But however furious and ruthless their attack, they cannot reach up to that summit of his being where his human mind, his rational will (*voluntas ut ratio*), has the dominion. A sinlessness is in it, an unshakable firmness such as has never been found in any other human will. In an act of free obedience Jesus surrenders himself to the Father. "Not as I will, but as thou wilt" (*Matt.* xxvi. 39). "Father, into thy hands I commend my spirit" (*Luke* xxiii. 46). "Whereas indeed he was the Son of God, he learned obedience by the things which he suffered" (*Heb.* v. 8). "Who, when he was reviled, did not revile: when he suffered, he threatened not: but delivered himself to him that judged him unjustly" (*I. Pet.* ii. 23). The purest and most perfect volition is set free in him. It is a will rising superior to all the powers of fallen nature, heroically subduing them, consecrate to the will of the Father to the last drop of blood and to the last breath. Yet it is a will springing wholly from human nature as its loveliest blossom, its noblest manifestation, and so wholly dedicate to mankind that it takes man's guilt upon itself and dies for it (*cf. I Pet.* ii. 24). A new thing has appeared, the sacrifice of a man without spot or blemish, rising from the frail foundation of humanity, limited yet overcoming all limitations, an acceptance of God so resounding and absolute that it drowns every negation of man. The sacrifice of all sacrifices is here, the highest, most spiritual, freest act of adoration and reparation, so incomparable in its content and dignity that it would still remain the purest and most perfect praise of the divine majesty, even if the whole world beside persist in unbelief and sin. As it is, this sacrifice became the means of redemption for all mankind, the inexhaustible source of every great achievement of holiness and of all true heroism.

It was the meritorious cause of our redemption. By accomplishing in the utmost moral freedom his act of obedience and suffering for the sake of mankind, Jesus made in the garment of our humanity that reparation which man owed to his Creator. And since it was the Son of God who for the sake of mankind took their suffering upon himself, there attaches to it an expiatory value transcending and overtopping all human perfection, a value which no guilt of man can ever lessen or destroy. And therefore its benefit extends to us all. Just as at the dawn of human history, it was not a single individual that by Adam's sin came under the ban of sin, but the whole commonalty of mankind, men as a totality, so it accorded with the divine love and wisdom that in the new man who is Christ the whole of redeemed humanity be set, that he should be the head and we his body. Hence Christianity can only display itself as a unity, as a communion of the redeemed, in other words as a Church. Thus from the same cross, against which the dread storm of the divine justice breaks, there flames up also God's infinite love and mercy. " For God so loved the world, as to give his only begotten Son ; that whosoever believeth in him, may not perish, but may have life everlasting " (*John* iii. 15). God so loved the world that " he spared not even his own Son : but delivered him up for us all " (*Rom.* viii. 32). We stand before a revelation of the divine love so incomprehensible, so utterly transcending all measures, that before this folly of God all human wisdom melts away, and a great silence enwraps it.

In fact, the speech of our faith is reverent silence, the tense listening for that glad and holy word spoken from the Cross to mankind : " We are redeemed." Ever since Christ died for us the malediction and anger of God, the horror of infinite, impardonable, hopeless guilt, and with it the despair of human existence, has been taken away. Human nature is once and for all rescued from itself and freed from its captivity and awakened to the supernatural and its riches. It is God's. It still bears, indeed, the traces of its former bondage to sin. There remain the consequences of sin—concupiscence, sickness, and death. But all the sting, all the hopelessness, is taken from them. They are no longer a brand of guilt but marks of old wounds left in the redeemed, which by the will of the all-wise God call us to humility and penance. They serve for our protection. In their infirmity our power is made perfect (*cf. II. Cor.* xii. 9). Like the glorious stigmata of the risen Lord, they will be henceforth the witnesses of our victory. And certain as it is that these scars remain, it is equally sure that their root-stock, our greatest guilt, has been torn up. Hence human nature no longer stands on this side the gulf which Adam's sin created, but on the other. Indeed, it has been in principle raised in the risen Lord to the life of God himself. Its true abode is where the Incarnate Son stands at the right hand of the Father. For it is not true that Christ only cleared away the encumbrances of our guilt and thus opened the way by which we could of ourselves go to meet God. The truth is that he himself is the way (*John* xiv. 6). "Having therefore, brethren, a confidence in the entering into the Holies by the blood of Christ : A new and living way which he hath dedicated for us through . . . his flesh" (*Heb*. x. 19 *sq*.). By killing our guilt he also gave us of his life. Thus he is for us not only the forgiveness of sins but also "justice and sanctification" (*I. Cor*. i. 30), and it is in the power of this sanctification alone that man is able to tread "the way of the Lord" (*cf. Matt*. iii. 3), the way of "abounding" justice, to which Jesus called special attention in his sermon on the mount. Jesus, therefore, not only created the conditions governing our approach to God, but also won for us the power to attain to the new life, in fact the new life itself. Wherever man is, there exists for him, because he is man, this new fundamental relationship as his right. This is true for the Jews also and for the heathen, even for the fool who says in his heart, there is no God. For those, too, the act of redemption was accomplished once for all.

Indeed, it is retrospective to the remotest generations. For somehow or other all are included in the benediction of Christ's Cross. The Cross sheds its light even on lifeless nature, on the whole of creation, which " groaneth and travaileth in pain even unto now." It is for the Apostle of the Gentiles a consoling certainty that " the expectation of the creature waiteth for the revelation of the sons of God," and that the day will come when " the creature itself shall be delivered from the servitude of corruption, into the liberty of the glory of the children of God " (*Rom.* viii. 22, 19, 21). It is the last and the happiest thing which the seer of the New Testament saw in his vision. " And I saw a new heaven and a new earth. For the first heaven and the first earth was gone, and the sea is now no more. And I John saw the holy city the new Jerusalem coming down out of heaven from God, prepared as a bride adorned for her husband. And I heard a great voice from the throne, saying : Behold, the tabernacle of God with men " (*Apoc.* xxi. 1 *sqq.*). We are redeemed.

*   *   *   *   *

The redemptive historical fact that Christ, through the sacrifice of himself on Golgotha, made full satisfaction to God for us, and that objectively and once and for all he thus paid the price of our redemption, is the postulate and foundation of all subjective Christian piety and of our own personal faith. How does this personal Christianity of ours originate ? How do we subjectively apply to ourselves this objective fact of the Redemption of mankind? From being an extra-personal, supra-personal event how does it become a personal reality to us, your salvation and mine? This is the last question we shall have to answer. It is the ultimate question for every human life.

The answer to this, too, can only come from God, by the light of his revelation. In this light nothing shines out more brightly than the truly regal and divine freedom of his mercy and love, that love which pours its sunshine and its rain on the just and on the unjust, which knows " no respect of persons " (*Rom*. ii. 11; *cf. Ep*. vi. 9; *Col*. iii. 25), which will not be hemmed in by any earthly constraints, but seeks out and surprises every individual soul. " For there is no distinction of the Jew and the Greek : for the same is Lord over all, rich unto all that call upon him " (*Rom*. x. 12). Thus in the infinite treasury of the divine love and providence, there lies a wealth of extraordinary ways of grace by which the Redeemer may approach those souls who live their lonely lives outside Christendom and the external organization of the Church, and are untouched by its influences. Those seeds of the divine word, spoken of by the Fathers, which fall everywhere, even in non-Christian and unbelieving hearts, are also life-germs of redemptive grace, born and nourished by Christ's blood. And these visitations of his grace are as individual and as countless as there are men on earth. They occur invisibly, possibly under the shroud of some curious legend or rite, entangled in a rank growth of superstition and erroneous conceptions, cumbered, too, by perverse habits and tendencies, but nevertheless finding soil in some earnest desire for truth, virtue, and blessedness. "They have sought me that before asked not for me, they have found me that sought me not" (*Is.* lxv. 1 ; *cf. Rom.* x. 20).

But multifarious and rich as the extraordinary ways of grace are, yet, since they work invisibly and from within, they lack the certifying, convincing weight of a power acting from without, nor do they give that objective certainty of salvation which guarantees peace to the soul. Therefore the same divine love which was visibly embodied in the Saviour has given us the grace of the Redemption under the veil of perceptible signs, through audible word and visible sacrament. Word and sacrament are ordained by God to be the ordinary, regular way by which Christ redeems us. While Christ's word, spoken by the Church, is ringing in our ears, his grace, according to the abounding measure of the divine justice and love, penetrates into our souls, startles us out of our bondage to the natural, and opens our eyes to the realm of the supernatural. It makes us believers. "For we confess with our mouth the Lord Jesus, and believe in our heart that God hath raised him up from the dead" (*cf. Rom.* x. 9). It is an act of the intellect which we perform, one of firm acceptance of supernatural realities as truths. But it is an act shuddering with the consciousness of our responsibility and guilt, permeated by awe in the face of God and his justice, and fired by our yearning for redemption.

It is a faith charged with contrition and penance and full of a hunger after justice, a faith which from the depths of human impotence pleads, as did those men at Jerusalem, " What shall we do, men and brothers ? " (*Acts* ii. 37). Such belief is the foundation and the root of our justification and redemption. It is only by being lifted up into the light of God's mysteries that we become capable of receiving the sacrament of our salvation. This sacrament is baptism.

Baptism is the nuptial gift of the risen Lord to his young bride the Church (*cf. Matt.* xxviii. 19), and was therefore from the beginning the first and immediate aim of all Christian mission work and a fundamental element of the Christian religion (*cf. Heb.* vi. 2). Under the simple symbolism of exterior cleansing, there is consummated in the name and by the power of the Holy Trinity the divine miracle by which a new thing is brought into being. We are cleansed of the stain of original sin in us. The objective redemption of human nature becomes the subjective redemption of our own person. We are freed from our natural solidarity with Adam and his sin and raised to a new, supernatural union with Christ and his life. We become members of Christ, united to him through his Holy Spirit, and in him and through him with all those who have received the same Holy Spirit in baptism. " For in one spirit were we all baptized into one body, whether Jews or Gentiles, whether bond or free " (*I. Cor.* xii. 13). A new unity and communion, a new humanity arises, namely man loosed from the chains of his fallen nature and born again to eternal life, in other words the Christian. Baptism is therefore the sacrament which is at the foundation of the Christian faith. Once and for all it makes us Christ's and through Christ the Father's. We are drawn from the world of the profane and become consecrate to God—saints, in the original biblical sense. Hence all the other signs of grace rest on it. Hence, too, the life of the Christian receives in baptism its peculiar stamp and its distinctive form, so that his Christian life actually may be called a prolonged baptism in Christ. St. Paul, in giving emphasis to this fact, is actually exuberant in his expressions. "We, who are baptized in Christ Jesus, are baptized in his death" (*Rom.* vi. 3), "buried together with him by baptism into death" (*Rom.* vi. 4; *cf. Cor.* ii. 12). "For if we have been planted together in the likeness of his death, we shall be also in the likeness of his resurrection" (*Rom.* vi. 5). The mysticism of baptism therefore dominates all Christian life. "For as many of you as have been baptized in Christ have put on Christ. There is neither Jew, nor Greek: there is neither bond, nor free: there is neither male, nor female. For you are all one in Christ Jesus" (*Gal.* iii. 27 *sq.*).

So thoroughly and effectively are we reshaped by baptism into the likeness of Christ, that in this new likeness and unity all natural differences fall away. Our natural being is wholly raised into the supernatural and has become Christ's. By receiving baptism with faith we are so truly and effectively transplanted into Christ

not only in our minds and wills, but also in the full
breadth and depth of our being that all our natural
functions, our living and acting and dying are in vital
connection with him. We are " always bearing about in
our body the mortification of Jesus, that the life also of
Jesus may be made manifest in our bodies " (*II. Cor.* iv.
10). In the life and death of the Christian there is repro-
duced and manifested in virtue of his baptism the life and
death of Christ, and in the hereafter his resurrection will
take place in us. Thus the life of the redeemed is a
life in and through Christ, springing up out of a supernatural, sacramental union with him and proving itself
in faith and love. By seeing all our ordinary, natural
being and acts, all that our everyday life brings to us,
our eating and drinking, our laughter and tears, our
thoughts and deeds, in their mysterious relation to
Christ ; by quickening all these things, great and small,
by the spirit of Jesus ; and by accepting sickness and
death in union with him, we live and die " in the Lord,"
in the " fulness of Christ," in the bliss of the redeemed.
There is nothing more simple and direct than such
a life. God's loving providence may, indeed, from
time to time call individual Christian souls to special
perfection and to extraordinary tasks, and therefore
lead them by an unusually steep road, beset by bitter
renunciation and grievous sacrifices. But it will always
pour out over life like this such a wealth of helping,
strengthening, consoling grace, that in spite of all Christ's
yoke will be sweet and his burden light. And these
renunciations and these tasks will be so woven into their

everyday lives, into the demands of the moment, that they will appear as obvious incidents on the road of life and will be gathered by such Christians as our Lord's silent reminders of himself. Thus Christianity emphatically does not involve a repressive ethic and unnatural mortification ; still less does it involve blustering combat and shrill sentiment. It is a secluded retirement in Christ, a *vita abscondita cum Christo in Deo* (*Col.* iii. 3). " I live, now not I ; but Christ liveth in me. And that I live now in the flesh : I live in the faith of the Son of God, who loved me, and delivered himself for me " (*Gal.* ii. 20). It may of course happen that anxious fears force their way into this seclusion, aye, and torturing cares, too ; and passionate struggles. This can happen, since even the redeemed still bears the stigma of concupiscence and remains exposed to the exterior powers of temptation. But though he falter and fall, he still remains as before Christ's own, and hence he is in a very special sense called to redemption. And after as before his fall it remains true that the price of redemption for his sin is already paid. In spite of every sin he is close to God's heart, infinitely closer than his former natural self, tainted by original and inherited sin. He may believe and hope. He may supplicate and pray. And never will his prayer be a lonely supplication ; for wherever a Christian prays, Christ, the head, prays with him. And wherever " one member suffer anything, all the members suffer with it " (*I. Cor.* xii. 26). In the union with the head and his members, in confession and penance, the glad

certainty will be brought home to him anew, that
" the blood of Jesus Christ cleanseth us from all sin "
(*I. John* i. 7).

Man and Christ face one another as question and
answer, as desire and fulfilment. Only he who sees in
Christ the answer to his question and the fulfilment of
his desires is redeemed. " There is no other name under
heaven, given to men, whereby we must be saved,"
save the name of Jesus (*Acts* iv. 12). For nigh on two
thousand years this gospel of Christ the Redeemer of
the world has been spread among men. It is being proclaimed clearly and nobly in our own day. And yet we
cannot evade the appalling realization, that at no period
have revolt from Christ and the supernatural and idolization of man and his nature been so noisily preached, so
audaciously organized, and carried into effect with such
terrible severity and such extensive display of power
as in these days in which we live. The era of the serpent
is near. Already its word, " You shall be as gods,"
may be heard in the streets and lanes. Did Christ die
in vain ? Was his work of redemption an immense
failure ? Has the serpent after all become lord over God ?
Sin over the Redeemer ? Man may thus blaspheme, but
God hears and laughs at him. There is a laughter of
God. It is more terrible than his anger. For it is the
infinite wrath of wounded love. It is a laughter which
freezes man and hardens him, so that his guilt becomes
ineradicable. " For it is impossible for those, who were
once illuminated, have tasted also the heavenly gift, and
were made partakers of the Holy Ghost, have more-

over tasted the good word of God, and the powers of the world to come, and are fallen away; to be renewed again to penance, crucifying again to themselves the Son of God, and making him a mockery " (*Heb.* vi. 4 *sqq.*). God is not mocked. Redemption does not mean that God humbles himself to be the blind slave of his love, that because a man is inexhaustible in his wickedness God also must be inexhaustible in his redemptive love, that he will subdue such wickedness by the superabundance of his love. Hence there will always be men sitting in the shadow of death, unredeemed, who, in rebellious self-deification, renounce the new objective relation of our nature to God in Christ and even their subjective filiation to God won in baptism, and descend into their fallen nature, into the world and its lusts. The spirit of Antichrist will ever take shape in such men. For " this is Antichrist, who denieth the Father and the Son " (*I. John* ii. 22). The fight of belief with unbelief will ever be the true theme of history. In this aspect Christianity is not a reconciliation, but a dividing of souls, not a universal appeasement of the world, but its cleansing and purification, the salt wherewith it shall be salted.

In every true Christian life this salt is working. The powers of the Redemption are in it. Silently and invisibly they accomplish their work. We cannot ask, Where are they? For they are neither here nor are they there (*cf. Luke* xvii. 21). They are in the hearts of men, where the Spirit of the Son calls Abba, Father (*cf. Gal.* iv. 6). But they are the powers of victory and of eternal life. And when hereafter the Son of man shall come with the clouds of heaven, they will become manifest and will overcome the world. For Jesus is the Christ.